THE NEW COMPLETE
GUITARIST

THE NEW
COMPLETE
GUITARIST

RICHARD CHAPMAN

LONDON, NEW YORK, MUNICH, MELBOURNE, DELHI

REVISED EDITION
US editor Christine Heilman
Project editor Anna Fischel
Art editor Edward Kinsey
Senior editor Neil Lockley
Senior art editor Kevin Ryan
DTP designer Rajen Shah
Production controller Sarah Sherlock

Managing editor Adèle Hayward
Managing art editor Karen Self
Category publisher Stephanie Jackson

This book is dedicated to Carol

ORIGINAL EDITION
Editors Laurence Henderson and Katie John
Project editor Terry Burrows
Managing editor Sean Moore
Designers Heather McCarry, Gurinder Purewall, and Dawn Terrey
Deputy art director Tina Vaughan
Deputy editorial director Jane Laing

Special Contributors:
Rack-mounted systems Jim Barber
Care and maintenance Bill Puplett
Sound and amplification John Seabury

Original edition produced and art directed in Great Britain
by Nigel Osborne, 115J Cleveland Street, London W1

Revised American Edition, 2003

Published in the United States by
DK Publishing, Inc.
375 Hudson Street
New York, New York 10014

First published in 1993 by DK Publishing, Inc.,
95 Madison Avenue, New York, New York 10016

First published in paperback 1994

03 04 05 06 07 08 10 9 8 7 6 5 4 3 2 1

A Cataloging-in-Publication record for this book
is available from the Library of Congress.

ISBN 0-7894-9701-8

Reproduced in Singapore by Colourscan
Printed in China by L.Rex Printing Company

Discover more at
www.dk.com

CONTENTS

INTRODUCTION

The guitar has established itself as the world's most popular musical instrument. It is adaptable, portable, and attractive, and its myriad forms and versatility have led to a vast range of fascinating music. The captivating sounds of the guitar can be heard in every corner of the world. Its unparalleled diversity ranges from indigenous folk music with simple homemade instruments through to sophisticated compositions and improvisation using electric guitars linked to computers.

Books of guitar music were popular as long ago as 1552

The guitar has ancient and mysterious origins. Stone-cut reliefs from central Turkey show guitars in the Hittite civilization from over 3,000 years ago. The emergence and widespread adoption of the instrument in Europe during the Middle Ages produced some of the first written references to the guitar and the earliest music we can hear and understand today. By the 16th century the guitar was firmly established in many European countries and had even reached the Americas. Primarily a small-bodied instrument with four or five strings predominantly arranged in pairs, it was played at all levels of society for songs and dances. Instrumental compositions were circulated, and the guitar started to evolve into its present form.

The earliest surviving guitars come from the end of the 16th century and the 17th century. They are fragile and often highly decorated. The guitar took an important step toward its modern-day form during the late 18th century, when instruments in Italy appeared with six single strings tuned EADGBE. During the mid-19th century, the Spanish maker Antonio de Torres built a large-bodied instrument, which is the template for modern classical and flamenco guitars. The United States became the center for guitar innovation in the late 19th century and 20th century, with a range of dramatic and revolutionary designs. These have established virtually all modern guitar designs with steel strings, ranging from flat-top steel-string acoustics to archtops, resonators, and amplified electric guitars. The guitar continues constantly to evolve with acoustic and electronic innovations.

GUITAR MUSIC

Today every type of music can be heard on the guitar. One of the strengths of the instrument is that it is not dominated by any one style or approach. Each genre has different facets and various areas of musical activity. Styles include classical, flamenco, blues, country, jazz, rock, pop, folk, and a whole range of music from around the world, such as Brazilian and African. There are also many indefinable hybrid crossovers. This explosion of styles took place during the 20th century. Before that, there was classical music, and popular songs and dances, flamenco, and various folk styles including early blues and gypsy music. Music has evolved both where the guitar is integral, as in, for instance, flamenco and modern rock and pop, and within sophisticated areas such as jazz, led and developed by saxophone and piano.

It is helpful and inspiring to listen to and be aware of different types of guitar music. There are many outstanding individuals from the past whose music can be appreciated on recordings. These range from the gypsy jazz genius Django Reinhardt through to the rock visionary Jimi Hendrix.

PLAYING THE GUITAR

At first, it is best to concentrate on and stay within a chosen area of music. With certain popular styles, such as rock and pop, it is possible to work and develop within a simple framework. To be creative and learn to improvise in a fully developed way, it is important to understand and play jazz. Different areas use widely divergent techniques and material, yet there are interesting possibilities for cross-fertilization when it comes to writing or improvising. Consider carefully the long term before choosing one style. Take classical music, for example. To play classical music, it is essential to use a proper nylon-string guitar

Five-course guitar dated around 1590

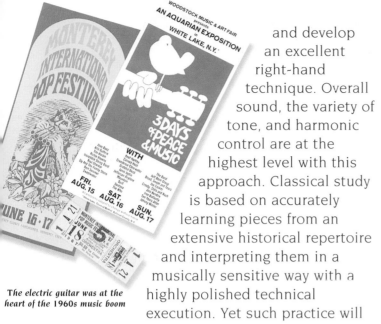

The electric guitar was at the heart of the 1960s music boom

and develop an excellent right-hand technique. Overall sound, the variety of tone, and harmonic control are at the highest level with this approach. Classical study is based on accurately learning pieces from an extensive historical repertoire and interpreting them in a musically sensitive way with a highly polished technical execution. Yet such practice will not prepare the guitarist for playing in other styles. To step outside classical music and develop creative and improvisational skills and techniques, it is necessary to study theory, composition, and jazz.

Every style and approach has different goals and values as well as strengths and weaknesses. Rock guitar can be incredibly limited but, with knowledge and inspiration, it is possible to absorb, adapt, and recreate ideas and techniques from anywhere. Blues is based on a small traditional vocabulary of chords and phrases, yet it can be profound and expressive. Jazz is an umbrella term for a wide range of different music from styles based on past eras to contemporary approaches. It is unlimited in its creative possibilities. The jazz area continues to produce much of the most advanced music as well as pointing to the future.

CHOOSING A GUITAR

Guitars can be divided into acoustic and electric. There are two general types of acoustic guitar: those with nylon strings and those with steel strings. Guitars with nylon strings are the only type for classical and flamenco music. They are also used in South American music, crossover styles, and certain other areas. Steel-string guitars are played in most popular styles. They are particularly widely used by singers to support the voice.

Most players start on an acoustic guitar of some type. This is a sensible choice, since it helps the guitarist to focus on playing with a real sense of touch and to develop a solid fingering technique. It also enables the guitarist to practice properly on the production of a good tone, and work at dynamics and nuance. From an acoustic, it is relatively easy to move over to an electric guitar at an early stage. Many players start on cheap small-bodied nylon-string or steel-string guitars.

Electric guitars are the mainstay of rock and pop as well as jazz, country, and blues. If you are particularly interested in music with electric guitars and want to eventually play in a group, obtain an electric guitar as soon as possible and learn to use this effectively with an amplifier and effects. Although it is not essential to play an acoustic guitar as well, it is strongly recommended. Regular acoustic practice, as well as electric, helps to develop strength, touch, and sensitivity for sound production and playing technique.

For those who are very young, it is best to start on a small instrument or one that is easy to play with a low string action. Avoid really poor instruments or those with flaws such as a bent neck. It is offputting to play on something that will never sound good!

On a personal note, I have written this book to provide a wide range of source material, ranging from all kinds of techniques to advanced theories. My aim is to enlighten and inspire guitarists at every level, from the beginner to the professional. I wish everyone the best of luck!

RICHARD CHAPMAN

John D'Angelico archtop guitar

Jimi Hendrix developed his own approach to playing, and produced some of the greatest guitar music

THE GUITAR

The contemporary guitar can be separated into four main types: the nylon-string classical, the steel-string acoustic, the archtop, and the solid-body electric. This section of the book traces the history of the instrument to the present day and details the principles on which each type of guitar is constructed.

CLASSICAL GUITARS

THE DESIGN AND CONSTRUCTION OF THE CLASSICAL GUITAR

Innovation
Many established makers are refining and adjusting their work within the classical tradition. Australian Greg Smallman and German Matthias Dammann have revolutionized the guitar with new bracing systems and the incorporation of carbon fiber.

Today's classical guitar is based on the traditional design of the Spanish maker Antonio de Torres (1817-92). In the mid-19th century he developed a new large-body guitar with a pleasing outline and standardized rectangular bridge. His guitars took construction and sound a step forward. The Torres guitar had extra volume and a good tone and was widely adopted by classical players. It replaced the small-body guitars of makers such as Panormo and Lacote.

Strings
Guitars were originally strung with gut treble and metal-wound silk bass strings. In the 1940s, nylon treble strings were introduced. Nylon strings are more consistent in quality, stronger, and may be used at high tension to produce a clear sound with good projection.

CHRISTOPHER DEAN CLASSICAL (BELOW)
One of the outstanding English guitar makers, Christopher Dean (b.1958) has been building guitars professionally for over 20 years. He is part of a tradition going back nearly half a century to the early work of David Rubio (1934-2000). Dean worked at one time with prominent maker Paul Fischer (b.1941), who in turn had worked with Rubio for a number of years. Dean continually strives to refine and enhance his sound. His guitars have a bright crisp string tone, and the body adds a pure resonance and depth. There is a good response in all registers. Dean's instruments are evolving within the tradition of European classical guitar building, influenced by Torres, Bouchet, Hauser, and the philosophy and approach behind English guitar-making. The guitars are used widely for performing and recording.

Materials Finished in 2003, the instrument is made principally of four woods: Indian rosewood for the body, bridge, and headstock facing, European spruce for the top, mahogany for the neck, and ebony for the fingerboard.

Bridge The rosewood bridge has a saddle set in a slot with a tie block for the strings. The internal bracing has five radiating fan struts and a cross bar under the saddle.

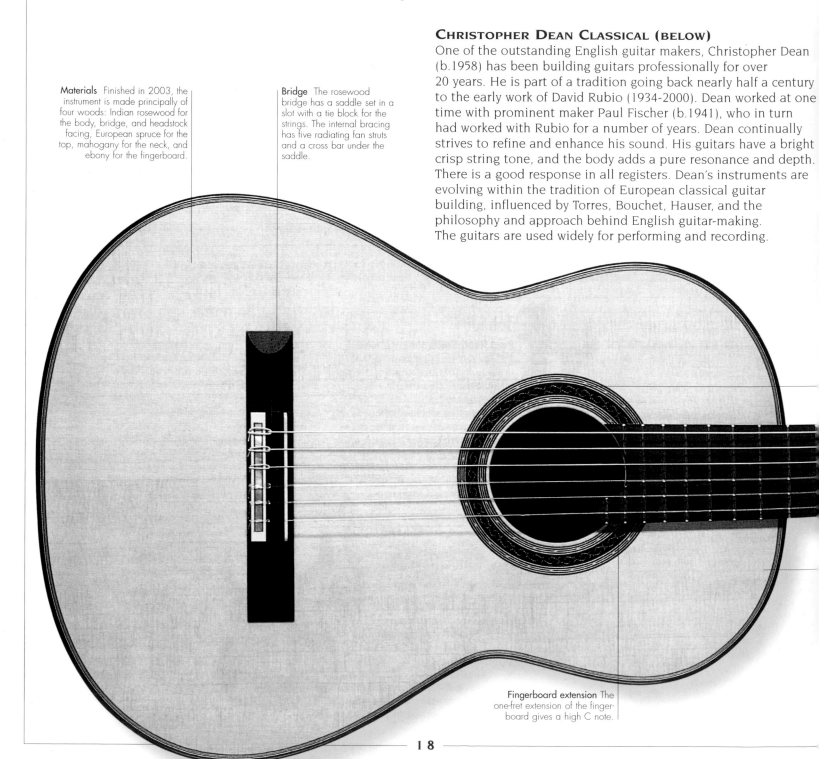

Fingerboard extension The one-fret extension of the fingerboard gives a high C note.

Flamenco feature The guitar has a *golpeador* plate to stop the top from becoming damaged from the *golpe*, the technique where the fingers use the top for percussive, rhythmic tapping.

Headstock The solid headstock with friction pegs is a feature of early instruments.

Construction Flamenco guitars have a thinner top than classical instruments to make them more responsive.

FLAMENCO GUITARS

The flamenco guitar is a classical guitar in outline, shape, and proportions, but it has a number of important differences in construction that give it its own particular tonal qualities. It has lighter internal bracing than a classical guitar, a thinner top with a transparent *golpeador* tapping plate, and a light-colored cypress-wood body with cedar neck. The string action is set lower. The overall effect is a warm, loose guitar with a pronounced string sound. Nevertheless, the

flamenco guitar player can produce a cutting attack from the instrument as well as a mellow, soulful quality.

The guitar featured here is the work of Domingo Esteso (1882-1937). His guitars are fragile, antique instruments, dating from the early 1900s, yet they are still valued for their remaining tonal qualities. There are many great makers in Spain today, among them the Hermanos Conde, successors to Esteso in Madrid, and Manuel Reyes in Cordoba.

Today, flamenco guitars have more in common with the modern classical guitar. Professional flamenco guitars have a slotted headstock with worm-and-gear tuners instead of pegs, which make the instrument difficult to tune. Many flamenco guitars are made with rosewood bodies, which give more power and density to the sound. Many leading guitarists today, including the great Paco de Lucía, have to amplify their guitars on stage, particularly in a group.

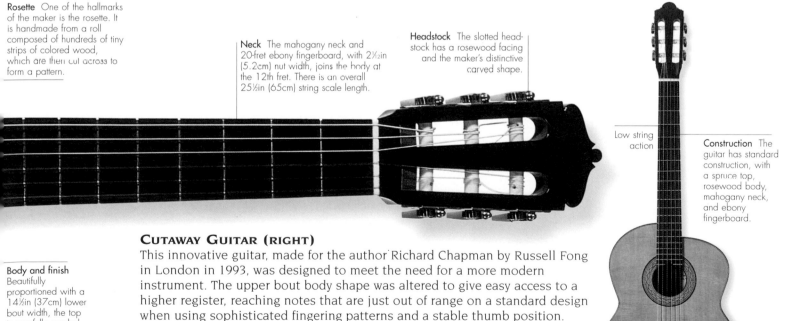

Rosette One of the hallmarks of the maker is the rosette. It is handmade from a roll composed of hundreds of tiny strips of colored wood, which are then cut across to form a pattern.

Neck The mahogany neck and 20-fret ebony fingerboard, with 2½in (5.2cm) nut width, joins the body at the 12th fret. There is an overall 25½in (65cm) string scale length.

Headstock The slotted headstock has a rosewood facing and the maker's distinctive carved shape.

Low string action

Construction The guitar has standard construction, with a spruce top, rosewood body, mahogany neck, and ebony fingerboard.

CUTAWAY GUITAR (RIGHT)

This innovative guitar, made for the author Richard Chapman by Russell Fong in London in 1993, was designed to meet the need for a more modern instrument. The upper bout body shape was altered to give easy access to a higher register, reaching notes that are just out of range on a standard design when using sophisticated fingering patterns and a stable thumb position. The neck joins the body one fret higher than normal, and a dropped shoulder on the treble side gives an extra two frets. The guitar has a rounded neck profile and the heel is cut in closer to the body than usual. Together, these structural changes let the player move three frets higher and play melodies, improvisation, and chords in a better register, similar to steel-string and electric guitars, while maintaining a beautiful full nylon-string sound.

Body and finish Beautifully proportioned with a 14½in (37cm) lower bout width, the top is carefully sanded for a superb tonal response. The instrument is finished with a light French polish made from shellac.

STEEL-STRING ACOUSTICS

THE DEVELOPMENT OF THE STEEL-STRING ACOUSTIC GUITAR

Steel strings
By 1928 steel strings had gained wide acceptance and replaced gut as the standard fitting on virtually all Martin models. Gut is virtually unknown today. Nylon strings, associated with classical guitars, appeared in the 1940s.

Steel strings have existed for centuries but were used widely only from the late 1800s. Their incisive cutting edge created an entirely new guitar sound, and their tone has became an integral part of American blues, folk, and country music as well as acoustic rock and pop. Today, these styles are played with steel strings throughout the world. The American acoustic guitar is differentiated from the classical and archtop guitars as a steel-string "flat-top" acoustic.

Bracing
Unlike the classical guitar, the American flat-top acoustic has an internal X-bracing, developed by Martin as a simple, effective support. German-born C.F. Martin moved to the US and founded his company, the premier American flat-top manufacturer, in 1833.

MARTIN 000-18 (BELOW)

With its mahogany body and functional design, the OOO-18 is one of the most popular mid-range Martin models. Its design changes describe the evolution of steel-string guitars. Small Style 18 guitars with a specific mix of woods and decoration were listed from 1857. In 1902 the demand for more volume led to the OOO body size with a 15in (38cm) lower bout width. The OOO-18 came out in 1911, with a rosewood body, cedar neck, and ebony fingerboard. It was offered primarily with steel strings from 1923. A solid headstock and 14-fret neck-to-body junction came in during 1934; a rosewood fingerboard from 1940. The modern OOO-18, with its metallic springy tone, has been popular with English folk guitarists such as Richard Thompson and Martin Carthy.

Saddle and bridge There is a compensating slanted saddle. The rosewood belly bridge has black pins with white eyes holding the strings.

Clear finish

Construction The spruce top is X-braced internally and has a round sound hole with three groups of black and white concentric ring inlays.

Body The OOO-18 was given a mahogany body and neck from 1917. The black binding came in during 1966. The lower bout width is 15in (38cm).

TWELVE-STRING ACOUSTICS

Guitars with doubled pairs of strings, termed courses, date from five centuries ago. After the ascendancy of six single strings, one of the few prominent guitars with 12 strings in the early 20th century was the interwar Stella instrument, used by many blues guitarists. Modern steel-string guitars with six pairs of strings became popular in the 1960s. The first 12-string guitar made by Martin in any numbers was the D12-20, which came out in 1964. The acoustic 12-string has a huge orchestral sound with a sensation of continual ringing. Folk virtuoso Leo Kottke and jazz and classical player Ralph Towner have used it to great effect.

MARTIN D12-28

The D12-28 was first produced in 1970. It has the Style 28 woods and decoration, and the D-shaped large body with square shoulders that was brought into full production by Martin in the 1930s. The guitar has the top two strings doubled at the same pitch. The four lower strings have an upper octave pair, which sits above the normal string and is struck first on a downstroke.

Large ebony pin bridge

Body The rosewood body has extra bracing to accommodate the increased string tension. The top is spruce.

Headstock with 12 tuners

Strings The overall string scale length is 25in (63.5cm).

Headstock The rosewood headstock facing has a gold Martin logo and tuners with metal buttons.

Sound There is a Fishman transducer pickup under the saddle and an internal microphone.

Neck The one-piece mahogany neck with a 20-fret unbound rosewood fingerboard with dot inlays joins the body at the 14th fret.

TAYLOR 714CE (RIGHT)

From 1931, Mario Maccaferri designed guitars with cutaways, played by Django Reinhardt. Gibson brought out a J160E acoustic with a fitted pickup in 1954, which the Beatles used. Yet acoustics with cutaways and fitted pickups did not become popular until the 1970s. The Taylor 714CE cedar-top electro-acoustic model from 1992 is high quality. The combination transducer and microphone gives attack and a full-bodied sound. It has a shimmering tone without strong bass, ideal for backing vocals and with other instruments. This guitar's Indian rosewood body has a sharp cutaway on the treble side, a two-piece back with center stripe, and a Western Red cedar top with a round sound hole with concentric ring inlays of koa wood and abalone.

ELECTRIC GUITARS

THE DEVELOPMENT OF THE ELECTRIC GUITAR

Manufacturers
Electric guitar making is dominated by Americans. After the Rickenbacker and Gibson models, the Fender Telecaster in 1950 triggered the manufacture of today's classic guitars in the 1950s and early 1960s. These include the Les Paul, 335, Stratocaster, and Flying V.

The electric guitar has become a design icon of the 20th century, instantly recognizable the world over as the mainstay of rock, pop, blues, jazz, and country music. The intitial experiments with electric guitars started in the 1920s, and the first full-production guitars were the Rickenbacker electro-Spanish models of 1932. In 1936 Gibson produced the ES-150, sparking a golden age of innovation and design in the 1940s and 1950s.

Fingerboard changes
In 1959 the Stratocaster acquired a rosewood fingerboard, which gives a slightly softer tone. Maple fingerboards returned as an option in the late 1960s.

FENDER STRATOCASTER (BELOW)

Launched in the spring of 1954 as the rock'n'roll era dawned, the Fender Stratocaster is the world's most famous electric guitar. Its aerodynamic shape suggested the advent of the space age. The guitar has been used by the most famous players in rock, blues, and pop, starting with Buddy Holly, Hank Marvin, and Buddy Guy. After the emergence of Jimi Hendrix, with his astonishing sounds and inspired playing, the Stratocaster was adopted by leading guitarists, such as Eric Clapton, Jeff Beck, Dave Gilmour, and, later, Mark Knopfler, Stevie Ray Vaughan, and Johnny Marr. Its sound ranges from thin, dry, and metallic through to a singing string that soars in the upper register with a colorful tone. Today, the Stratocaster is available in forms ranging from models that follow the look of the classic early series to extravagant "Custom Shop" models.

Bridge and tailpiece Six height- and length-adjustable metal saddles sit on the bridgeplate and tailblock assembly which tips forward and backward as a tremolo unit. It is held by two adjustable anchor posts.

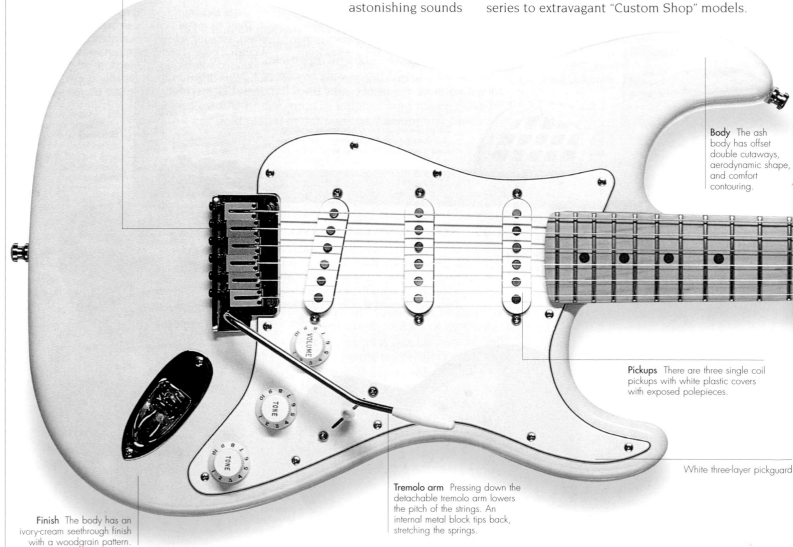

Body The ash body has offset double cutaways, aerodynamic shape, and comfort contouring.

Pickups There are three single coil pickups with white plastic covers with exposed polepieces.

White three-layer pickguard

Finish The body has an ivory-cream seethrough finish with a woodgrain pattern.

Tremolo arm Pressing down the detachable tremolo arm lowers the pitch of the strings. An internal metal block tips back, stretching the springs.

FENDER TELECASTER (BELOW)

The first mass-produced solid-body electric guitar, the Telecaster and its single pickup version the Esquire, were launched in 1950. Initially called Broadcasters, the name Telecaster came in during 1951. It is still a popular classic, particularly favored by country players and one of the major instruments in pop. Roy Buchanan, Albert Lee, James Burton, Danny Gatton, Keith Richards, Andy Summers, and Jonny Greenwood have all used Telecasters. The guitar has a tonal range from a plangent throaty twang to a cutting and chunky metallic edge ideal for rhythm. The construction of the Telecaster is straightforward. It has a flat solid body made from ash with a single cutaway. The solid maple neck

with an asymmetric headstock and cambered fingerboard has 21 frets and inset black dot markers. The neck is attached to the body with a rectangular metal neckplate held by four screws. A dark "skunk stripe" appears down the back where the neck is routed for a strengthening truss rod. The string scale length is 25½in (65cm). In the 1950s the guitar acquired a lighter cream finish and a white pickguard replaced the black one. In 1959 a rosewood fingerboard was introduced. Maple fingerboards came back in the late 1960s, and today Telecaster models reflect differing 1950s and 1960s classic designs. There was also a 1960s Custom model and a Thinline model from 1968 to 1978.

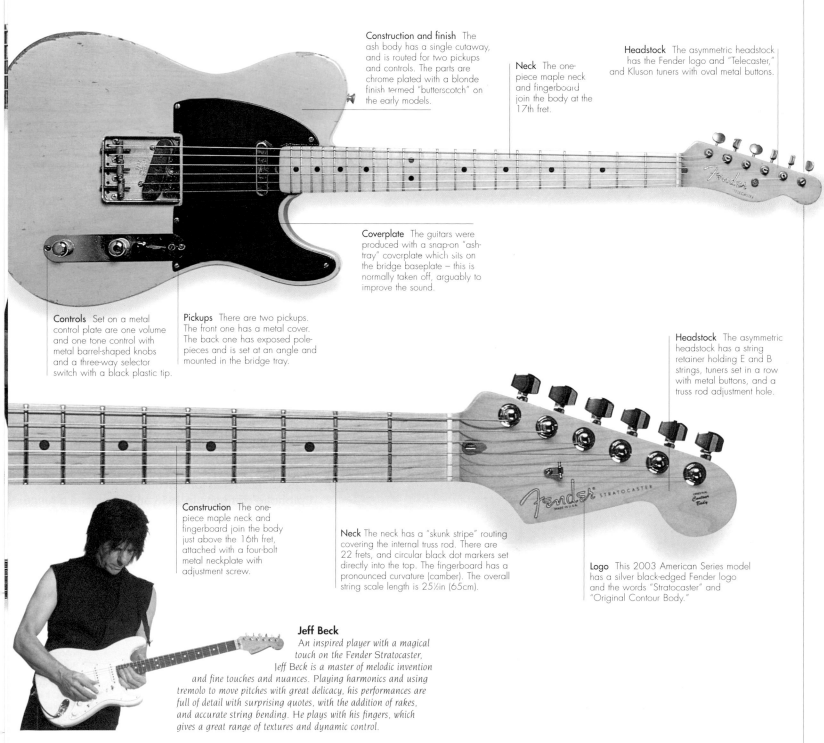

Construction and finish The ash body has a single cutaway, and is routed for two pickups and controls. The parts are chrome plated with a blonde finish termed "butterscotch" on the early models.

Neck The one-piece maple neck and fingerboard join the body at the 17th fret.

Headstock The asymmetric headstock has the Fender logo and "Telecaster," and Kluson tuners with oval metal buttons.

Coverplate The guitars were produced with a snap-on "ash-tray" coverplate which sits on the bridge baseplate – this is normally taken off, arguably to improve the sound.

Controls Set on a metal control plate are one volume and one tone control with metal barrel-shaped knobs and a three-way selector switch with a black plastic tip.

Pickups There are two pickups. The front one has a metal cover. The back one has exposed pole-pieces and is set at an angle and mounted in the bridge tray.

Headstock The asymmetric headstock has a string retainer holding E and B strings, tuners set in a row with metal buttons, and a truss rod adjustment hole.

Construction The one-piece maple neck and fingerboard join the body just above the 16th fret, attached with a four-bolt metal neckplate with adjustment screw.

Neck The neck has a "skunk stripe" routing covering the internal truss rod. There are 22 frets, and circular black dot markers set directly into the top. The fingerboard has a pronounced curvature (camber). The overall string scale length is 25½in (65cm).

Logo This 2003 American Series model has a silver black-edged Fender logo and the words "Stratocaster" and "Original Contour Body."

Jeff Beck

An inspired player with a magical touch on the Fender Stratocaster, Jeff Beck is a master of melodic invention and fine touches and nuances. Playing harmonics and using tremolo to move pitches with great delicacy, his performances are full of detail with surprising quotes, with the addition of rakes, and accurate string bending. He plays with his fingers, which gives a great range of textures and dynamic control.

SOLID-BODY ELECTRIC GUITAR CONSTRUCTION

After more than forty years of production, the Telecaster, inspired by Leo Fender's early Broadcaster guitar, remains an industry standard – a tribute to its creator and the excellence of its simple design. The straight-sided, single-cutaway slab body carries the hardware and pickups, and the detachable rock-maple neck is secured by four woodscrews. The single-sided headstock allows the strings to run straight over the nut to the machine heads: a *string tree* is required on the 1st and 2nd strings to provide sufficient angle over the nut. The strings are threaded from the back and pass through the body over the six individual saddles, allowing height and intonation adjustment for each string. Early Telecasters had only three saddles, which led to a compromise on intonation accuracy. The ball-ends of the string rest in six string *ferrules* in the back of the body. There have been many different types of Telecaster produced, including those with humbucking pickups, tremolo arms, and the semi-hollow "thinline" body style.

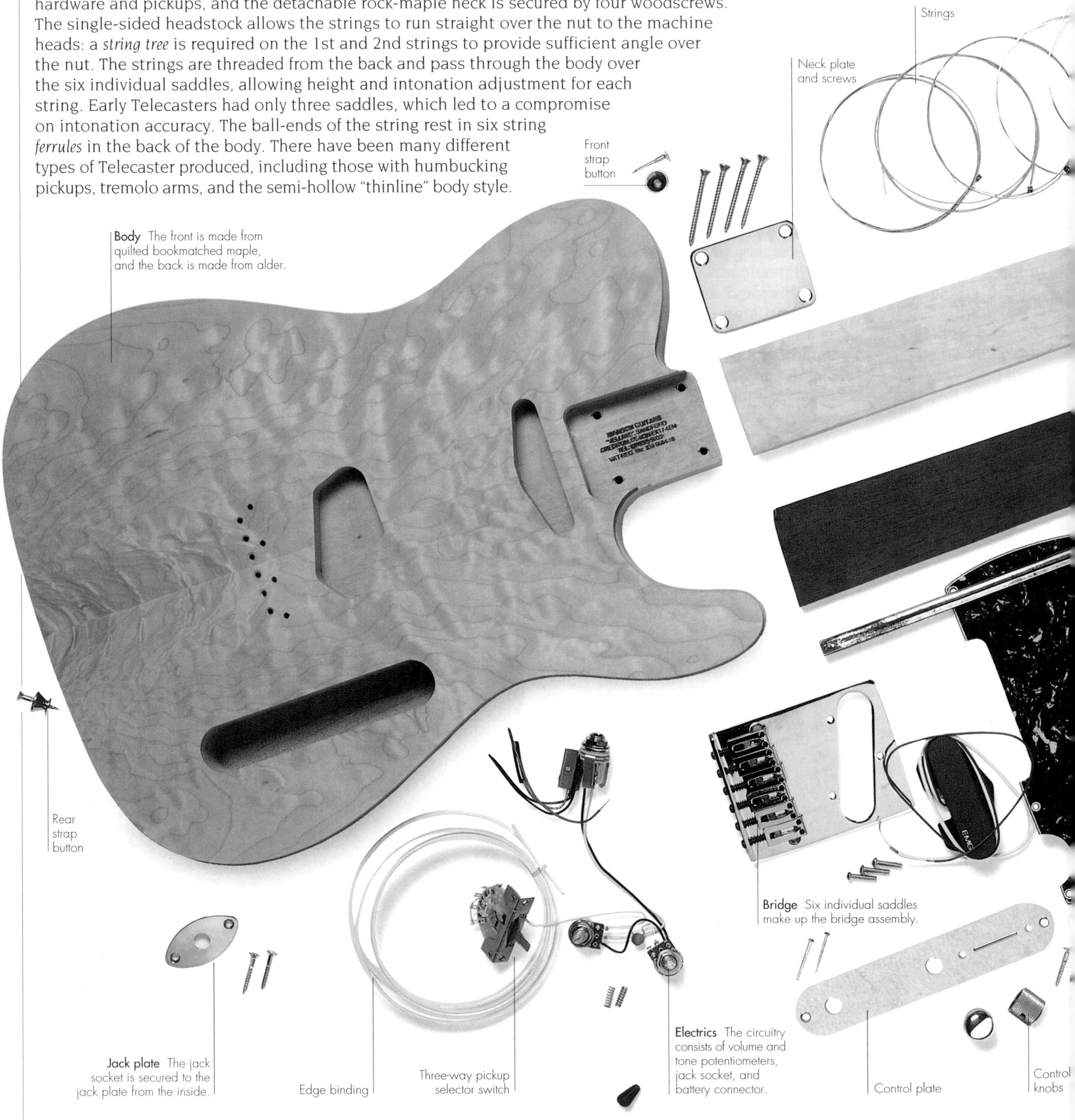

Strings

Neck plate and screws

Front strap button

Body The front is made from quilted bookmatched maple, and the back is made from alder.

Rear strap button

Bridge Six individual saddles make up the bridge assembly.

Jack plate The jack socket is secured to the jack plate from the inside.

Edge binding

Three-way pickup selector switch

Electrics The circuitry consists of volume and tone potentiometers, jack socket, and battery connector.

Control plate

Control knobs

Schaller machine heads

Neck The neck is made from hard rock maple.

Nickel silver frets

Ebony fingerboard

Truss rod

Pickup

Custom-made guitars
Hand-built instruments can usually be custom-ordered to meet a player's specific requirements. For example, the controls and pickups may be back-routed so that they are set into the body without a mounting plate or a pickguard surround.

Tortoiseshell scratch plate

CONTEMPORARY TELECASTER DESIGN

On this model, produced by Hugh Manson, Telecaster styling is combined with modern refinements that include 22 frets, a compound radius fingerboard, and a graphite nut. The alder body has a maple front with a vintage sunburst finish of hand-polished lacquer. Regular Telecaster pickups are replaced by a set made by EMG that give a low-noise, low-impedance output and impart harmonic sweetness, to which the ceramic magnets add clear, bright treble notes. The bridge allows for the adjustment of individual string height and intonation, and the Schaller machine heads facilitate precise tuning. The hardware on this instrument is chrome-plated.

String tree

Graphite nut

Neck This guitar features neck made from "Bird's-eye" maple.

String ferrules

ELECTRICS
The Telecaster has two pickups – a small single-coil unit (*rhythm* pickup) which sits near the end of the neck, and a larger single-coil unit (*lead* pickup) set at an angle into the bridge assembly to balance treble and bass response. This pickup provides the famous cutting treble "Tele" sound. The pickups are controlled by a three-way selector switch allowing the use of either or both pickups. There is one volume control and one tone control. When a guitar is fitted with a traditional passive pickup, a treble bleed capacitor is wired to the volume control. This prevents treble being lost as the volume is turned down.

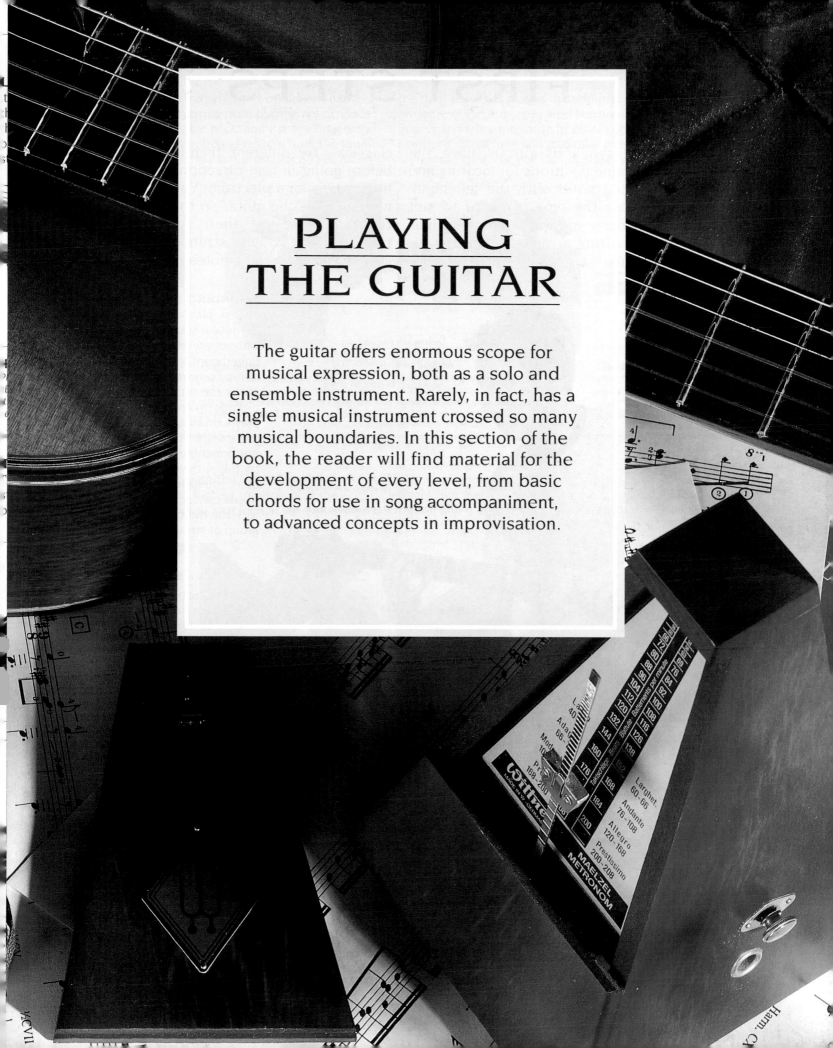

PLAYING THE GUITAR

The guitar offers enormous scope for musical expression, both as a solo and ensemble instrument. Rarely, in fact, has a single musical instrument crossed so many musical boundaries. In this section of the book, the reader will find material for the development of every level, from basic chords for use in song accompaniment, to advanced concepts in improvisation.

FUNDAMENTALS

UNDERSTANDING THE GUITAR

To play the guitar, you need to understand the fingerboard and recognize note positions. Standard guitars have six strings running along a fingerboard: they provide the means to play notes. Metal frets sit at intervals all along the fingerboard: they divide the smallest degree of pitch between each note. When you press a string against a fret and strike it with the right hand, it vibrates between the fret and the bridge. The length, thickness, and tension of the string set the frequency of the soundwaves.

Easy learning
Most of the musical examples in this book are in the key of C major and its related minor key. As a framework for memorizing and comparing sections of music, C major is one of the simplest keys. As soon as you understand elements in this key, follow the suggestions for repeating the material in all other keys.

NOTES AND SYMBOLS ON THE STAVE

Music is written down using a five-line grid called a stave. Each line and space is used to place a symbol that represents the pitch and time-value of a note. The first seven letters of the alphabet, A to G, are used to name the notes. A stylized letter G

(𝄞) – known as a treble clef – fixes the second line of the stave as the note G. Notes that sit above and below the stave are placed on ledger lines. To make guitar music easy to read, the notes on the fingerboard are written one octave (C to C, for instance) higher than their actual

pitch. Middle C occurs on the 1st fret of the 2nd string, not on the 3rd fret of the 5th string. When reading music not written specifically for the guitar, remember to play it one octave higher. The octave change is particularly apparent if you play melodies too low.

Notes on the treble stave
*Memorize the notes on the treble stave and their positions with simple mnemonic phrases. The notes **on** the stave lines are, from bottom to top, E-G-B-D-F. Remember them by the first letter in each word of the phrases "**E**at **G**ood **B**read **D**ear **F**ather" or "**E**very **G**ood **B**oy **D**eserves **F**avour". The notes in between the stave lines are F-A-C-E, spelling the word "**FACE**".*

The stave and open strings
*The six open-string (using right hand only, with no left-hand fret position) notes on the guitar can be placed on the stave using symbols. The lowest note **E** corresponds to the open 6th string on the guitar. **A** is the open 5th string; **D** the open 4th string; **G** the open 3rd string; **B** the open 2nd string; and **E** is the open 1st string.*

RANGE OF THE GUITAR

The full range of notes available in standard tuning is shown on the stave. The top notes of an acoustic guitar normally range between B and D. Electric guitars have a higher range, which varies from C# to E. On many Fender guitars, C# is the top note. On 22-fret guitars (such as Gibsons) the top note is D. 24-fret electric guitars have a top note of E.

Fret The metal fret determines the pitch of the note. The letter shows the note played when the finger sits below it on the "fret position."

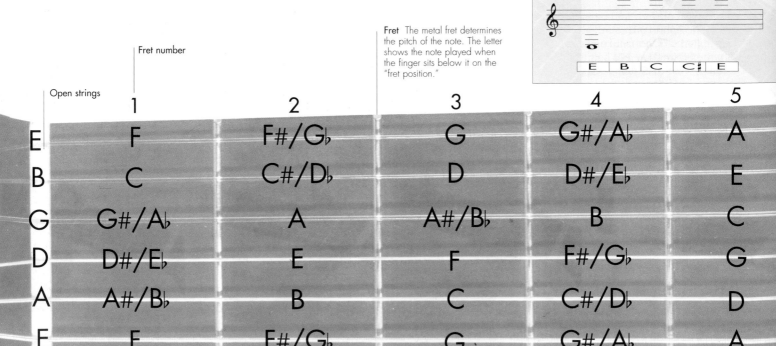

SCALE ON THE 5TH STRING

The interval between any 12 chromatic steps on the fingerboard, such as the open 1st string and the 12th fret of the 1st string, is an octave. Each of the 12 steps is called a semitone. An interval of two frets is called a tone. To name every semitonal step, the letters A to G have intermediate names: they are raised by adding sharps (#), and lowered by adding flats (♭). A natural (♮) cancels a sharp or flat. The interval between B and C is a semitone. A tone is twice the interval, such as F to G. Using the 5th string as an example, the order of note names runs from the open string (the note A), through the chromatic series up to the 12th fret, when it is repeated on the octave. The octave here is the note A, which vibrates at twice the frequency of the open string A, giving a higher register of the same pitch.

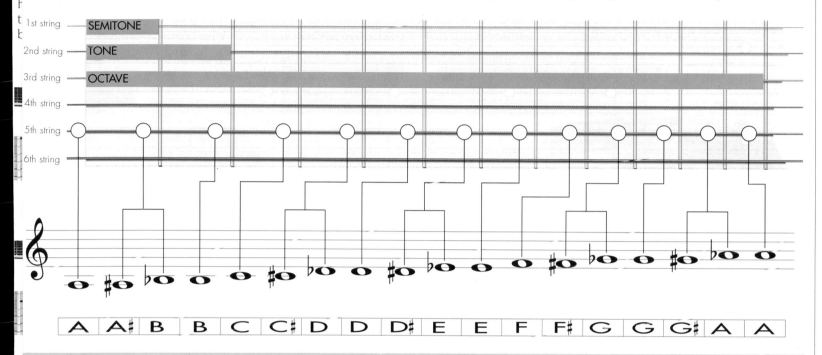

| A | A♯ | B | B | C | C♯ | D | D | D♯ | E | E | F | F♯ | G | G | G♯ | A | A |

NUMBERS AND LETTERS

Below is a standard guitar fingerboard with the fret numbers indicated above. Every open string and fret position has its own letter name, corresponding to the 12 chromatic semitones (steps) of an octave on the fingerboard. Every semitone is the musical interval between one fret.

So each string runs in a chromatic series of 12 semitones from its open note up to the 12th fret. At this point the series is repeated. Playing these notes is one way to ascend through a series of semitones on the guitar. The same notes also occur at other points on the fingerboard, and in higher and lower octaves.

12th fret The series of notes repeat themselves with the open E occurring one octave higher. The same series of notes starts again with F from the 13th fret upward.

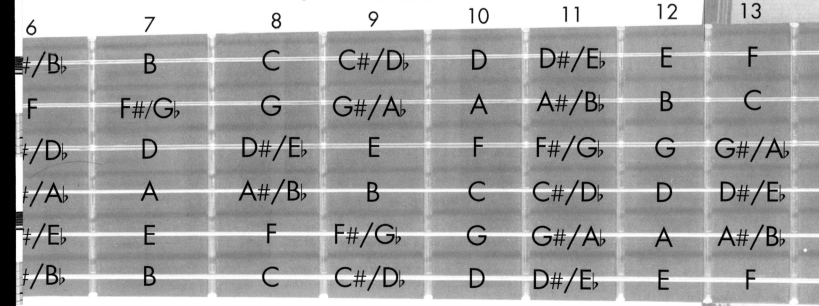

PLAYING POSITIONS

ADOPTING THE CORRECT POSTURE FOR PLAYING THE GUITAR

Playing different instruments
The type of guitar affects ease of playing. For example, a classical guitar with large, heavy strings and a high action, and a modern electric with light-gauge strings and a low action require completely different levels of pressure when the notes are fretted.

When playing the guitar, it is essential to adopt a relaxed and comfortable position. For beginners, the sitting positions are easiest. Most guitarists rest the instrument in their lap, supporting it with either the left or right leg for stability and control. Many live performers, though, play standing up, with the guitar supported by a strap. To an experienced electric guitarist, this can become the most natural way to play.

Stretching the hand
Nearly all guitar music requires left-hand stretching that initially feels awkward and causes difficulties. As an exercise to prepare the hands for playing, open out the fingers of the left hand, stretching them gently.

Acoustic posture
The standard posture is to rest the guitar on the right leg. This allows the guitarist to sit in a comfortable and relaxed position.

Head Beginners need to look down at the strings.

Right arm
Pressure from the right arm holds the guitar steady.

Shoulders
Relax the shoulders.

Legs Keep legs parallel, feet flat on the floor.

POSTURE WITH A CLASSICAL GUITAR
When sitting down, classical players rest the waist of the guitar's body on the left leg. The neck is angled upward so that the left arm can easily reach the fingerboard. The right arm rests on the edge of the upper rim of the body. The left foot is often placed on a small stool to bring the left leg up to a higher position. In this standard posture, the weight of the instrument is well supported. Some players in other styles use this or a similar position.

Head Look ahead or at the strings, whichever is comfortable.

Right arm
The forearm is parallel to the floor.

Right leg
Point the right leg out at a comfortable angle.

Footstool
Use an adjustable footstool so you can find the best leg height.

ACOUSTIC GUITAR POSITION
A popular and natural sitting position for playing acoustic guitars is with the instrument resting on the right leg. The inside of the right arm keeps the guitar in place and prevents it from tipping forward or sideways. The right arm is drawn back, resting against the guitar with the forearm diagonal to the strings. The neck is close to the player's body. This gives a comfortable left-arm position for playing any guitar.

Classical posture
The orthodox classical posture is for the waist of the instrument to rest on the left leg. To achieve the correct neck angle, raise your left foot on a footstool or other support. This raises the height of the guitar, helping the left-arm position and your overall posture.

STANDING UP

With the support of a strap, any type of guitar can be played in a standing position. It is important to let the instrument hang from the strap, with its weight against the body and a good center of gravity. This leaves the hands and arms free for easy access and comfortable movement. With many modern pop players, it is fashionable to place the guitar in a low position. Although this may be visually desirable, it makes the instrument harder to play and is not recommended for beginners.

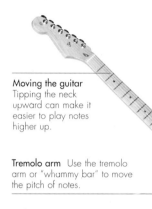

Arm The right arm is crooked to form a triangle.

Strap support Standing up should feel comfortable when the guitar is supported by a strap.

Thumb You can place the thumb on the upper edge of the neck for some playing positions.

Legs Keep the weight on both feet when standing still.

Electric guitar posture
All electric guitars are designed primarily for a performance-style standing position. For a practical left-hand position, tilt the neck upward. The posture should feel comfortable when a strap supports the electric guitar.

Sitting down with an electric guitar
Small electric solid-body guitars have a low playing position, close to the body. Larger electric guitars with acoustic proportions are played with a more normal posture. You may need a strap even when sitting down to support and balance the weight of the guitar.

PLAYING LEFT-HANDED

For the many left-handed musicians, it is entirely acceptable to play with the guitar the other way around. Try the guitar both ways – even some left-handers prefer to play right-handed. It is a matter of which way feels instinctively correct and which gives easier control and hand coordination. If you play a symmetrical acoustic guitar or a right-handed electric guitar upside down, change the strings. The thinnest, high-pitch strings must be at the bottom.

Moving the guitar
Tipping the neck upward can make it easier to play notes higher up.

Tremolo arm Use the tremolo arm or "whammy bar" to move the pitch of notes.

Standing posture
There are guitars designed specially for left-handed people. They are made and strung so that they are mirror images of right-handed guitars. Whether left- or right-handed, standing up with the guitar can give a creative feeling of freedom and rhythmic movement. There is nothing wrong with playing "air guitar" with the real thing.

Express yourself Many players find it exciting and inspiring to move around with an electric guitar.

Mirror image
The chord below is the chord of E minor for the left-handed player looking down at the fingerboard. It is a mirror image of the chord on the right, which is a right-hander's view of E minor. Throughout the book, left-handers should treat all images of guitar necks, chord boxes and superimposed scale patterns as mirror images.

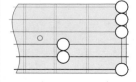
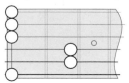

STARTING TO PLAY

PLAYING YOUR FIRST CHORD SEQUENCE ON THE GUITAR

Numbering
The fingers on the left hand are given numbers from one to four, starting with the index finger. The diagrams for playing include numbers that represent the fingerings used for playing chords and single notes. The numbers are shown inside circles, which are positioned just below the fret. Circles without numbers, over the nut, represent open strings.

When two or more notes are played at the same time, the effect is called a *chord*. One of the simplest ways to begin playing is to construct basic chord shapes on open-string positions. The strings are tuned so that standard chords can be produced when the fingers are placed in certain set patterns. *Harmony* is the term used for the arrangement of notes and chords in a musical structure. It is very easy to produce chordal harmony by brushing the right-hand fingers across the strings. The left-hand fingers press strings against the fingerboard to create fretted notes. This action will make the fingertips sore at first, but the problem will soon pass; with practice, the skin will harden and the muscles of the left hand will become stronger.

First notes
Play the individual guitar strings by picking one string at a time. Without playing any fretted notes or chords, pick the 1st string with the index finger of the right hand. Pick each string from the 1st to the 6th, and as each open string note is plucked, try not to hit any other strings.

INTRODUCTION TO FINGERING

Chords are formed by using one or more fingers to press the strings down on a fretted position. With *open-string* voicings, the fretted notes are combined with open strings. The fingers must remain in the correct position behind the fret so that the notes ring clearly without buzzing. Forming chords tends to stretch the hand and fingers into uncomfortable positions at first. Depending on the size of the hand, reaching some notes can be difficult. On many of the chord shapes, the fingers may feel bunched together. The third and fourth fingers will have less strength than the first two; extra practice and patience are needed to develop accuracy in using them. The fingers must hold the pressure on the notes after they have been played to keep them ringing.

1 *Play an A on the open 5th string. Put the second finger on the 2nd fret of the 5th string and play the note B.*

2 *Add the third finger next to the second finger, placing it on the 2nd fret of the 4th string to play the note E.*

3 *Holding the two notes down firmly, strum across all six strings with the first or second finger of the right hand.*

Forming an E minor chord

Before attempting to play the full E minor chord, build up to the chord shape by playing each fretted element separately. Pick the open A on the 5th string carefully either with an upstroke of the first or second finger of the right hand, or with a downstroke of the thumb. Place the second finger of the left hand on the 2nd fret of the 5th string, forming the note B. Play this note and then take the finger off the string. Now place the third finger of the left hand on the 2nd fret of the 4th string, forming the note E, and play this with the right hand. Take the third finger away. Place both the second and third fingers back on these note positions at the same time and strum all six strings with a downstroke. This is a full E minor chord. With practice, you will be able to place the fingers of the left hand on a chord position as one movement.

TABLATURE

The tablature system is widely used when writing down guitar music and is often included as a complement to the staff. Tablature indicates the positions for playing notes and chords and the order in which they are to be played. Some systems add symbols to indicate time, rhythm, and techniques. The guitar strings are depicted as six horizontal lines running from left to right. Numbers placed on the lines show the fret positions. For example, the number 3 on the top line represents the 3rd fret of the 1st string. A group of numbers running along the lines indicates a series of notes that are to be played one after the other in sequence.

Chords in tablature

The lines and numbers shown on a tablature diagram correspond to the individual strings and the fret numbers found on the fingerboard. Whenever the numbers are shown in a vertical line, play all the notes indicated at the same time; i.e., play them as a chord.

Arpeggios in tablature

Whenever numbers in tablature are written from left to right, play the notes one after the other in sequence. The tablature diagram below shows an E minor chord with each of the notes sounded separately. This way of playing a chord is termed an "arpeggio."

Single-note movements

It is also possible to indicate single-note movements in tablature by writing the numbers from left to right. In the sequence shown below, begin by playing an open A, followed by B on the 2nd fret, C on the 3rd fret, and an open D. These movements constitute a simple four-note scale.

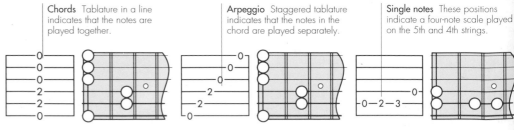

Chords Tablature in a line indicates that the notes are played together.

Arpeggio Staggered tablature indicates that the notes in the chord are played separately.

Single notes These positions indicate a four-note scale played on the 5th and 4th strings.

INTRODUCING CHORDS

Using only a small number of chord types, it is possible to develop a basis for playing with other instruments or accompanying songs. Each of these chords should be learned, both visually and by name. At first, building a chord one note at a time is useful, but eventually the chord must be formed by placing the fingers accurately in position at the same time. Every note in the chord should ring clearly: notes must not buzz against the frets, and open strings must not be muffled by adjacent fingers.

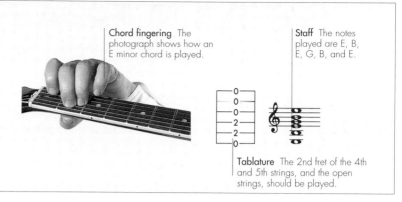

Chord charts
The chord notation system used in this book features a fingerboard photograph, a diagram that shows fingering positions, a small block of tablature, and the notes of the chord on a traditional staff. Circled numbers on the diagram show which fret to play on and which finger to use when playing notes on the fingerboard.

Chord fingering The photograph shows how an E minor chord is played.

Staff The notes played are E, B, E, G, B, and E.

Tablature The 2nd fret of the 4th and 5th strings, and the open strings, should be played.

E MINOR The E minor chord shape consists of the notes E, B, E, G, B, and E. All six strings are played at the same time.

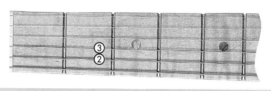
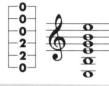

E MAJOR The E major chord shape consists of the notes E, B, E, G♯, B, and E. All six strings are played at the same time.

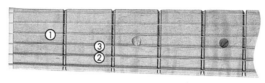
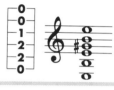

A MINOR The A minor chord shape consists of the five notes A, E, A, C, and E. The 5th to the 1st strings are played.

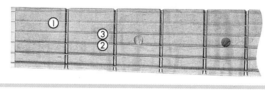
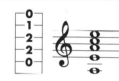

D MAJOR The D major chord shape consists of the four notes D, A, D, and F♯. The 4th to the 1st strings are played.

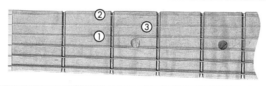
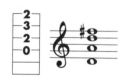

PLAYING A CHORD SEQUENCE

The exercises on the right show the chords learned above linked together in a short musical sequence. In each case, voicings and names should be memorized. To begin with, chord changes should be practiced slowly and speed built up gradually. The first movement simply changes an E minor to an E major by adding the first finger to the shape. Once this change can be made smoothly, the second chord change – to an A minor – should be tried. This shape is the same as E major, with the E fingering simply moved across to the 2nd, 3rd, and 4th strings. The final chord change – from A minor to D major – requires the biggest jump in technique and should be practiced separately. A common mistake when first playing D major is to strike the 5th and 6th strings, which are not part of the chord, but this will be remedied by practice.

E minor
Place the second finger on the 5th string 2nd fret, and the third finger on the 4th string 2nd fret. This forms E minor. Strum the chord gently downward with the right hand.

E major
While still holding down the E minor chord, change it to E major by adding the first finger to the 1st fret of the 3rd string. Again, strum the chord downward with the right hand.

A minor
Take the three fingers away from the E major position and move this shape across from the 3rd, 4th, and 5th strings to the 2nd, 3rd, and 4th strings to form the A minor chord.

D major
Take the fingers away from the A minor shape. Place the first finger on the 3rd string 2nd fret, the second on the 1st string 2nd fret, and the third on the 2nd string 3rd fret.

E MIN	E MAJ	A MIN	D MAJ

SCALES AND TIMING

AN INTRODUCTION TO FORMING SCALES AND UNDERSTANDING TEMPO

Introducing scales
Melody and harmony are based on the organization of individual notes into an ordered succession. This sequence is termed a *scale*. Most scales used in western classical music are made up of a pattern of seven notes, with fixed intervals within an octave.

Having linked together a series of chords, the next step is to pick out individual notes and play them as scales. To play any sort of scale structure, or *melody*, it is important to develop the ability to play notes evenly and build timing control. To play a scale, the left hand must be able to pick out each individual note clearly. To be effective, the right hand must be coordinated with the left. These skills are vital in laying the foundations for playing correctly.

Scale positions
The guitar is constructed in such a way that the same notes can be played in different positions on the fingerboard. The same scale can be played by moving along one string or across different strings. This choice can lead to difficulties in positional thinking.

FINGERING ON ONE STRING
The first step toward developing single-note technique is to play a five-note chromatic scale on the top string of the guitar. For this exercise, each finger is used for a fret. As each new note is played, any previous note held is released.

Fingering technique
The scale on the left is composed of semitone intervals running from the open top E string to the G♯/A♭ on the 4th fret. This series of intervals is not melodic but provides an ideal starting point for the development of technique by building toward an equal facility with each finger of the left hand. Break the scale down to a one-note movement between each of the fingers.

E

F

F♯

G

G♯

G

F♯

F

E

C MAJOR SCALE
The major scale is the primary order of tones and semitones. Each note is termed a *degree* of the scale, the first note of the scale being the first degree, or *keynote*. The major scale always has the following ascending order of tones and semitones: tone-tone-semitone-tone-tone-tone-semitone. This sequence of intervals can be repeated in any octave. A major scale pattern can be built from any note on the fingerboard. The notes in the C major scale have letter names without sharps (♯) or flats (♭) – they are the same as the white notes on a piano keyboard. These notes occur in all registers of the fingerboard. To play a C major scale on the guitar, the lowest C – the 3rd fret of the 5th string – must be located. The seven-note scale ascends from this point.

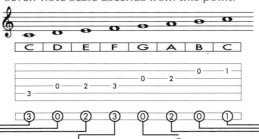

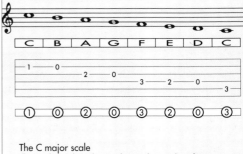

The C major scale
The scale is played as a descending order of notes from the key note C on the 1st fret of the 2nd string.

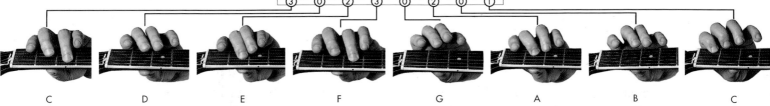

C

D

E

F

G

A

B

C

MELODY EXERCISES
By varying the sequence of notes in the C major scale, a series of patterns and melodies may be created. Two passages are shown as examples on the right. After carefully picking them out, try to create your own single-note lines.

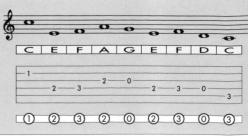

RHYTHM AND TIMING

Rhythm and time is the framework within which the notes are placed to define their character and effect. Up until now, chords and scales have been played as a sequence of movements without any sort of strict time value. However, virtually all music is played or written down using an ordered system for the duration and position of musical sounds. Once the left hand has become reasonably comfortable when forming the E major and A minor chord shapes, the next logical step is to develop smooth and even movement between chords, creating a basic rhythmic structure. With practice, coordination between the hands will gradually improve, paving the way for playing chord changes in a set period of time.

TEMPO AND QUARTER-NOTE SPEED

As the beat in music can vary in speed, the amount of time between each beat changes: this is referred to as the *tempo*. The *quarter note* is often used as a reference point for tempo. A quarter note written with a number next to it indicates how many are played during each minute. For example, if a quarter note is marked as ♩=60, the rate of movement in the music is one quarter-note beat per second.

METRONOMES AND SOUND SOURCES

Using a source to provide an even beat can be of great help when trying to acquire basic rhythmic coordination. The "click" from a metronome, or a regular beat from a drum machine or sequencer, can be adjusted to provide a comfortable speed to strike chords and individual notes. This will help to develop the ability to coincide right-hand movement with the beat.

Playing in time

Play the eight quarter-note beats slowly and evenly, counting to four seconds between each chord. Still counting at the same speed, play a chord every two seconds – this doubles the tempo. Working up to playing a chord every second requires practice. Playing along with a metronome or drum machine helps develop timing.

Quarter notes

This bar contains four quarter notes. It represents the note A played four times with an equal lapse of time between each note.

Time signature of four beats to the bar.

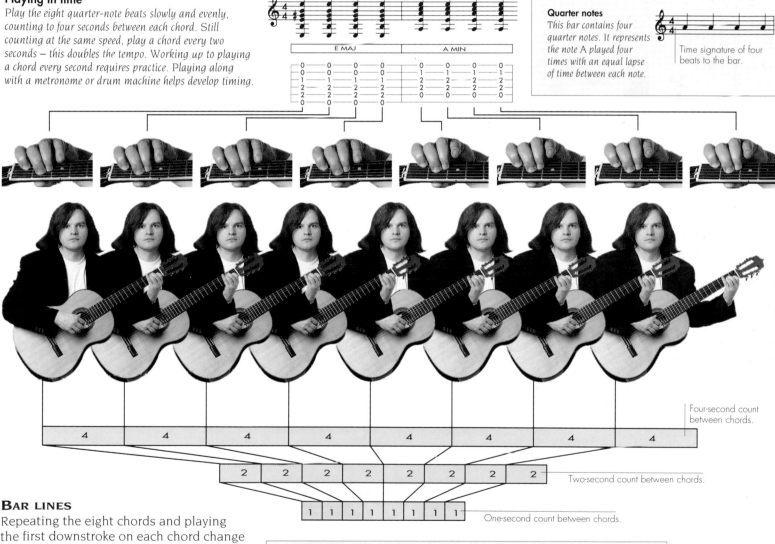

Four-second count between chords.

Two-second count between chords.

One-second count between chords.

BAR LINES

Repeating the eight chords and playing the first downstroke on each chord change with a greater volume gives an accent to each group of four beats. Each of the accented groups is separated by a bar line that denotes its overall rhythmic length and structure. The two numbers at the beginning of a bar show the *time signature* – a grouping of four quarter-note beats is 4/4 (*four-four*) time. Groups of three notes (3/4), and two notes (2/4) can also be played.

Time signature of 2/4

The top figure (2) represents the number of beats in the bar, and the bottom figure (4) represents quarter notes.

Time signature of 3/4

There are three quarter notes per bar, implying a structure with three beats. This time signature is termed "waltz" or "triple" time.

FLATPICK TECHNIQUE

DEVELOPING RIGHT-HAND PLAYING TECHNIQUE

Pick types
Picks are produced in a wide variety of shapes, sizes, and materials. The shape of a pick can influence your technique and movement. The size and thickness of a pick affects the tone and color produced from contact with the strings. Try the various types available. Acoustic players often favor a thin pick, whereas thicker, rigid types are usually preferred for soloing on an electric guitar.

The standard pick, or plectrum, is a flat, triangular piece of plastic held between the first finger and thumb. The majority of electric and steel-string acoustic guitarists use picks. Many of the sounds and styles in popular music stem from the use of the pick, which lends itself naturally to the block chords and solos associated with blues, jazz, and rock. Its use is essential for fast soloing and achieving the texture, nuances, and tone on an electric guitar. The pick is also used to create tightly played, percussive, rhythmic chordal patterns. As the point of contact with the strings, playing with a pick produces a strong, clear, and even tone.

Picking direction
The key to developing a good pick technique is mastering the upstroke and downstroke. In the diagrams shown throughout this book, stroking directions are shown below the staff and tablature. The symbol "⊓" represents a downstroke, and "v" represents an upstroke. A passage of notes can be played using different combinations of pick strokes depending on the desired effect or musical context.

HOLDING THE PICK

Accurate pick movement with a relaxed position is essential for playing with any degree of control and for eliminating tension. Guitarists tend to play by swiveling the wrist and forearm, and moving the joints of the thumb and fingers. Picking technique uses a combination of these elements to varying degrees.

Pick position
The pick must be pointed directly down, toward the body of the guitar. It is important that you do not allow it to turn around as you use it to pick the strings. Keep the flat body of the pick in line with the strings in order to ensure free movement and control.

Gripping the pick
Hold the pick between the side of the top joint of the first finger and the bottom of the first joint of the thumb. Your grip should be firm enough to stop the pick moving out of position as it strikes the strings. The second, third, and fourth fingers should be curved inward.

Stability
Rest the inside of the right arm on the guitar, keeping the right hand away from the body to give free movement to the arm. Alternatively, to give more stability, rest the side of the hand or fingers on either the body, pickguard, or bridge. Take care to avoid accidentally muting strings.

Striking the string
Play the top E string with a downstroke. The tip of the pick should touch the strings evenly and make just enough contact with the string to produce a full tone. If you hit the string with too much body, it can impede movement when passages of notes are being played.

Parallel position
Ensure that the tip of the pick is parallel to the strings. This produces a clear attack on the note and makes pick movement easier to control during fast passages. Turn the pick to an angled position in relation to the strings to produce a fuller sound with more color.

PICKING TECHNIQUE

To control picking technique properly it is important to be able to play a series of single notes on the guitar using all types of directional movement. Fast passages of notes are played much more economically by using alternate strokes – an upstroke after a downstroke as a single movement. Speed and fluency are developed in this way to achieve a high level of control for playing scales, melodies, and improvised solos. The ability to play a series of repeated downstrokes or upstrokes is also necessary for controlling tone, rhythmic phrasing, and other advanced playing techniques. The exercises on the right are designed to develop a thorough grounding in pick control. At this stage, simple downstrokes, upstrokes, and then more advanced combinations of both are played on an open string.

Downstrokes
Play four downstrokes, using similar volume and attack for all of them. As you position the pick for the repeat downstroke, avoid hitting the string.

Upstrokes
Play four upstrokes with a similar level of volume and attack. The upstroke movement is important for balancing the overall control of the pick.

Alternating
Pick a downstroke, then an upstroke. Repeat, using an even motion. Passages are usually played with alternating strokes for economy of movement.

Directional control
Play two downstrokes followed by two upstrokes. Using different directional movements is important when single notes are played across the strings.

PICKING A SCALE

A short succession of notes, such as part of a scale or a melody, can be played using a combination of alternate pick movements on a single string. When moving from one string to another, it is helpful if the pick is on the correct side of the string just played, ready to play the next adjacent string.

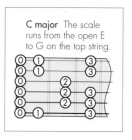

C major The scale is built on the four middle strings only.

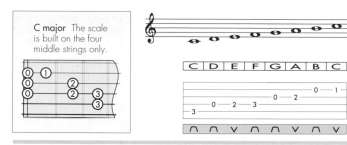

Picking C major

Play C and D as downstrokes, then E and F using alternate picking. Play the open G as a downstroke followed by A as an upstroke. Play the open B as a downstroke, and complete the movement with an upstroke on C.

Extending C major

The C major scale on the right has been extended to cover all the notes on the open-string position. Play up and down this extended scale with the pick. Take small sections of two- and three-note movements from any position and work on achieving a smooth, comfortable action. If possible, play these scale movements against a drum machine or metronome. This will help you to develop an accurate, balanced technique.

C major The scale runs from the open E to G on the top string.

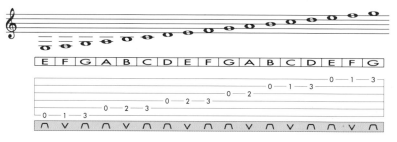

CHORD STRUMMING TECHNIQUE

Some of the basic principles of movement for playing single notes with a pick are applied to strumming. The pick should be parallel to the strings, and the arc of movement should not take the hand too far away when a stroke has been played. The hand should not rest against the face of the guitar. The inside of the forearm can rest on the edge of the body, but the hand and forearm must be free to make a sweeping movement across the strings.

The downstroke

Downstroke technique is important for strumming chords: a fast downward sweep, playing every note, is the main method of playing vertical harmony with a pick. Play a full downstroke across the open strings, followed by the E major chord.

E major down The order of notes when E major is played with a downstroke is E, B, E, G#, B, and E.

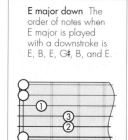

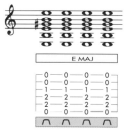

Downstrokes The E major chord is played as a series of four downstrokes.

The upstroke

Play an upstroke, using a movement similar to the downstroke. Build up control by playing the same series of single note directional exercises shown on the previous page. Start with loose alternate strumming and then move on to disciplined strokes.

E major up The order of notes when E major is played with an upstroke is E, B, G#, E, B, and E.

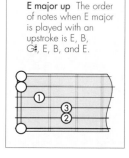

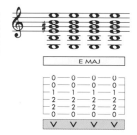

Upstrokes The E major chord is played as a series of four upstrokes.

Alternating strokes

Play four downstrokes followed by four upstrokes. Reduce this to two of each, moving back to alternate strumming. Now play E to A minor, first using downstrokes, then with upstrokes, and finally with alternate movements.

E major Play all the notes of the E major chord on both the downstroke and the upstroke.

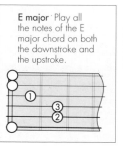

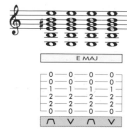

Alternating E major is played as a downstroke followed by an upstroke.

FURTHER TECHNIQUES

Move the pick slowly across the E major chord, so that each note can be heard separately. This sound is called an arpeggio – a succession of chord notes. Variations can be played by picking out individual notes to form patterns of arpeggios. The first exercise below is based on a pattern on the E major arpeggio.

Arpeggio on an E major chord

Using a series of downstrokes, play the 6th, 4th, and 3rd strings. Repeat the 4th string, this time as an upstroke. Pass over the 3rd string and play the 2nd string as a downstroke. Finally, play an upstroke on the 3rd string. This style of breaking a chord into single notes can be used to develop a number of melodic variations.

Bass notes with a chord

Using a downstroke, play the 6th string, then pass over the 5th string and strum the top four strings together with a downstroke. Then, using a downstroke, play the 5th string, and then strum the top four strings together with a downstroke. Repeat this sequence, trying to keep even time. This style of playing is commonly heard in country music or as an accompaniment to popular ballads.

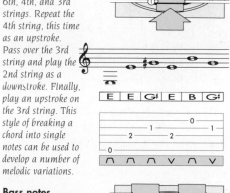

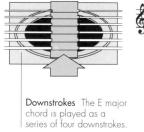

BASIC CHORDS

EXTENDING YOUR CHORD VOCABULARY

Chords can be constructed with two or more notes, using any combination of positions on the guitar. Every chord has a letter name and a short definition of its harmonic structure. Most guitar chords are named from the root, which is usually the lowest-pitched note. The root is the reference point from which a chord is built. The open-string position forms an initial area for playing where basic chord types can be formed, using fretted notes and open strings. A small group of chord types are commonly used in guitar music, primarily the major, minor, and dominant seventh chords.

C MAJOR Built from the notes C, E, G, C, and E, this chord uses three fretted and two open strings. Only the top five strings are played.

 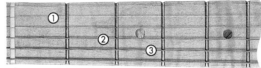

D MINOR This consists of the notes D, A, D, and F, using three fretted notes and one open string. Only the top four strings are played.

D DOMINANT SEVENTH Formed from the notes D, A, C, and F♯, this uses three fretted notes with one open string. Only the top four strings are played.

 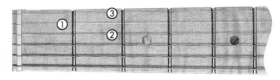 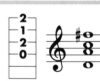

E DOMINANT SEVENTH The notes for this chord are E, B, D, G♯, B, and E, played on two fretted and four open strings. All six strings are used.

  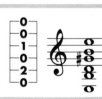

F MAJOR This chord is formed from the notes F, A, C, and F. All of these notes are fretted. The first finger holds the 1st and 2nd strings.

G MAJOR The notes that make up this chord are G, B, D, G, B, and G. All the strings are used; three of them are fretted, and three are open.

 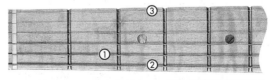

G DOMINANT SEVENTH This chord consists of the notes G, B, D, G, B, and F, using three fretted and three open strings. All six strings are played.

 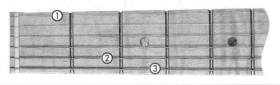

A Major Formed from the notes A, E, A, C♯, and E, this chord uses three fretted and two open strings. Only the top five strings are played.

A dominant seventh This consists of A, E, G, C♯, and E, played on two fretted and three open strings. Only the top five strings are used.

B diminished The chord is formed from the notes B, F, B, and D. Only the four middle strings are played, and all of the notes are fretted.

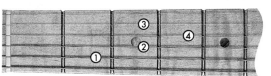

B dominant seventh B, D♯, A, and B, on the four middle strings, are used for this chord. Three of the strings are fretted, and the other is open.

B major This chord is made up of the notes B, F♯, B, and D♯, using four fretted strings. Only the four middle strings are played.

MOVING A SHAPE ACROSS THE FINGERBOARD

Every chord has a distinctive shape, made from its constituent notes, which forms a pattern referred to as a voicing. When a chord with a fixed voicing is moved, for example from a 6th-string to a 5th-string root, it cannot retain the same shape. This is because the 2nd string has a smaller tuned interval – the open strings on a guitar are tuned with intervals of a fourth between each, except for the 3rd and 2nd strings, where the interval is a major third. The chord shape has to alter in order to compensate for this smaller interval, and the note on the 2nd string moves up by one fret. Similarly, when a 5th-string chord shape is moved across the fingerboard to a 4th-string root, the note on the 2nd string is shifted up by one fret.

MOVING A SHAPE UP THE FINGERBOARD

When chord shapes are moved up and down the fingerboard, they retain their voicings, but the finger positions change because fretted notes are used instead of open strings. One shape can be used to play the same chord type on each fret. The root name changes on each position.

E major, A major, D major
The E major chord built from the 6th string has the same type of voicing as A major on the 5th string and D major on the 4th string. The A major chord uses only the top five strings, and D major uses only the top four strings.

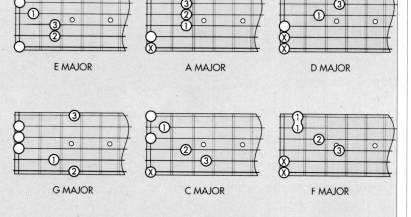

E MAJOR   A MAJOR   D MAJOR

G major, C major, F major
The chord shapes for G major, C major, and F major have the same type of structure on the fingerboard. The chord voicing for G major has a set order of notes in relation to the root. The C major chord with the root on the 5th string and F major on the 4th string share the same order of notes in relation to their roots.

G MAJOR   C MAJOR   F MAJOR

D major, E♭ major, E major
The D major chord shape can be moved up and down the fingerboard. When D is moved up one fret to E flat, the new fingering can be used to play any of the ascending major chords. For example, holding the shape and moving it one fret up forms E major.

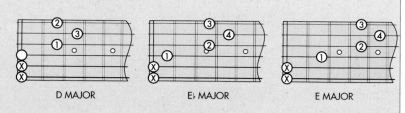

D MAJOR   E♭ MAJOR   E MAJOR

SONG SEQUENCES

PUTTING CHORDS TOGETHER

Count and strum
At first, try to get used to counting the numbers under the chords and playing them at the same time. You can lightly emphasize 1, the first beat. Count and play evenly and rest on the point where it states 1 & HOLD. To play the strings, either pluck them with the fingers or strum them with the thumb. With a plectrum, play downstrokes.

One of the primary roles of the guitar is to accompany songs. To set you on your way to playing an accompaniment, learn how to put the most common sentences of chords together. This section introduces formulas for songs and full sequences that shape or underlie innumerable pieces. The easiest way for the beginner to play chord sequences and understand how they work is to learn a basic vocabulary of related chords in C major. This section will build up to six standard chords in C major with a series of additional chords. Simple movements start with playing just pairs of chords.

Building sequences
Use these chords to make songs as well as learning to busk around simple sequences for backing songs in one key. It will be necessary to learn many further chords and other keys to build up a practical vocabulary of chords. Songs in C often use various chords with notes outside the scale, such as D major, which uses an F#, or F minor, which uses an Ab.

NUMBERING CHORDS
Roman numerals (**I-VII**) often denote the position of a chord in relation to the first note, **I** (one). So, 5 is **V**, still called "five."

C	D	E	F	G	A	B	C
I	II	III	IV	V	VI	VII	I
1	2	3	4	5	6	7	1

BASS NOTES
Learn names and fingerboard positions for C, D, E, F, G, A, and B. The lowest position of each note is the chord bass note. So, the lowest C is on the 3rd fret of the 5th string and matches the C note in the chord voicing. Use open D above for the D minor chord. Drop down to the bottom open string for E minor. Move up through F, G, A, and B for the other bass notes.

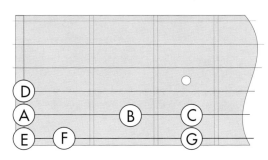

F major
In the sequences below, a full F major chord is written out in the chord box. The full chord requires the use of a "barre" with the first finger, which is covered on pages 90-94. For now, try this simpler version.

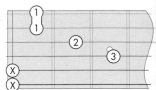

C MAJOR (I) TO G MAJOR (V)
Start by just moving from the C major chord to the G major chord and back to C. Practice this in your own time without trying to rush the change to the following chord at first. If you find C and G are difficult as full shapes, simply hold as many of the upper string notes as you can. Later on, try playing the full chord.

C MAJOR				G MAJOR				C MAJOR
1	2	3	4	1	2	3	4	1 & HOLD

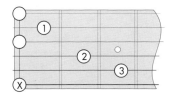
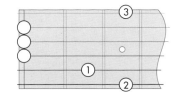
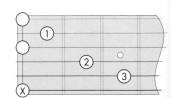

C MAJOR (I) TO F MAJOR (IV)
Now move from C major to F major. At first play F as a chord on the top four strings only if you find the shape difficult, or start building from the bass note upward. Practice it slowly and keep going – F major is an important chord and it is essential to persevere with it.

C MAJOR				F MAJOR				C MAJOR
1	2	3	4	1	2	3	4	1 & HOLD

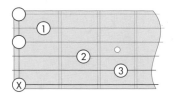
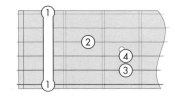
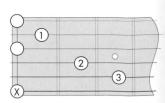

I-IV-V-I and I-IV-I-V

Combine C, F, and G chords in short sentences, practicing a smooth transition between them. Count and play C, F, G and a return to C in the first exercise; C to F, C to G in the second exercise. Notice that the G sounds unresolved and needs to go back to C.

C MAJOR	F MAJOR	G MAJOR	C MAJOR
1 2 3 4	1 2 3 4	1 2 3 4	1 & HOLD

C MAJOR	F MAJOR	C MAJOR	G MAJOR
1 2 3 4	1 2 3 4	1 2 3 4	1 & HOLD

I-V-IV-I

This sequence is light and jaunty. It moves around the chords in another direction and is in 3/4: each bar has three beats instead of four. Strum each chord evenly three times, emphasizing the chord on the number 1.

C MAJOR	G MAJOR	F MAJOR	C MAJOR
1 2 3	1 2 3	1 2 3	1 & HOLD

THREE-CHORD SONGS AND SEQUENCES

With three chords you have a basis for playing a three-chord 12-bar blues and simple rock sequences. Many simple folk and popular songs are also based on combinations of three chords in various keys. Chuck Berry's *Johnny B. Goode*, James Brown's *I Got You*, and the Carter Family's *Wildwood Flower* all use harmony based on various versions of three chords in different keys. Listen for the chord changes in songs to develop an ear for basic chord movements. The three **I**, **IV**, and **V** chords occur in all 12 keys. For example, in G major the notes are G (**I**), A (**II**), B (**III**), C (**IV**), D (**V**), E (**VI**), F# (**VII**). Therefore, the three chords are those on the the first, fourth, and fifth degrees (a degree is a step of the scale). In G major they are G major (**I**), C major (**IV**), and D major (**V**). G major is one of the most common keys for all types of music played on the guitar. In this key it is possible to play the three full chords without using a barre.

Auld Lang Syne
This famous Scottish song played on New Year's Eve can be supported with just three chords of C, F, and G. Play two or four strums in the bar. The chord structure is eight bars, repeated.

Amazing Grace
Written in England in the 18th century, this song can be played with the three basic chords. It is in 3/4. Try strumming three downbeats in the bar. Repeat the entire 16-bar structure.

Blues in C
These sequences are three of the basic versions running over 12 bars: they are all "12-bar blues." At first, just get used to the rate of change between the three chords before trying a rhythmic feel.

INTRODUCING MINOR CHORDS

With the three major chords of C, F, and G mastered, it is time to add the three minor chords in C major. They are A minor on the sixth (**VI**) degree of the scale, D minor on the second degree (**II**), and E minor on the third degree (**III**). This practical group of chords widens your palette of color and mood and lets you play more sequences. Try the first example of C major (**I**) to A minor (**VI**).

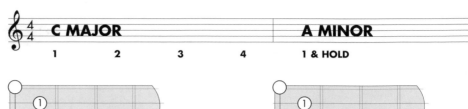

Adding D minor

Move from C major (**I**) to D minor (**II**), and down to G major (**V**). Resolve the sequence by moving back to C major (**I**). The movement from D minor (**II**) to G major (**V**) back to C major (**I**) is a common chord movement.

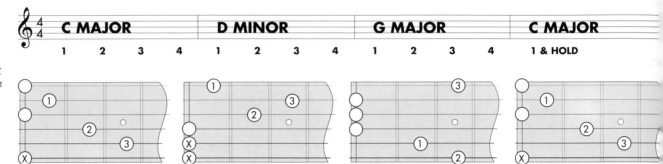

Adding E minor

Move from C major (**I**) to A minor (**VI**). Drop down to the low six-string E minor (**III**) chord and rest on it. Notice how it has a dark, sad quality.

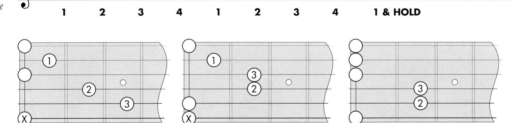

Major with minor chords

Here the three major chords already encountered, together with the three new minor chords, are combined in common four-bar sequences that form the introduction, or part, of many songs. The first sequence **I-VI-IV-V** and the variant **I-VI-II-V**, sometimes referred to as "turnarounds," are common as endings that lead back to the beginning of a song. The third sequence **I-VI-III-V** has a more somber sound, while the last sequence **I-V-VI-IV** is uplifting.

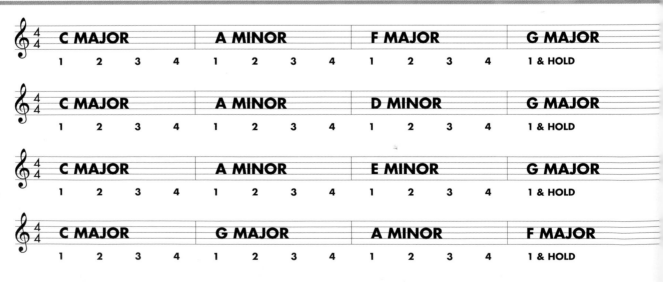

Two-chord vamp

*Sequences can start on any chord in C major and function without the C major chord. D minor (**II**) to G major (**V**) is repeated as a rhythmic "vamp" that can go around and around behind a solo.*

D MINOR	G MAJOR	D MINOR	G MAJOR
1 2 3 4	1 2 3 4	1 2 3 4	1 2 3 4

Step movements

Without strumming the four beats in the bar, move up the scale with chords. Go from C major to D minor then, rather than going up to an E, drop an octave for the E minor and up to F. In the second example, go from C up to G major, then resolve back to C major.

C MAJOR	D MINOR	E MINOR	F MAJOR

C MAJOR	D MINOR	E MINOR	F MAJOR	G MAJOR	C MAJOR

Cycle movements

Natural chord cycles, moving in fourths up or fifths down, can be used for all six chords. Count the bass notes as four notes up or five notes down. The first example uses four chords and the second all six.

A MINOR	D MINOR	G MAJOR	C MAJOR

E MINOR	A MINOR	D MINOR	G MAJOR	C MAJOR	F MAJOR

USING THE B BASS NOTE

The seventh degree, B (**VII**), has a diminished chord with the notes B, D, and F. As a simple chord voicing, this can sound dissonant and so has been left out for the moment. However, it is a highly important chord and is fundamental in jazz. Simple pop song sequences often use one of the existing chords with a B in the bass, called an inversion and written as a "/" chord, for instance, G major/B.

The first example uses an inversion of G major with B in the bass to link C major with A minor. The second sequence shows C major moving down to E minor with B in the bass, which acts as another link to A minor. Play both sequences the other way around, too, as A minor going up to C major via the two inversions.

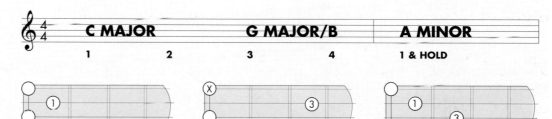

C MAJOR	G MAJOR/B	A MINOR
1 2	3 4	1 & HOLD

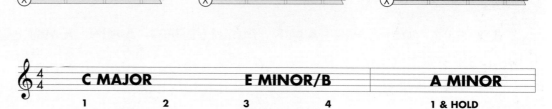

C MAJOR	E MINOR/B	A MINOR
1 2	3 4	1 & HOLD

The scale in chords

Both sequences have a bass movement, the first going down the scale and the second up. A different chord inversion is used in each for the B bass note.

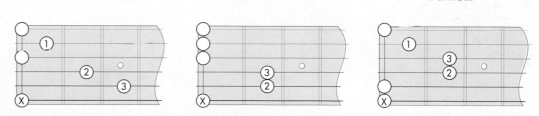

C MAJ	E MIN/B	A MIN	G MAJ	F MAJ	E MIN	D MIN	C MAJ

C MAJ	D MIN	E MIN	F MAJ	G MAJ	A MIN	G MAJ/B	C MAJ

THE MINOR SYSTEM

The notes or chords from A to A in C major are also a harmonic system with Roman numerals. A minor, the 6th chord (**VI**) of C, is the pivotal home note one (**I**) chord.

A	B	C	D	E	F	G	A
I	**II**	**III**	**IV**	**V**	**VI**	**VII**	**I**
1	2	3	4	5	6	7	1

A MINOR TO D MINOR

In the first example, the A minor (**I**) chord moves to the D minor (**IV**) chord. Practice the chords until the transition is smooth.

| A MINOR | D MINOR | A MINOR |

A MINOR TO E MINOR

In the second example, practice moving smoothly from the A minor (**I**) chord to the E minor (**V**) chord.

| A MINOR | E MINOR | A MINOR |

A MINOR TO E MAJOR

The E minor (**V**) chord is often altered by adding a G# to make it an E major (**V**) chord, giving a **V-I** release.

| A MINOR | E MAJOR | A MINOR |

THREE MINOR CHORDS

Play A minor (**I**), move up to D minor (**IV**), and play two bars of E minor (**V**). Move smoothly from one to the next.

| A MINOR | D MINOR | E MINOR | E MINOR |

MINOR BLUES

Blues is essentially a minor-scale music. The minor chord system has its own 12-bar blues sequences based around **I**, **IV**, and **V**. The first example below has an outline movement that is similar to major chord rock-blues sequences. As a variation, it can be played with an E minor chord in the tenth bar instead of a D minor chord. The second sequence uses E major chords as the (**V**) chord in bars nine and ten. There are other movements of chords using minor chords. Try this interesting alternative sequence with a different order of minor chords, retaining the distinctive blues feeling: A-A-E-E-A-A-D-D-A-E-A-A.

| A MIN | A MIN | A MIN | A MIN | D MIN | D MIN | A MIN | A MIN | E MIN | D MIN | A MIN | A MIN |

| A MIN | A MIN | A MIN | A MIN | D MIN | D MIN | A MIN | A MIN | E MAJ | E MAJ | A MIN | A MIN |

Mixing minor and major chords

Bring major chords into the minor framework. The three majors C, G, and F function as chords revolving around A minor. This turns the chords into a system with its own harmonic flavor.

| A MINOR | G MAJOR | A MINOR |

| A MINOR | C MAJOR | G MAJOR | A MINOR |

| A MINOR | G MAJOR | F MAJOR | G MAJOR |

| A MINOR | G MAJOR | F MAJOR | E MAJOR |

| F MAJOR | E MINOR | A MINOR | A MINOR |

PENTATONIC ROCK SYSTEM

Rock, blues, and pop use a hybrid minor system with major chords. Take five chords, **I**, **II**, **III**, **IV**, and **V**, in the minor system and play them as a blues-style pentatonic (five-note) scale. Below this system (right) are all five as major chords. Major and minor chords in various mixtures can follow pentatonic bass lines. This open harmonic interchange is not strict or fixed.

A MINOR	C MAJOR	D MINOR	E MINOR	G MAJOR	A MINOR
I	**III**	**IV**	**V**	**VII**	**I**
1	3	4	5	7	1

| A MAJOR | C MAJOR | D MAJOR | E MAJOR | G MAJOR | A MAJOR |

ROCK MOVEMENTS

Powerful chord sequences can be put together using the combination of minor and major chords with an outline pentatonic movement or framework. With this way of approaching harmony, major chords can replace any minor chord.

Such sequences are sometimes presented as a type of major system. A major (**I**) is the major home chord and the rest are C major

(♭**III**) instead of C# minor, D major (**IV**), E major (**V**), and G major (♭**VII**) instead of G# diminished. In other words, there are the three fundamental **I**, **IV**, and **V** chords in A major with C major as a flattened third (**III**) chord and G major as a flattened seventh (**VII**) chord. In fact, it is not a proper major system but a type of hybrid blues-scale minor system. Coincidentally, these five chords are

often used as a beginner's system for learning the five open-string major shapes with the acronym "**CAGED**" to remember the group.

The sequences below show a number of common rock movements. All the examples have an instantly recognizable blues-rock sound. Try chords with just two notes, using the root and fifth note as chords – they are neither major nor minor.

Three chord moves
*Run up and down three major chords: A (**I**), C (**III**), and D (**IV**). The 2/4 beat helps the rhythm.*

2/4	A MAJOR	C MAJOR	D MAJOR	C MAJOR	A MAJOR
	1 2	1 2	1 2	1 2	1 & HOLD

Three chord I-IV-III-I
*In 4/4, go from A major (**I**) up to D major (**IV**), and down through C major (**III**) to A major (**I**).*

4/4	A MAJOR	D MAJOR	C MAJOR	A MAJOR
	1 2 3 4	1 2	3 4	1 & HOLD

Four chord IV-III-I-VII-I
*From the D major (**IV**) chord, go down to C (**III**), pause on A (**I**), then down to G (**VII**). Emphasize the final A major (**I**) chord.*

2/4	D MAJOR	C MAJOR	A MAJOR	G MAJOR	A MAJOR
	1	2	1 2	1	2

Three chord I-VII-IV-I
*Catchy and memorable – go from A (**I**) down to G (**VII**) to D (**IV**) before returning to A major (**I**).*

4/4	A MAJOR	G MAJOR	D MAJOR	A MAJOR
	1 2	3 4	1 2	3 4

Three chord I-IV-V
Treat this three-chord sequence as a major or minor blues movement.

4/4	A MAJOR	D MAJOR	E MAJOR
	1 2 3 4	1 2 3 4	1 & HOLD

CHORD AND MELODY RELATIONSHIPS

The A minor pentatonic scale can be used as a framework for movements of major chords or a mixture of chords for three-chord or pentatonic-type rock

sequences. In this case, the "one" (**I**) chord, whether it is a simple A major, A7, or A minor, relates melodically to the minor scale called the Dorian mode (scale). It is the A minor scale (called the

Aeolian mode) with the F raised a semitone to F#, creating the Dorian mode notes A, B, C, D, E, F#, G, A. This also applies to blues where the Dorian mode and blues scales can be combined.

House of the Rising Sun
This famous traditional bluesy minor song has major chords added, including F. Strum it in 3/4 and also play it 6/8. The dots at each end are repeat signs.

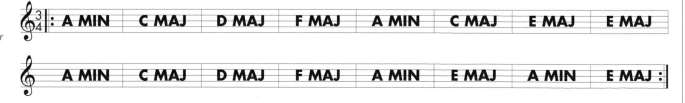

3/4	A MIN	C MAJ	D MAJ	F MAJ	A MIN	C MAJ	E MAJ	E MAJ
	A MIN	C MAJ	D MAJ	F MAJ	A MIN	E MAJ	A MIN	E MAJ

PLAYING RIFFS

REPEATING SHORT CATCHY PHRASES WITH THE GUITAR

Varying riffs
The examples below are in simple downbeat crotchet form. Try doubling to quavers or even semiquavers, and add upbeats with certain notes. Bluesy dotted quavers and triplets also work well.

Riffs are greatly enjoyable to play on the electric guitar, particularly with distortion and effects. As catchy introductions and motifs, they recur in breaks to uplift and strengthen the music. Riffs are usually based around pentatonic-type scales, rhythmically propelled and emphasized by down- and upbeats. Short and focused, riffs can run over just two bars.

Control and expression
To control staccato, quickly release the left-hand pressure on the notes. The outer edge of the palm of the right hand can rest on the strings near the bridge to mute the sound, which can give a strong and effective texture.

Pentatonic and blue note
Move up the pentatonic scale playing A-C-D-E-G-A, then down playing A-G-E-D-C-D. Give the notes an emphatic dynamism for a blues-rock sound. Break the notes into groups of three and four, starting from any note, and try making up riffs. Now play the same scale, adding an E♭. This is a strong "blue note," sometimes called a flat five. Experiment with short phrases using the new note. Now try to play all of this material starting on A on the 5th fret of the bottom string and staying in the middle of the fingerboard.

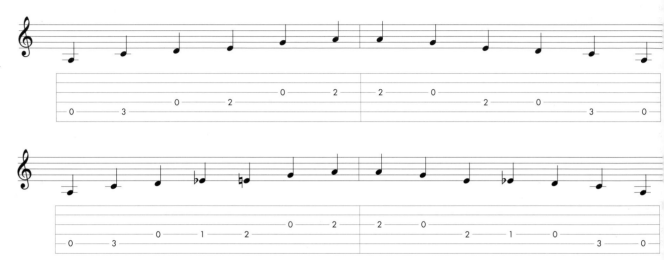

Phrases
Try playing the ascending phrase as even notes. The fall from the top E to C and A gives it a rock-blues character. Now try the ascending phrase that answers it. The move from E up to the note G complements the first phrase. The two work together as a call and response. Give the phrases a strong rhythmic framework, turning them into a long riff. In the four-bar example the first two notes are repeated and there are now 16 notes on the beat.

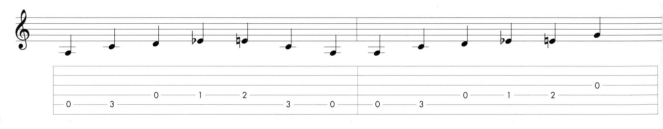

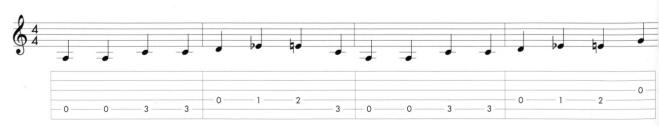

Double-stopped riffs
Now try the A pentatonic scale from the first, top example, with a note a fourth underneath it. Each note has an additional one on the same fret four steps lower. The technique is sometimes called "double stopping," from violin terminology, where two notes are held by the left hand.

Fourths above

Now try a completely different sound, the pentatonic scale with fourths above. This means an additional note four steps above each note. The notes are on the same fret position apart from the top two, G with C and A with D.

Fifths above

Try the same idea with fifths above. It is harder to control with open-string positions. Once you are used to fretting one pair of fifths on adjacent strings, move up and down the lower strings as a fixed pattern with the left hand.

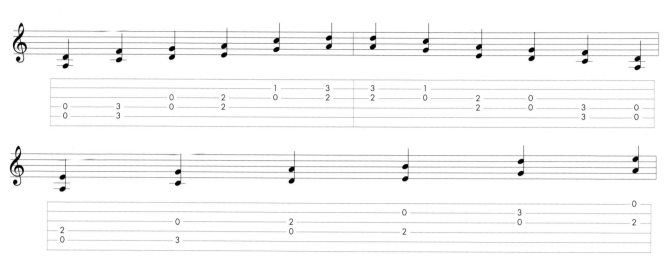

RIFFS WITH DROPPED TUNING

A particularly popular and effective approach to playing pairs of double-stopped notes is to tune the bottom string down a tone or two half steps to D. Play the open D 4th string and detune the bottom E string until the notes resonate together smoothly as an octave D pair. Alternatively, tune down until the note on the 7th fret of the bottom string matches the open A. This gives a powerful, exciting effect, and it is instantly possibly to play the entire series of pentatonic double-stopped notes up and down the bottom two strings. These pairs of notes, which are in fact two-note chords, can be made into bigger chords by playing or fretting across all three bottom strings to give D5, F5, G5, and the other chords ("5" means the chord is roots and fifths only).

Free movement

Try playing up and down, strumming open lower strings and fretting notes on the pentatonic with one finger. Instant rock sequences come out. Try other frets such as the 2nd or 9th to give different chords and movements.

CHORD RIFFS

Another way to approach riffs is to apply some of the above ideas to playing chords. Short, pithy chord movements, sometimes with muting and rhythmic emphasis, are termed chord riffs if they are used to give a song a particular flavor. Simple harmonic movements within chords are also sometimes thought of as riffs. Try experimenting with two-note and three-note chords, using the low bass note and the adjacent note, and try two-and three-chord movements. These can be played on any guitar. The use of distortion and effects on electric guitars thickens the texture and enhances sustain, both of which can dramatize the chord riffs.

Chord riffs G to E

Play G and B with the first and second finger. Lift off the second finger to sound the open E with the B. This is one of the simplest chord riffs based on G major and an E5 voicing.

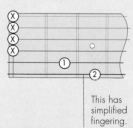

This has simplified fingering.

Open strings

Strum open strings and hammer-fretted chords such as E major while the notes are ringing. Play the open string and quickly press down the E major on an emphatic downbeat.

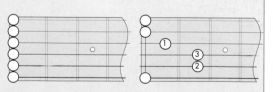

Chord extension

Similar in outline to the open-string riff idea, chord extensions are more practical musically. Hold the A major chord and play an extension with two notes to give it a melodic movement. You can resolve the extension back down to the major chord.

Suspended note

This example starts with a major chord with the addition of a D "suspended" note, written as A sus 4 or A sus 11. The suspended note creates a strong need to be resolved down to the C#. Try playing all the examples over a metronome, drum machine, or computer sequencer.

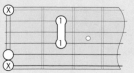
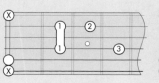

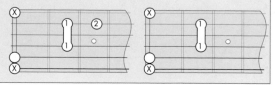

PLAYING MELODIES

STARTING TO PLAY SONGS AND MELODIES

Note lengths
The crotchets are one beat. Hold the minims for two beats. Hold the dotted crotchets over to the first half of the next beat and play the quaver note on the upbeat.

Songs and melodies are both appealing and memorable sentences of notes. When written down as music they should be phrased and interpreted sensitively. The three well-known English folk songs here are sung and played traditionally and have also been arranged as melodies for orchestra by the British composers Ralph Vaughan Williams and Frederick Delius.

Technique
Play with a finger per fret. Play all 1st fret notes with the first or index finger, all 2nd fret notes with the second or middle finger, and all 3rd fret notes with the third or ring finger. Tablature fret numbers coincide with finger numbers.

BRIGG FAIR

Like all good melodies, this 16-bar folk song is characterized by attractive groups of notes, which form phrases that make up the song. Brigg Fair has an opening four-bar phrase and succeeding phrases. It uses the notes of C major in 3/4, running throughout a one-octave range from C to C. The tune starts on an A and ends on a D and has a tendency to pivot around D. C is not the "tonal center," although it is written with C major notes. Brigg Fair has a D Dorian modal flavor – the series of notes from D to D within C major acts as a mode (scale) with its own shape. The song has been moved down to an easier position and so is played lower than normal. The rhythm has been slightly simplified.

LOVELY JOAN

This also uses the notes of C major. Lovely Joan is a lively eight-bar folk song in 4/4, which runs throughout a range from C to D. It starts on D and ends on a D. As with Brigg Fair, C is not the tonal center, although it is written with C major notes. It is in the minor mode of D Dorian. At the beginning, a pair of notes lead into the first bar, called an anacrusis. To play the anacrusis, count four beats. On the fourth beat, play the two notes on the downbeat and upbeat. Lovely Joan is also simplified rhythmically and moved on to the lower strings and positions.

GREENSLEEVES

This well-known melody is 16 bars long and has been written in 6/4 instead of the standard 6/8 to make it easier to read. *Greensleeves* has a range of notes running from E on the 2nd fret of the 4th string to G on the 3rd fret of the 1st string. It is in A minor Dorian as well as A minor with the use of an

F# and G# and G natural. It starts on A as an anacrusis (lead-in), similar to *Lovely Joan*, and ends on an A. The melody has an F# on the 4th fret of the 4th string, which should be played with the fourth finger. As in previous two examples, tablature fret numbers are the same as finger numbers. Chord

symbols have been placed underneath so that the melody can be played in a duo, or solo fingerstyle. To learn *Greensleeves* as a piece with chords, start by adding just the bass note under the melody note. Fill out with chord notes. Where there is one chord in the bar, you can play it twice, on the first and fourth beats.

FINGERSTYLE

THE TECHNIQUES USED IN CLASSICAL AND NYLON-STRING PLAYING

Naming the fingers
The fingers of the right hand have letters derived from their Spanish names. The thumb is **P** (pulgar); the first, or index, finger is **I** (índice); the second, or middle, finger is **M** (medio); and the third, or ring, finger is **A** (anular). The little finger, when used, is **X** (or **E**). **PIMA** notation is used to direct fingering for playing all types of scales, chords, and arpeggios. **PIMA** directions are written above the staff.

The guitar has evolved mainly as a chordal instrument, played with the thumb and fingers of the right hand. Using the fingers opens up the entire vocabulary of musical movement on the guitar. Chords can be played with arpeggiated variations, bass movements, or melody lines. Two or more parts can also be played simultaneously. Classical guitar playing is based entirely on a fingerstyle approach that has developed to a point where it has become standardized. Flamenco playing and some of the steel-string styles of music based on fingerpicking have their own distinctive techniques and traditions. The classical right-hand technique shown here can provide the basis for stylistic variations. Fingerstyle also enables chord sequences to be played without imposing technical limitations.

Nails with steel strings
Guitarists do play on steel-string acoustic and electric instruments with right-hand fingernails. However, the main problem is simply that nails are easily damaged by regular contact with metal strings, and they wear down quickly. Playing with nails on nylon-string guitars is important for producing a good tone. The composition and tension of the steel strings makes this kind of tone control difficult.

RIGHT-HAND NAIL TECHNIQUE

In the past, a number of outstanding classical instrumentalists have played without fingernails. However, today virtually all nylon-string players use them. Fingernails must be maintained at a shape and length that provide optimum playing control and tone production. Guitarists cut and file their nails in a number of different ways – some use a rounded nail shape, and others prefer a straighter edge, where the nail plucks the string. However, the preferred length of nail varies greatly. Many guitar players have badly formed or weak nails that split or break. Wear caused by playing on nylon strings with a high level of attack exacerbates the problem. To overcome such difficulties, artificial nails are sometimes used.

Arm position
Rest the inside of the forearm on the upper edge of the guitar, keeping the hand at an angle to the strings. The shoulder and arm should be relaxed and the hand in a position to reach all of the strings comfortably.

Hand height
Your hand should not touch the soundboard or the bridge. If it is too close to the strings, the movement of the fingers is impeded. Your wrist should be about 2.75 in (7 cm) above the strings. This will enable the fingers to move freely.

Playing action
Move the thumb down to play the bass strings, and the fingers up to play the middle and top strings. The fingers should be curved slightly inward. Strike the notes with a flowing movement through the strings.

Using PIMA
The arrows show the playing direction of the thumb and fingers. The circles indicate the order in which the fingers move. For clarity, the points at which the strings are played in relation to the soundhole are exaggerated. The correct positions are shown at the left.

LEARNING TO PLAY PIMA

When playing, the thumb is referred to as "**P**," the first finger as "**I**," the second finger as "**M**," and the third finger as "**A**." In the following exercise, **P** plays the 6th string and **I**, **M**, and **A** play the 3rd, 2nd, and 1st strings, respectively. The fingernails strike the strings over the soundhole toward the side closest to the bridge. The strings should be sounded with a *downward* movement of the thumb and an *upward* movement of the three fingers. After striking the notes, the fingers and thumb should move up and away without hitting or resting on any of the other strings. This action is termed *free stroke movement*. Once the exercises have been played on the open strings, they can be repeated using chord shapes.

Playing PIMA
*Begin by playing the 6th string using the thumb (**P**), followed by the 3rd, 2nd, and 1st strings with the **I**, **M**, and **A** fingers.*

Playing PAMI
*Play the 6th string with the thumb, the 1st string with the **A** finger, the 2nd string with the **M** finger, and the 3rd string with the **I** finger.*

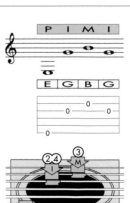

Playing PIMI
*Play the 6th string using **P**, the 3rd string using **I**, the 2nd string using **M**, returning to play the 3rd string with **I**.*

Playing PIMAMI
***P** plays the 6th string, **I** the 3rd, **M** the 2nd, and **A** the 1st. Return to the 2nd and 3rd strings using **M** and **I**.*

PIMA WITH CHORDS

Hold down an E major chord hand and play the first set of open-string **PIMA** variations. Take the left hand away from the E major chord, and hold down an A minor chord. Repeat the same set of variations, this time playing the bass note on the 5th string with the thumb. Keep the finger movements on the right hand as even as possible. Play these exercises accurately, gradually increasing the tempo.

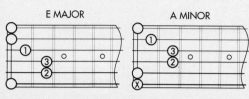

E MAJOR   A MINOR

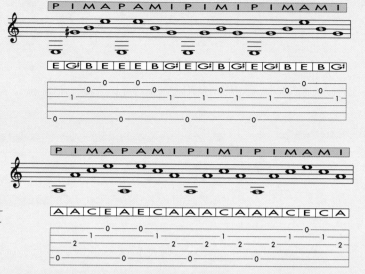

PIMA using E major

The notes on the 4th and 5th strings should not be played. Try playing E major with the 1st finger of the left hand holding G♯ and the 2nd and 3rd fingers removed.

PIMA using A minor

Play the A minor chord with a different fingering. The 1st and 2nd fingers hold down the notes C and A, and the 3rd finger is removed. In these exercises, the note on the 4th string is not played.

PIMA VARIATIONS

The following variations are all based on the E major chord. They will help to build flexibility of movement and the control of arpeggiation. There are many variations with the **I**, **M**, and **A** fingers. Play the exercises and then work on the **IMA** part of each one without the bass note. In these examples, **I** always plays the 3rd string, **M** the 2nd string, and **A** the 1st string.

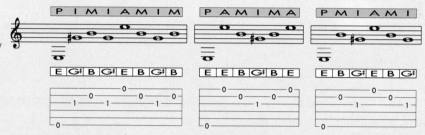

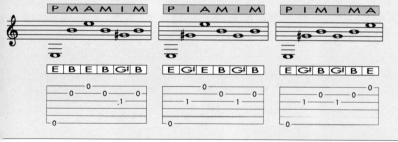

Alternatives

Repeat the exercises in A minor with **P** playing the 5th string, and **I**, **M**, and **A** repeating on the 3rd, 2nd, and 1st strings.

MOVING THE THUMB

Thumb movement is a vital part of right-hand technique. To begin with, it is useful to play the exercises using only the open strings of the guitar. Using **P**, play an open 6th string followed by open 5th and 4th strings. Move back and forth across the three lower strings, building up alternate movements between the 6th and 5th, 5th and 4th, and the 6th and 4th strings. The exercises on the right should be played holding a standard open-string E major chord, moving **P** from the open 6th string to the other strings. Play the **IM** and the **IMAMI** arpeggio with **P** moving from the 6th to the 5th, and then to the 4th strings. Independent thumb movement is built up in this way, using arpeggio patterns with the bottom notes played individually by the thumb on the lower strings.

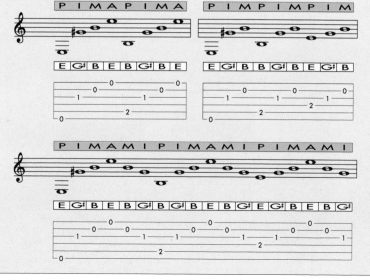

IMA and IM exercises

In the first bar, play the 6th string followed by **IMA** and the pattern from the 5th string: **PIMA** is played twice. In the second bar, play the 6th string followed by **IM** and then the pattern from the 5th and 4th strings: **PIM** is repeated three times.

PIMAMI exercise

In the third bar, play the 6th string followed by **IMAMI** and then the pattern from the 5th and 4th strings. The sequence **PIMAMI** is repeated three times. Play each pattern as a continuous cyclical movement.

OTHER THUMB MOVEMENTS

The thumb can be used to play more than one note in a five-note arpeggio. Play the first *and* second notes with the thumb. Complete the arpeggio using the **I**, **M**, and **A** fingers. The thumb can be also be used to move from the bass strings to play notes usually played by the fingers.

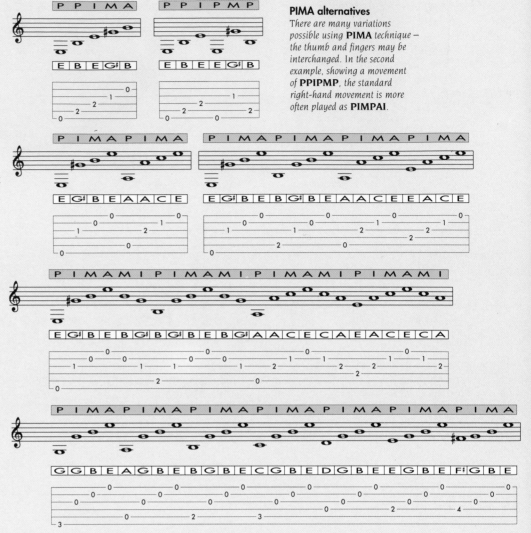

PIMA alternatives
There are many variations possible using **PIMA** *technique – the thumb and fingers may be interchanged. In the second example, showing a movement of* **PPIPMP***, the standard right-hand movement is more often played as* **PIMPAI***.*

POSITION ON CHORD CHANGES

It is important to maintain control during chord changes. In this exercise, when E major is changed to A minor, be sure that the thumb hits the correct bass string as the chord changes. Play **P** on the 6th string followed by **IMA**, then **P** on the 5th string followed by **IMA** as the chord changes.

CHORD MOVEMENTS

This exercise will develop overall stability and independence of the thumb. Play the **IMAMI** finger sequence continually as the chord changes. To perform this exercise well, the chord changes must be made quickly. To improve speed and control, practice **P** and **IMA** independently.

ARPEGGIO WITH THUMB SCALE

The thumb can also be used to play scales and melodies *below* arpeggios. In this exercise the thumb is used to play notes from the G major scale against a pattern on the open top strings. Play **IMA** on its own before adding the scale that ascends from the 3rd fret of the 6th string.

STRUMMING WITH PIMA

When a chord of more than four notes is played quickly with the right-hand fingers, the thumb (**P**) is used to play more than one string. For example, when an E major chord is played on the bottom five strings, in order to sound all the notes together, **IMA** plays the 4th, 3rd, and 2nd strings, and the thumb strikes the 6th and 5th strings at the same time. Similarly, with a full six-string voicing, the **I**, **M**, and **A** fingers play the top three strings, and the thumb plays the bottom three strings.

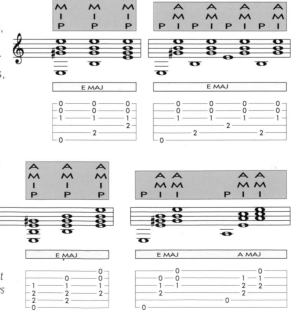

Block chord exercise
Further control of the thumb and fingers can be developed with the four variations on the right. Chords can be broken up into sections and played with different bottom notes. The thumb can be used to play bass notes and the **I**, **M**, *and* **A** *fingers to play a section of the chord. Try playing all chords in sections.*

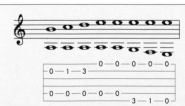

Voice movement
"Oblique motion" refers to a note being held while a second moves in relation to it. Repeat an A while playing the scale ascending from B to E. Then repeat E while playing the bass notes descending from A to E.

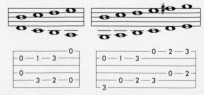

Contrary motion
Play the two scales that ascend from B to E, and descend from D to A.

Parallel motion
Play the two ascending scales at the same time. They run from B to G, and from G to E.

STRUMMING WITH THE THUMB

Mastering a combination of downstrokes and upstrokes with the thumb enables the player to develop a relaxed and loose wrist, and gives control when playing rhythms. In the thumb exercise below, combinations of strokes are used. Strumming with the side of the thumb may also be used as an alternative technique.

STRUMMING WITH THE INDEX FINGER

When strumming with the index finger, the movement should be made by the finger itself, rather than by the entire wrist. In the exercises below, when using alternating strokes, care should be taken to prevent the nail from catching the strings and impeding movement on the upstroke. The exercises can also be played with the **M** finger.

TREMOLO TECHNIQUE

The **I**, **M**, and **A** fingers can be used to play a continually repeating pattern on one note. This is known as *tremolo* and is widely used in classical and flamenco styles. Try playing tremolo slowly on the top string while playing the open 6th or 5th string below with the thumb. When these notes are played faster, the effect should be an even, rippling sound.

AMI movement
Play the open E string with **A**, **M**, *and* **I**. *Repeat the sequence slowly and evenly. Build up speed and play as a continuous pattern, eventually connecting each* **AMI** *movement without stopping between the* **I** *and* **A**.

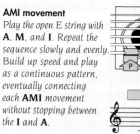

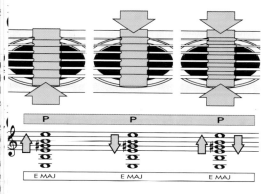

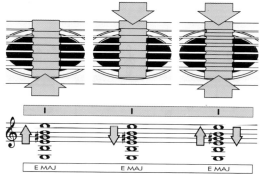

RIGHT-HAND SCALE TECHNIQUE

Acquiring a good scale technique is one of the most important priorities in learning to play the guitar. There are different approaches to playing scales with the right-hand fingers on a nylon-string guitar. Most players alternate the **I** and **M** fingers. An alternating **IMA** technique for some passages may also be used. Play the passages below with both combinations of fingers. Ascending and descending passages sometimes use different combinations of fingers. The use of **IM** and **IMA** depends on the number of notes on a string. For example, with a five-note scale, two notes on a string will be played by **IM** or **MI**, and three notes on an adjacent string will use **IMA** or **AMI**.

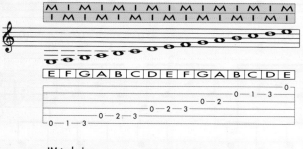

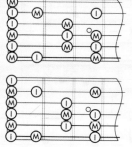

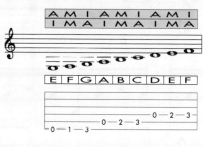

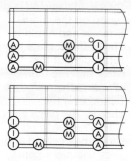

IM technique
The scale above is a two-octave modal scale that uses fifteen notes in C major, starting on the bottom E and ascending to the E on the top string. Play this scale starting with the **I** *finger, and play the next note with the* **M** *finger. Play the entire scale, alternating right-hand fingers. The scale should then be played starting with the* **M** *finger, alternating the fingers the other way.*

Scale order The chart above shows which right-hand fingers play the notes held down by the left hand.

IMA technique
The scale shown above is a shortened version of the E scale. Use the **A**, **M**, *and* **I** *fingers to play groups of three notes on the 6th, 5th, and 4th strings. Then strike the notes in reverse, using the fingers in* **IMA** *sequence. Because of the length of the* **M** *finger, playing with* **IMA** *or* **AMI** *on the lowest strings of the guitar may be difficult to begin with.*

IMA sequence The chart above shows which right-hand fingers play the notes held down by the left hand.

Thumb scales
The thumb is often used to play scales. Play the lower part of the C major scale shown below.

Rest stroke using IMA
The rest stroke is used to play notes with greater volume and a fuller tone. When a note is struck, the finger plays down toward the body of the instrument and completes its movement by resting on an adjacent string.

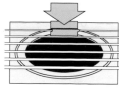

Rest stroke using the thumb
The thumb can also be used to play rest strokes. Play with a downward movement, resting on the adjacent string after the completion of the stroke. Rest strokes can be played with considerable volume.

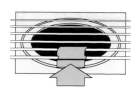
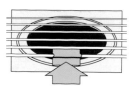

THE MAJOR SCALE

UNDERSTANDING THE INTERVALS THAT MAKE UP SCALES

The "sol-fa" system
Each note of the major scale has a sol-fa series of note names. They are **do**, **re**, **mi**, **fa**, **sol**, **la**, and **ti**. These one-syllable words can help the player to memorize the sound of intervals. A useful exercise is to sing each note as it is played on the guitar. This helps the ear to recognize notes and melodies.

The major scale is formed from a series of fixed intervals and provides the framework for many harmonic and melodic structures. The tones and semitones in the major scale can also be used to form any intervals: the distance between a perfect fifth and the root is three tones and a semitone. Every note on the scale is assigned with a name that denotes its relationship to the root note. These names, running from one *tonic* to the next octave, also identify the seven notes both as individual tones and as roots for chords.

Naming major scale notes
The formal name of a note on the major scale describes its relationship to the **tonic** (root) and the **dominant** (fifth). The **supertonic** is the note above the tonic. It is followed by the **mediant** (midway between the tonic and the dominant), **sub-dominant**, **dominant**, **sub-mediant**, and **leading note**.

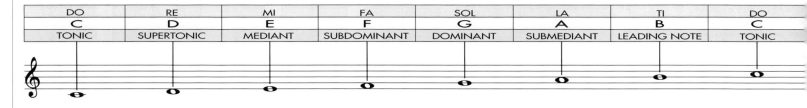

DO	RE	MI	FA	SOL	LA	TI	DO
C	D	E	F	G	A	B	C
TONIC	SUPERTONIC	MEDIANT	SUBDOMINANT	DOMINANT	SUBMEDIANT	LEADING NOTE	TONIC

INTERVALS ON THE MAJOR SCALE

The intervals on any scale occur between individual notes. The series of tone and semitone steps on the major scale are termed major and minor seconds. For example, C to D is a tone or a major second and E to F is a semitone or a minor second. Larger steps between notes of the major scale also have an interval name to identify the number of scale notes and the size of the space between them. Compare the names used to determine the interval between individual notes and the root note of the scale. For example, C to E is a major third and C to F is a perfect fourth.

THE SCALE OF C MAJOR

There are several ways to play a scale from its root to its octave note. The C major scale is usually played across the strings. To illustrate the intervals from the root, the C major scale is shown here played on the 5th string.

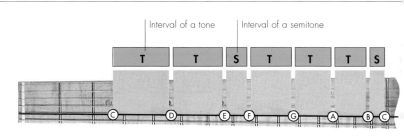

Interval of a tone   Interval of a semitone

| T | T | S | T | T | T | S |

C major shape
Compare the arrangement of the notes in C major both on the 5th string and in the standard position. The scale on the 5th string shows the relationship of the notes as a series of tone and semitone steps.

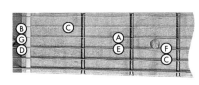

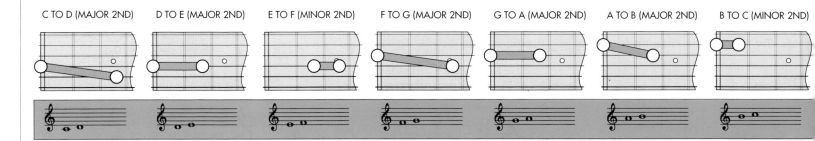

| C TO D (MAJOR 2ND) | D TO E (MAJOR 2ND) | E TO F (MINOR 2ND) | F TO G (MAJOR 2ND) | G TO A (MAJOR 2ND) | A TO B (MAJOR 2ND) | B TO C (MINOR 2ND) |

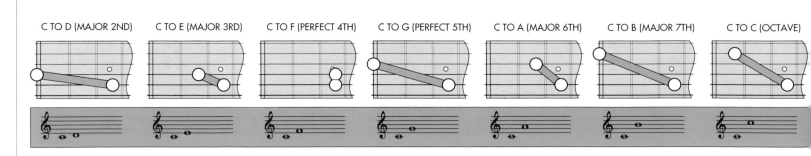

| C TO D (MAJOR 2ND) | C TO E (MAJOR 3RD) | C TO F (PERFECT 4TH) | C TO G (PERFECT 5TH) | C TO A (MAJOR 6TH) | C TO B (MAJOR 7TH) | C TO C (OCTAVE) |

OTHER SCALE POSITIONS

The C major scale has already been played from the 5th string to the 2nd using a combination of open strings and fretted notes (see p. 48). However, it can also be played from several other positions. One of the most widely used standard patterns starts on the 3rd fret of the 5th string and moves across the fingerboard to the higher octave C on the 5th fret of the 3rd string. This pattern is played using the fourth finger to fret notes. The fingering pattern can also be moved to start the scale on the 8th fret of the 6th string, and extended across the fingerboard to an upper octave.

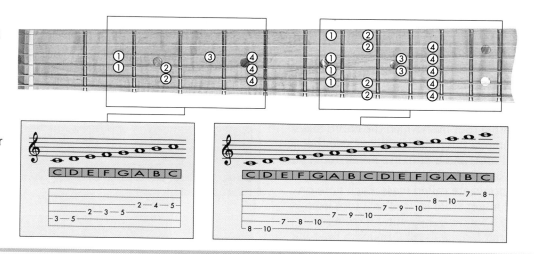

CHROMATIC INTERVALS

The diagram on the right uses the note C as a fixed point and shows a one-octave chromatic scale that includes all seven notes of the major scale as well as the five unused notes outside the scale. The notes are shown on the 5th string from the 3rd fret to the 15th fret, along with the names for all the intervals. There are twelve chromatic intervals before the octave is reached. Remember that an interval may have more than one name.

Major scale intervals
The C major scale is shown ascending the 5th string. The intervals, labeled with their relationship to the root, are found on the 5th, 7th, 8th, 10th, 12th, 14th, and 15th frets.

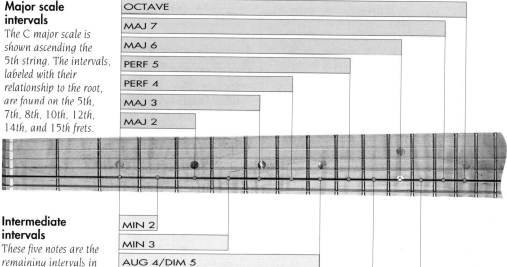

OTHER MAJOR INTERVALS

All the different types of intervals occur in the major scale when other notes are used as a reference point. For example, in the key of C major, the intervals running from the note A are major, minor, and perfect. The intervals from the note B are all minor, perfect, or diminished.

Intermediate intervals
These five notes are the remaining intervals in the octave. They occur on the 4th, 6th, 9th, 11th, and 13th frets, between the frets for the major scale intervals.

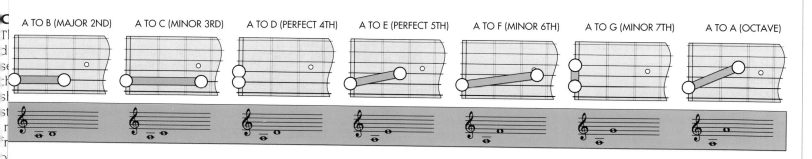

A TO B (MAJOR 2ND) — A TO C (MINOR 3RD) — A TO D (PERFECT 4TH) — A TO E (PERFECT 5TH) — A TO F (MINOR 6TH) — A TO G (MINOR 7TH) — A TO A (OCTAVE)

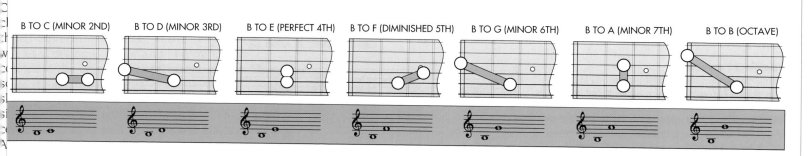

B TO C (MINOR 2ND) — B TO D (MINOR 3RD) — B TO E (PERFECT 4TH) — B TO F (DIMINISHED 5TH) — B TO G (MINOR 6TH) — B TO A (MINOR 7TH) — B TO B (OCTAVE)

CHORDS AND SCALES

CHORDAL VARIATIONS USING NOTES FROM THE MAJOR SCALE

Chords from scales
The chords based on the seven degrees of the C major scale can be viewed in relation to the other notes in the scale. They are shown below, with the C major scale superimposed, using black dots for the notes that are not part of the chord. Each chord can be seen as a shape within C major, and altered by adding scale notes to create chordal variations.

Any chord on the fingerboard can be visualized as a shape that consists of a group of notes sitting within a scale position. The majority of players look at the fingerboard and relate chord shapes to scale positions. It is important to understand this relationship. The first step to acquiring these skills is to work on the guitar using chords and a scale position in one key. This enables the player to add melody, extend harmony, and move around the fingerboard, combining single notes and chords. Linking notes with chords is an important step toward playing solo pieces and learning composition and improvisation.

Building chords
Triads are extended by using extra notes from related scales. One of the most common additions to a major or minor chord is the seventh. These additions have already been encountered with the dominant seventh (see p. 62). In the first octave, fourths and sixths are often added. In the second octave, ninths, elevenths, and thirteenths may also be used.

C MAJOR The notes taken from the C major scale are C, E, and G.
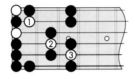

C MAJOR 7TH The note B, a major seventh above the root, is added.
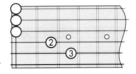

C MAJOR 6TH The note A, a major sixth interval above the root, is added.
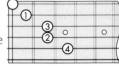

D MINOR The notes taken from the C major scale are D, F, and A.
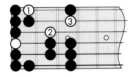

D MINOR 7TH The note C, a minor seventh above the root, is added.
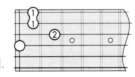

D MINOR 9TH The note E, a major ninth interval above the root, is added.

E MINOR The notes taken from the C major scale are E, G, and B.
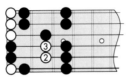

E MINOR 7TH The note D, a minor seventh above the root, is added.
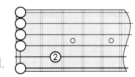

E MINOR 7TH The note D, an extra seventh, is added on the 2nd string.
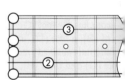

F MAJOR The notes taken from the C major scale are F, A, and C.
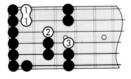

F MAJOR 7TH The note E, a major seventh above the root, is added.
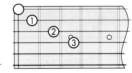

F MAJOR 6TH The note F, a major sixth interval above the root, is added.

G MAJOR The notes taken from the C major scale are G, B, and D.

G DOMINANT 7TH The note F, a minor seventh above the root, is added.

G MAJOR 6TH The note E, a major sixth interval above the root, is added.
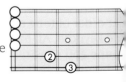

A MINOR The notes taken from the C major scale are A, C, and E.
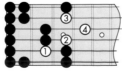

A MINOR 7TH The note G, a minor seventh above the root, is added.
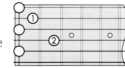

A MINOR 9TH The note B, a major ninth interval above the root, is added.

B DIMINISHED The notes taken from the C major scale are B, D, and F.

B MINOR 7 FLAT 5TH The note A, a minor seventh above the root, is added.
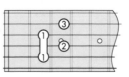

B MINOR 11 FLAT 5TH The note E, an eleventh above the root, is added.
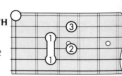

ADDITIONS WITHIN ONE OCTAVE

Adding a note a third above the fifth on every triad using the C major notes creates a seventh chord on every degree. On the C major chord, for example, C, E, and G have the note B added, a third above G and a major seventh above C. This is similar to adding the minor seventh on the dominant chord (see p. 62). Each triad on the C scale has a seventh added. When the sixth is added to a triad, the major sixth on the three major chords C, F, and G and the major sixth with the D minor chord are the most common harmonic additions. A suspended fourth can be used with C major and G major: this type of chord is constructed without a third in order to balance the voicing.

Adding sevenths

*The chords shown below, constructed as triads on each degree of the major scale, can all be extended by adding a seventh. This is placed a third above the fifth of each chord – this is seven notes above the root. In C, the seventh on the chords of C major (**I**) and F major (**IV**) are major seventh intervals from the root. The seventh on D minor (**II**), E minor (**III**), G major (**V**), A minor (**VI**), and B diminished (**VII**) have a minor seventh from the root.*

Adding sixths

*The four chords shown below, constructed on the major scale, can be extended by adding a sixth. In C, the sixth on the chords of C major (**I**), F major (**IV**), and G major (**V**) are major sixth intervals from the root. The sixth on the chord of D minor (**II**) is also a major sixth.*

Suspended fourths

*The two chords shown below – C major (**I**) and G major (**V**) – can have a perfect fourth added. Do not play the major third.*

COMPARING SEVENTHS

There are four main types of seventh chords on the major scale. The *major seventh* is a major triad with a major seventh addition. This occurs on the first (**I**) and fourth (**IV**) degrees of the scale. The *dominant seventh* chord is a major triad with a minor seventh that occurs on the fifth (**V**) degree of the scale. The *minor seventh* chord is a minor triad with a minor seventh addition, built on the second (**II**), third (**III**), and sixth (**VI**) degrees of the scale. The *minor seventh flat five* chord is a diminished triad with the addition of a minor seventh built on the seventh (**VII**) degree of the scale. The structure of the major scale determines the shape and combination of the intervals in a seventh chord on each degree.

C major seventh

This chord is composed of a major third between the root and the third, a minor third between the third and the fifth, and a major third between the fifth and the seventh. The two major sevenths on the C major scale are C major 7 and F major 7.

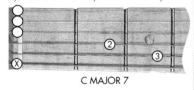

C MAJOR 7

THIRD

FIFTH

SEVENTH

C major
The C major seventh chord is composed of the first, third, fifth, and seventh notes.

G dominant seventh

The dominant seventh chord is composed of a major third between the root and third, a minor third between the third and the fifth, and a minor third between the fifth and the seventh. G7 is the only dominant seventh on the C major scale.

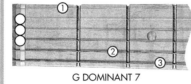

G DOMINANT 7

THIRD

FIFTH

SEVENTH

C major from G
The G dominant seventh chord is composed of the first, third, fifth, and seventh notes.

D minor seventh

This chord has a minor third between the root and the third, a major third between the third and the fifth, and a minor third between the fifth and the seventh. The three minor sevenths on the C major scale are D minor 7, E minor 7, and A minor 7.

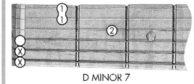

D MINOR 7

THIRD

FIFTH

SEVENTH

C major from D
The D minor seventh chord is composed of the first, third, fifth, and seventh notes.

B minor seventh flat five

This chord has a minor third between the root and the third, a minor third between the third and the fifth, and a major third between the fifth and the seventh. There is only one minor seventh flat five chord in the C major scale: B minor 7♭5.

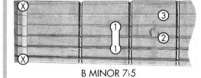

B MINOR 7♭5

THIRD

FIFTH

SEVENTH

C major from B
The B minor seventh flat five chord is composed of the first, third, fifth, and seventh notes.

MAJOR SCALE SEQUENCES

AN INTRODUCTION TO CHORD MOVEMENTS WITHIN THE MAJOR SCALE

Other keys
The Roman numeral system is used in every key with the same order of major, minor, and diminished chords. The major scale is constructed below from A and D, using two sharps in D major and three in A major.

Chords are constructed on the major scale using each note as a separate root. These *scale tone* chords are each assigned a Roman numeral. For example, the key of C major has the scale tone chords C major (**I**), D minor (**II**), E minor (**III**), F major (**IV**), G major (**V**), A minor (**VI**), and B diminished (**VII**). Many common sequences are built around the tonic (**I**), subdominant (**IV**), and dominant (**V**) chords.

The perfect cadence
The term **cadence** describes a movement between melody notes or chords. The **perfect** cadence is a movement from the dominant **V** chord to the tonic **I** chord. It is often used as a "full close" at the end of a section or a piece of music.

C MAJ	D MIN	E MIN	F MAJ	G MAJ / G DOM 7	A MIN	B DIM	C MAJ
I	II	III	IV	V / V⁷	VI	VII	I

PRIMARY MOVEMENTS IN C

The three primary major chords that are built on the first, fourth, and fifth degrees of the major scale have a close musical relationship to each other, and are often used together to form chord sequences and progressions. Each movement from chord to chord has an effective sound and harmonic quality. In the key of C major, the chords are C, F, and G major. G major is often modified with an added seventh when playing a movement from **V** to **I**.

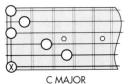
C MAJOR

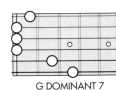
G DOMINANT 7

Movements in C
Play each of the three movements shown on the left. Play them using both the G dominant 7 chord and G major.

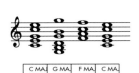

C MAJ	F MAJ	G MAJ	C MAJ
I	IV	V	I

C MAJ	F MAJ	G7	C MAJ
I	IV	V7	I

C MAJ	G MAJ	F MAJ	C MAJ
I	V	IV	I

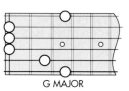
G MAJOR

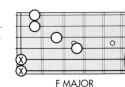
F MAJOR

G MAJ	A MIN	B MIN	C MAJ	D MAJ / D DOM 7	E MIN	F# DIM	G MAJ
I	II	III	IV	V / V⁷	VI	VII	I

MOVEMENTS IN G

The type of movement shown above in the key of C major can be played in other keys. In G major the primary chords are G major (**I**), C major (**IV**), and D major (**V**).

The chord progression C-F-G-C (**I-IV-V-I**) in the key of C major therefore becomes G-C-D-G (**I-IV-V-I**) in G major. These progressions may easily be transposed to D major and A major by writing out the major scales and using the three primary major chords in each key. All of these sequences can be played in other keys by using the major scale and selecting the three primary major chords in that particular key.

Movements in G
The movements in the key of C major are played in G major with voicings that use the open strings of the guitar.

 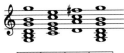 

G MAJ	C MAJ	D MAJ	G MAJ
I	IV	V	I

G MAJ	C MAJ	D7	G MAJ
I	IV	V7	I

G MAJ	D MAJ	C MAJ	G MAJ
I	V	IV	I

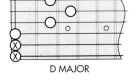
D MAJOR

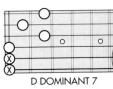
D DOMINANT 7

D MAJ	E MIN	F# MIN	G MAJ	A MAJ / A DOM 7	B MIN	C# DIM	D MAJ
A MAJ	B MIN	C# MIN	D MAJ	E MAJ / E DOM 7	F# MIN	G# DIM	A MAJ
I	II	III	IV	V / V⁷	VI	VII	I

OTHER TRANSPOSITIONS

The progressions that are used in C major and G major can be constructed in D major and A major. For example, the progression **I-IV-V-I** in C major becomes D-G-A-D in the key of D, and A-D-E-A in the key of A.

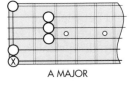
A MAJOR

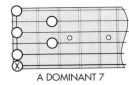
A DOMINANT 7

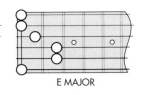
E MAJOR

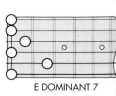
E DOMINANT 7

C MAJ	D MIN	E MIN	F MAJ	G MAJ / G DOM 7	A MIN	B DIM	C MAJ
I	II	III	IV	V / V⁷	VI	VII	I

ADDING THE RELATIVE MINOR IN C

On the major scale, the submediant minor chord positioned on the sixth degree (**VI**) is known as the relative minor. This is the most important of the secondary chords. In C, the relative minor chord is A minor. A minor has a close harmonic relationship to C major. Both chords have the notes C and E in common.

Adding A minor

The addition of A minor to the three primary major chords extends the range of progressions and movements. One of the most widely used progressions is I-VI-IV-V:
C major, A minor, F major, G major.

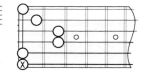

C MAJ	A MIN	F MAJ	C MAJ
I	VI	IV	I

The A minor (VI) links C major (I) to F major (IV).

C MAJ	G MAJ	A MIN	F MAJ
I	V	VI	IV

A minor (VI) links G major (V) and F major (IV).

Compare A minor with C major. They share notes and are often combined in chord movements.

OTHER SECONDARY MINOR CHORDS IN C

The secondary minor supertonic and mediant chords are found on the second (**II**) and third (**III**) degrees of the scale. In C these are D minor and E minor. They are used to extend and vary sequences. The **II** chord is frequently used before the **V** chord, as **II-V-I**, in a further development of the perfect cadence. The **III** chord often moves to **VI**, and is used in the progression **III-VI-II-V-I**. The **II** and **III** chords move up the scale in the movement **I-II-III-IV**. Play through the following sequences in C using the scale tone chords.

Using secondary minor chords

*In the first bar (top staff), the **II** chord links **I** and **V**. In the second bar (top staff), the **VI** chord links **I** to **II**. In the third bar (middle staff), the **II** and **III** chords link **I** and **IV**. In the fourth bar (middle staff), the movement **III-VI-II** leads to **V**. In the fifth bar (bottom staff), the **II** chord links **IV** and **V**. In the sixth bar (bottom staff), the **III** chord links **I** and **IV**.*

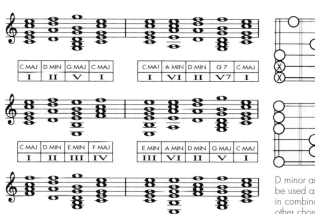

C MAJ	D MIN	G MAJ	C MAJ
I	II	V	I

C MAJ	A MIN	D MIN	G 7	C MAJ
I	VI	II	V⁷	I

C MAJ	D MIN	E MIN	F MAJ
I	II	III	IV

E MIN	A MIN	D MIN	G MAJ	C MAJ
III	VI	II	V	I

F MAJ	D MIN	G MAJ	C MAJ
IV	II	V	I

C MAJ	E MIN	F MAJ	G 7	C MAJ
I	III	IV	V⁷	I

D minor and E minor can be used as related minors in combinations with the other chords.

THE DIMINISHED CHORD IN C

The diminished chord **VII** is built on the major scale leading note. In C, this is the note B. Diminished chords often resolve to the tonic. They have a dissonant sound with the interval between the root (B) and the diminished fifth (F). The diminished chord sometimes replaces the dominant **V**, in this case G or G7. B diminished **VII** completes the series of chords on the major scale.

Adding B diminished to a movement

*In the first bar (top staff), the **VII** chord resolves to the **I** chord linking **II** and **I**. In the second bar (top staff), the **VII** chord links **VI** and **I**. In the third bar (bottom staff), the **VII** chord replaces **V** in the sequence **I-VI-II-V-I**.*

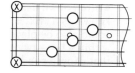

C MAJ	D MIN	B DIM	C MAJ
I	II	VII	I

C MAJ	A MIN	B DIM	C MAJ
I	VI	VII	I

C MAJ	A MIN	D MIN	B DIM	C MAJ
I	VI	II	VII	I

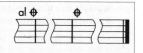

B diminished; the triad contains B, D, and F which are the 3rd, 5th, and 7th of G dominant 7.

REPEAT SIGNS, D.C., D.S., AND CODA

Music is often written down with repeat signs. Abbreviated signs are also used to direct the player to different sections. The signs are shown on the right; a chord sequence demonstrating their use is shown below.

Playing a standard sequence

Play the "intro" chord and the first twelve bars. On seeing the repeat sign at the end of the "first-time" bar, return to the repeat sign at the beginning and play the first eleven bars through to the "second-time" bar and the middle section. At the D.S. al coda sign, go back to %% and play until you reach ⊕. Then move to the coda section, ending with "fine".

Repeat signs
A repeat sign faces in the direction of the two dots. A section of bars is repeated between the dots.

Repeat the previous bar

"Da capo" (D.C.)
When the D.C. letters appear, the music is played through again from the beginning. Da Capo is Italian, and means "from the head."

D.C.

"Dal segno" (D.S.)
D.S. directs the player back to the point where the D.S. sign (%%) appears. Dal Segno means "from the sign."

D.S. %%

"Al coda"
The ⊕ sign indicates that the music moves on to a section marked by another ⊕ sign. Al coda means "to the tail."

al coda ⊕

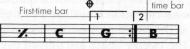

First-time bar / Second-time bar

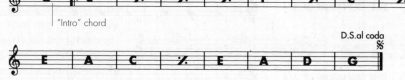

"Intro" chord

THE CYCLE OF KEYS

UNDERSTANDING THE RELATIONSHIPS BETWEEN RELATED KEYS

Modulation and transposition
Two terms are widely used to describe movements between keys. *Modulation* occurs when a passage of music moves into another key. A melody in C that moves into a section containing F♯ has *modulated* to the key of G major. The second term, *transposition*, refers to a section or piece of music repeated at a different pitch, retaining its form and structure.

Major scales are built on each note of the twelve chromatic degrees. Each scale is formed with a fixed pattern from the key note on which it is based: the sequence of intervals is the same for all twelve keys. When major scales start from notes other than C, sharps (♯) and flats (♭) are used to adjust letter names and intervals so that they conform to the major scale pattern. Sharps and flats are shown on the staff at the start of a bar. C major has two modal scales, on the fourth and fifth degrees (F and G), similar in shape to major scales. One note in each may be changed to form a new major scale.

Learning key signatures
Key signatures can be read quickly to find the correct key note by looking at the sharps and flats at the beginning of the bar. With a group of sharps, the symbol on the far right is the leading note of the key: the key note is one semitone above. With a group of flats, the symbol second from the right is on the line or space that is the key note.

C MAJOR TO G MAJOR

The scale ascending from the dominant fifth note of C major runs from G to G. It has the following order of intervals: tone-tone-semitone-tone-tone-semitone-tone. The seventh degree needs to be raised a semitone with the addition of a sharp to form the major scale of G.

C MAJOR TO F MAJOR

The scale running from F to F, which ascends from the sub-dominant fourth note of C major, has the following order of intervals: tone-tone-tone-semitone-tone-tone-semitone. In order to form the major scale of F, the fourth degree must be lowered a semitone with the addition of a flat.

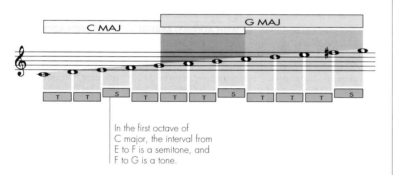

In the first octave of C major, the interval from E to F is a semitone, and F to G is a tone.

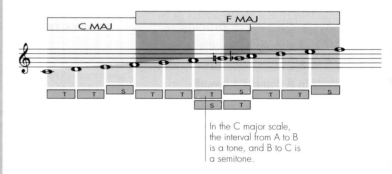

In the C major scale, the interval from A to B is a tone, and B to C is a semitone.

MIXOLYDIAN

The scale running from G to G in the key of C is termed *Mixolydian*. It shares the same notes as a G major scale, except for the seventh degree, which is an F natural.

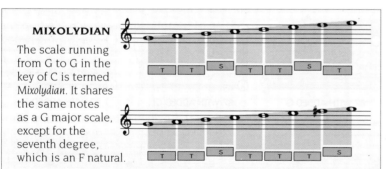

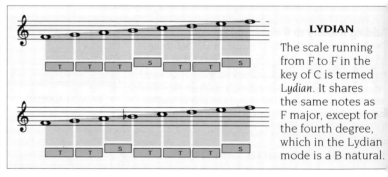

LYDIAN

The scale running from F to F in the key of C is termed *Lydian*. It shares the same notes as F major, except for the fourth degree, which in the Lydian mode is a B natural.

G MAJOR ROOTS

From the note C, at any level of pitch, there are two adjacent positions at which the first note of a G major scale can be found. G major can start either five notes above C or four notes below. The G roots are a perfect fifth above or a perfect fourth below C.

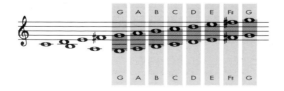

F MAJOR ROOTS

From the note C, at any level of pitch, there are two adjacent positions at which the first note of an F major scale can be found. F major can start either four notes above C or five notes below. The F roots are a perfect fourth above or a perfect fifth below C.

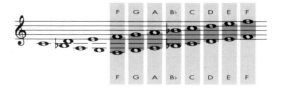

SHARP AND FLAT KEYS

Each of the major scales has two modal patterns that can be adjusted with the addition of a sharp (♯), flat (♭), or natural (♮) to form related major scales. The two major scales built from modal scales of C – G major with one sharp, and F major with one flat – can each in turn be modified to build a further major scale. C major moves to F major with one flat a fourth away.

F major, in turn, moves to B♭ major with the addition of the extra flat, or it can return to C major with a natural. The movement of fourths, using flats, runs in the following way: C-F-B♭-E♭-A♭-D♭-G♭-C♭. C major moves to G with one sharp a fifth away, and G major in turn changes to D major with the addition of an extra sharp. The movement of fifths, using sharps, runs in the following way: C-G-D-A-E-B-F♯-C♯. Each major scale

can move either backward or forward, through the cycle. By forming new keys, a scale can be transposed using all twelve keynotes, forming a cycle that finally returns to the original key. The cycle of keys moving in fifths continually raises the seventh degree of the new scale by adding a sharp. The cycle of keys moving in fourths adds a flat by flatting the fourth degree of the new scale.

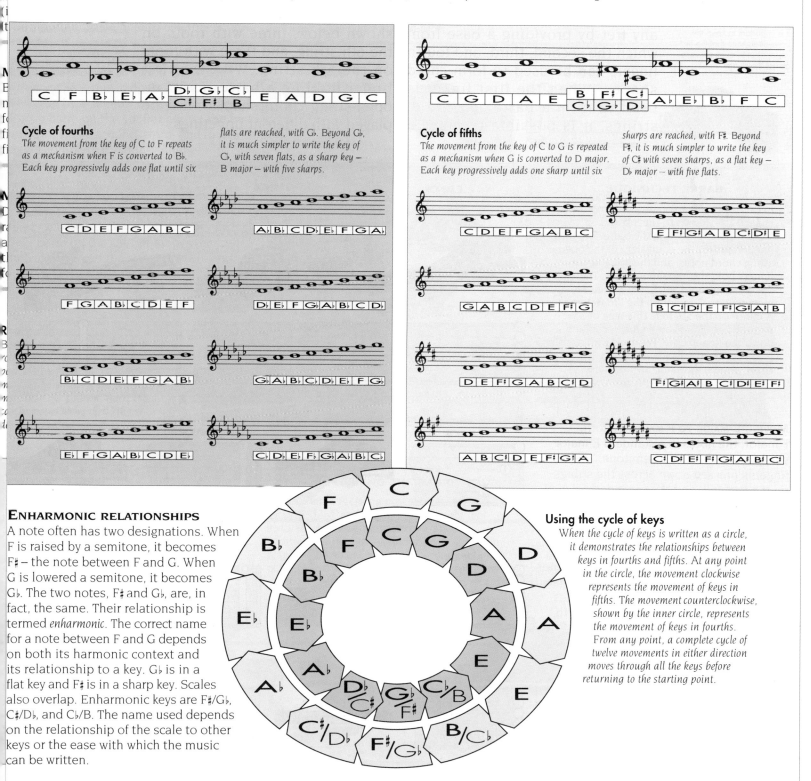

Cycle of fourths
The movement from the key of C to F repeats as a mechanism when F is converted to B♭. Each key progressively adds one flat until six flats are reached, with G♭. Beyond G♭, it is much simpler to write the key of C♭, with seven flats, as a sharp key – B major – with five sharps.

Cycle of fifths
The movement from the key of C to G is repeated as a mechanism when G is converted to D major. Each key progressively adds one sharp until six sharps are reached, with F♯. Beyond F♯, it is much simpler to write the key of C♯ with seven sharps, as a flat key – D♭ major – with five flats.

ENHARMONIC RELATIONSHIPS

A note often has two designations. When F is raised by a semitone, it becomes F♯ – the note between F and G. When G is lowered a semitone, it becomes G♭. The two notes, F♯ and G♭, are, in fact, the same. Their relationship is termed *enharmonic*. The correct name for a note between F and G depends on both its harmonic context and its relationship to a key. G♭ is in a flat key and F♯ is in a sharp key. Scales also overlap. Enharmonic keys are F♯/G♭, C♯/D♭, and C♭/B. The name used depends on the relationship of the scale to other keys or the ease with which the music can be written.

Using the cycle of keys
When the cycle of keys is written as a circle, it demonstrates the relationships between keys in fourths and fifths. At any point in the circle, the movement clockwise represents the movement of keys in fifths. The movement counterclockwise, shown by the inner circle, represents the movement of keys in fourths. From any point, a complete cycle of twelve movements in either direction moves through all the keys before returning to the starting point.

MORE BARRE TECHNIQUES

The second and third methods use the first finger to hold a full barre over all six strings. At first the full barre position can be rather uncomfortable; varying approaches can assist in the development of this technique. The examples below show how to build the fingering for an F major chord in stages.

In the first example, the chord is formed by adding notes to the first-finger barre. As a useful starting exercise, place the first finger across a fret and clearly strum all the notes held by this position. In the second example, the other fingers are stabilized *before* the barre is added. It is worth noting that the 1st fret is

a difficult position on which to play barre chords. At this position on the fingerboard, fret spacing is at its widest, and there is also considerable string tension next to the nut. Moving the chord shape half-way up the fingerboard can be easier when first practicing barre technique.

Full barre position
Begin by placing the first finger across the 1st fret of the fingerboard. Strum all six strings as a chord. Gradually add the other three fingers to form the major chord shape, and play all six strings. When you are comfortable with this technique, try playing on other fret positions.

1 Begin by holding the barre firmly and evenly across the 1st fret of the fingerboard.

2 Start to form the chord shape, placing the second finger on the 3rd string.

3 Continue building the chord by placing the third finger on the 5th string.

4 Complete the major chord by placing the fourth finger on the 4th string.

Adding the barre to a chord
Another technique for forming the barre is to first play an open E major shape with the second, third, and fourth fingers. Move the basic shape one fret up the

fingerboard. When the fingers feel comfortable and stable, add the barre to the 1st fret with the first finger. This chord movement is sometimes used in Spanish flamenco music.

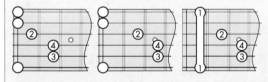

E MAJOR   F MAJOR OVER E   F MAJOR

Basic E major chord shape with the first finger clear of strings

Place the first finger barre only when the other fingers are comfortable

1 Begin by playing an E major chord with the second, third, and fourth fingers.

2 Move the shape up a fret and play the chord using the six fretted and open strings.

3 Add the barre to the 1st fret, converting the chord to an F major barre shape.

BARRE SEVENTH CHORDS
The major seventh, dominant seventh, and minor seventh chords can also be played on the main barre positions simply by adding the seventh note to major and minor chord shapes. With the addition of these new seventh shapes, the guitarist has a much larger vocabulary of chords available. Using the barre positions with the root on the 6th string, the major and

minor chords are converted to sevenths by removing the fourth finger. When this finger is moved from a note that doubles the root, the seventh note in the chord is held by the first finger on the barre. The major seventh can be played by refingering the barre chord. The doubled root on the major shape is replaced by the seventh a semitone below. Using the root on the 5th string, the doubled octave note is

removed, and the seventh in the chord is held by the barre. This applies to all of the shapes apart from the first example, where the B♭ major chord is changed to B♭ major 7 and refingered with the seventh held by the second finger. Practicing the movement of major and minor chords to sevenths is an effective way to learn new shapes. The standard barre shapes are shown below with their seventh voicings.

F DOMINANT 7TH F major is converted to a dominant 7th by taking the fourth finger away from the 4th string. The 7th is held by the barre on the 1st fret of the 4th string.

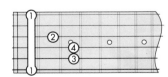

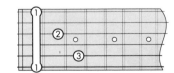

F MINOR 7TH F minor chord is converted to F minor 7th by removing the fourth finger from the 4th string. The 7th is held by the barre on the 1st fret of the 4th string.

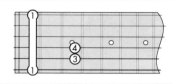

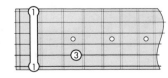

Bb MAJOR 7TH Bb major is converted to a Bb major 7th by replacing the second finger with the third and placing the second finger on the 2nd fret of the 3rd string.

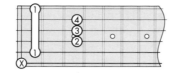 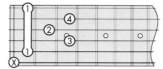 

Bb DOMINANT 7TH Bb major is converted to a Bb dominant 7th by placing the second finger on the 3rd fret of the 4th string. The 7th is held by the barre on the 3rd string.

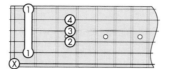 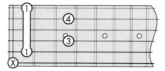 

Bb MINOR 7TH Bb minor is converted to a Bb minor 7th by taking the fourth finger away from the third string. The 7th is held by the barre on the 1st fret of the 3rd string.

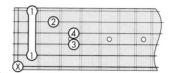 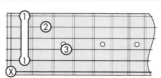 

Db MAJOR 7TH Db major is converted to a Db major 7th by taking the second finger away from the 2nd string. The 7th is held by the barre on the 1st fret of the 2nd string.

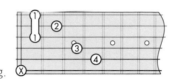 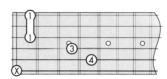 

CHORD POSITIONS

The same chord voicing can be played in different places. For some players, this can make choosing chords for a sequence confusing. Below are three ways of playing D major with the chord notes at the same pitch. The three chords contain exactly the same notes. Each chord has a distinct tonal color from its position on the fingerboard, and this creates a varied musical effect. The choice of chord position depends on technical requirements or the context in a sequence. Learning all the positions for a chord voicing enables chord sequences to be played in different areas of the fingerboard. With a full barre-chord vocabulary, sequences using 5th- and 6th-string roots can be played in any register without having to move the left hand more than four frets in either direction.

D major extended

The two higher shapes have extra chord voices available. The D major chord with the root on the 5th fret of the 5th string has the extra 1st string available. A doubled fifth note (A) can be added on the 5th fret of the 1st string if a barre is placed across the 5th fret. The D major chord with the root on the 6th string has both the 1st and the 2nd strings available for the addition of chord notes. The doubled 5th (A) can be played on the 10th fret of the 2nd string, with the extra D on the 1st string if a full barre is placed across the 10th fret.

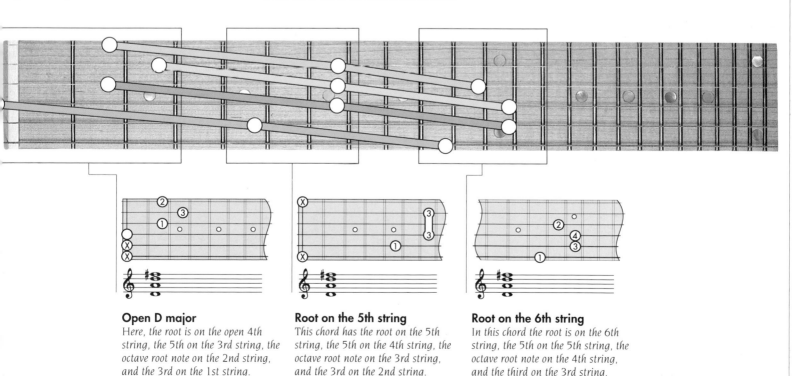

Open D major
Here, the root is on the open 4th string, the 5th on the 3rd string, the octave root note on the 2nd string, and the 3rd on the 1st string.

Root on the 5th string
This chord has the root on the 5th string, the 5th on the 4th string, the octave root note on the 3rd string, and the 3rd on the 2nd string.

Root on the 6th string
In this chord the root is on the 6th string, the 5th on the 5th string, the octave root note on the 4th string, and the third on the 3rd string.

MOVEMENTS ON THE CYCLE OF KEYS

The cycle of keys is an ideal aid to the development of chord technique and movement. Any chord type can be played in every key with all twelve root notes, creating a full and balanced vocabulary. Chords frequently move in fourths or fifths: one of the most commonly used groups is C, G, and D major, when playing in the key of G. The chords C, G, and D are related harmonically and can be found on either side of G in the cycle of keys. By playing around the cycle, each chord is placed next to its related chords an interval of a fourth or fifth away. Acquiring the technique of moving from any chord to an adjacent shape on the cycle of keys is important for playing all types of music.

Playing through exercises based on the cycle of keys is also a highly effective way to learn all the roots for chord shapes and their positions. This can be achieved by playing the different chord types – majors, minors, and sevenths – encountered so far, in movements of fifths and fourths around the cycle. There are various possible routes for the same sequence of chords: playing a sequence from C major in fifths or fourths can use a number of different positions. This gives alternative voicings for many of the chords.

POSITIONAL PROBLEMS

One of the most important things to remember is that a movement from one chord in one position, using the cycle movement, may appear confusing because of the position of the next root step in relation to the frets and strings. This may lead to a series of similar-sounding names being used for movements and positions. For example, when C major is moved from a 3rd fret position on the 5th string to F major, using the cycle of keys in fourths, the next chord (F) is a fourth *above* the C chord with roots on either the 5th or the 4th string. The F shape is also a fifth *below* C with the root on the 6th string. When C major is moved from its 3rd fret position on the 5th string to G major, using the cycle of fifths, the next chord (G) is a fifth *above* C major on the 5th or 4th string. The G shape is also a fourth *below* C with the root on the 6th string.

Major chord movements in fifths

You can play the twelve major chords using two shapes: a major voicing from the 5th string root, and a major voicing from the 6th string root. There are a number of combinations of fret positions for moving on the cycle of fifths. Play the first example, changing position from C to G on the third fret, and move up the fretboard, two frets at a time, to C on the 15th fret. The second example follows the same movements through to B major, then goes to F♯ major on the 2nd fret and moves up the fingerboard, ending with C major on the 8th fret.

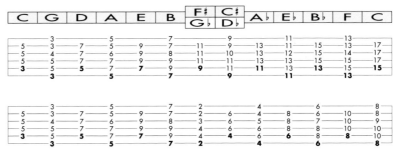

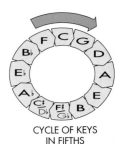

CYCLE OF KEYS IN FIFTHS

Major chord movements in fourths

The cycle can now be played moving around the other way in fourths. The first example uses the change of position from C on the 3rd fret to F on the 1st fret and moves around the fingerboard before returning to C on the 3rd fret. The second example starts with C on the 8th fret, moving to F on the 8th fret. This movement in chord position descends two frets at a time, until B is reached on the 2nd fret. B moves up to E major on the 7th fret, and the cycle descends from E, down the fingerboard, ending with C on the 3rd fret.

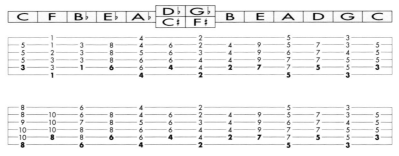

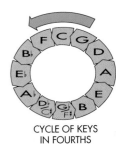

CYCLE OF KEYS IN FOURTHS

Minor seventh movements in fourths and fifths

Every chord type may be played around the cycle of keys in both directions. Following the exercises on the right, play a series of minor seventh shapes around the cycle in fifths, starting with the C minor seventh with its root on the 3rd fret of the 5th string. Starting from the same position, play around the cycle of keys in a movement of fourths. Playing the cycle of fifth positions in reverse order provides an alternative route for the cycle of fourth positions. Now play through the cycles and movements, beginning with C minor seventh with its root on the 8th fret of the 6th string. The cycle of chords moving through each of the keys may be started off from any point. Finally, try playing a complete series of dominant seventh chords through the cycle of fourths, starting from the A chord. The sequence A7-D7-G7-C7-F7-B♭7-E♭7-A♭7-D♭7-G♭7-B7-E7-A7 makes up the complete movement. Play this sequence in fifths.

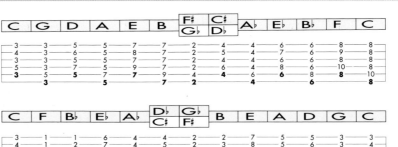

FIFTHS

FOURTHS

Enharmonic equivalents

In the cycle of fifths, the two minor seventh chords in the middle are labeled F♯ and C♯. In the cycle of fourths, the chords can use the enharmonic equivalents of G♭ and

D♭. When they are treated as a relative minor chord, or as a minor on the second degree of the scale (see p. 69), C♯ minor seventh and F♯ minor seventh are the correct scale note names.

TRANSPOSING CHORDS

PLAYING CHORD MOVEMENTS IN DIFFERENT KEYS

Roman numerals
The Roman numeral system for naming scale degrees can be used for chordal movements. In each major key, the numerals I to VII are used as a shorthand method to indicate the position and movement of chords. The same chord can be assigned different numerals depending on the key. For example, C major is a I chord in the key of C major, a IV chord in the key of G major, and a V chord in the key of F major.

A piece of music may be moved from one key to any other key; this is referred to as *transposition*. This is used for vocal ranges and instrumentation, or it may occur as part of a piece of music. Each key has the same type of structure: a scale and a group of chords that are based on a fixed system of harmonic relationships. As we have seen on page 68, each of the seven degrees of any key is labeled with a Roman numeral from I to VII. In the scale of C major, C major is the I chord, and G major is the V chord. Therefore, if a piece of music is transposed from the key of C major to the key of G major, the I chord beomes G major, and the V chord becomes D major.

Cycles of transposition
C major is the starting point for the cycle of transpositions in fifths using sharps and the cycle of fourths using flats. In the chart below, the chords line up vertically, enabling the player to compare the same type of movement in each of the keys. The chart below is divided into two sections: a partial cycle of fifths that moves through the sharp keys, and a partial cycle of fourths that moves through the flat keys.

TRANSPOSITION IN FIFTHS

In the key of C major, the sequence **I-VI-II-V** consists of the chords C major, A minor, D minor, and G major. This movement can be repeated in the key of G major by transposing all roots and chord types by a perfect fifth. This is repeated when G is transposed to D, and for all succeeding key movements in fifths.

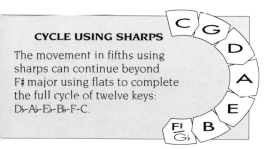

CYCLE USING SHARPS

The movement in fifths using sharps can continue beyond F♯ major using flats to complete the full cycle of twelve keys: D♭-A♭-E♭-B♭-F-C.

TRANSPOSITION IN FOURTHS

The relationship between the chords in the key of C major is repeated in the key of F major by transposing all the note names and the chord types by a perfect fourth. The I chord, C major, becomes F major, and the other elements also move by a fourth. When F major is transposed to B flat major, the transposition by a fourth is repeated. All the succeeding movements through the keys are the same.

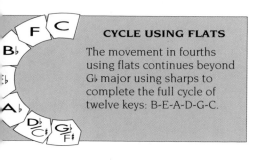

CYCLE USING FLATS

The movement in fourths using flats continues beyond G♭ major using sharps to complete the full cycle of twelve keys: B-E-A-D-G-C.

	I – V		I – IV		I	VI	II	V
C MAJOR	C MAJ	G MAJ	C MAJ	F MAJ	C MAJ	A MIN	D MIN	G MAJ
G MAJOR	G MAJ	D MAJ	G MAJ	C MAJ	G MAJ	E MIN	A MIN	D MAJ
D MAJOR	D MAJ	A MAJ	D MAJ	G MAJ	D MAJ	B MIN	E MIN	A MAJ
A MAJOR	A MAJ	E MAJ	A MAJ	D MAJ	A MAJ	F♯ MIN	B MIN	F MAJ
E MAJOR	E MAJ	B MAJ	E MAJ	A MAJ	E MAJ	C♯ MIN	F♯ MIN	B MAJ
B MAJOR	B MAJ	F♯ MAJ	B MAJ	E MAJ	B MAJ	G♯ MIN	C♯ MIN	F♯ MAJ
F♯ MAJOR	F♯ MAJ	C♯ MAJ	F♯ MAJ	B MAJ	F♯ MAJ	D♯ MIN	G♯ MIN	C♯ MAJ
C MAJOR	C MAJ	G MAJ	C MAJ	F MAJ	C MAJ	A MIN	D MIN	G MAJ
F MAJOR	F MAJ	C MAJ	F MAJ	B♭ MAJ	F MAJ	D MIN	G MIN	C MAJ
B♭ MAJOR	B♭ MAJ	F MAJ	B♭ MAJ	E♭ MAJ	B♭ MAJ	G MIN	C MIN	F MAJ
E♭ MAJOR	E♭ MAJ	B♭ MAJ	E♭ MAJ	A♭ MAJ	E♭ MAJ	C MIN	F MIN	B♭ MAJ
A♭ MAJOR	A♭ MAJ	E♭ MAJ	A♭ MAJ	D♭ MAJ	A♭ MAJ	F MIN	B♭ MIN	E♭ MAJ
D♭ MAJOR	D♭ MAJ	A♭ MAJ	D♭ MAJ	G♭ MAJ	D♭ MAJ	B♭ MIN	E♭ MIN	A♭ MAJ
G♭ MAJOR	G♭ MAJ	D♭ MAJ	G♭ MAJ	C♭ MAJ	G♭ MAJ	E♭ MIN	A♭ MIN	D♭ MAJ

MOVING CHORDS

DEVELOPING MOBILITY WITH OPEN-STRING AND BARRE CHORDS

The primary chords
In the major keys, the primary major chords are those built on the tonic (I), subdominant (IV), and dominant (V). They are related to one another with a series of strong musical movements. When combined, these chords may be used to create music and melody of considerable variety.

Music is frequently built around a few closely related chords. G major, C major, and D major are the I, IV, and V chords from the key of G. They may be played easily by using open-string voicings and are commonly found in all styles of music. Combining open-string and fretted barre voicings creates many variations on these chords. Playing the three chord types through the variations below will help develop a basic understanding of primary chord movements.

Primary chord movements
A thorough understanding of the primary major chords in every key forms a secure foundation on which to build a comprehensive vocabulary for accompanying songs and improvisation. There are a number of positions for each chord, and these may be played in many different way

ROOTS ON THE 6TH AND 5TH STRINGS

With the exception of D major in the open-string voicing, the chords in this section are placed with their lowest root note on either the 6th or the 5th string. The numbers in circles show the fingers to be used; circles without numbers represent optional notes.

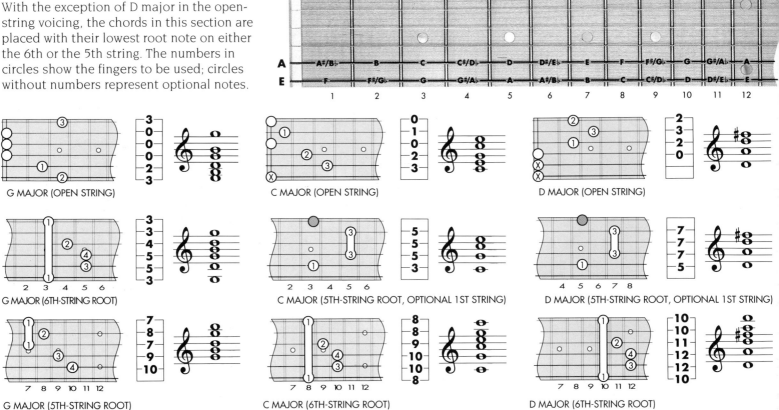

G MAJOR (OPEN STRING)

C MAJOR (OPEN STRING)

D MAJOR (OPEN STRING)

G MAJOR (6TH-STRING ROOT)

C MAJOR (5TH-STRING ROOT, OPTIONAL 1ST STRING)

D MAJOR (5TH-STRING ROOT, OPTIONAL 1ST STRING)

G MAJOR (5TH-STRING ROOT)

C MAJOR (6TH-STRING ROOT)

D MAJOR (6TH-STRING ROOT)

VARIATIONS ON G-C-D

Play through the three chord variations using G, C, and D major. Use all of the different voicings shown above to create as many combinations as possible. The order of the three chords can also be altered to give D-G-C, D-C-G, and C-G-D. Practice all the combinations using minor and seventh chords. Playing each of these combinations will help you develop chordal technique. One way to play through the three-chord examples is to use four downstroke beats on each of the first two chords and eight on the last chord. Doing so extends the chords into a four-bar sequence of 4/4 time.

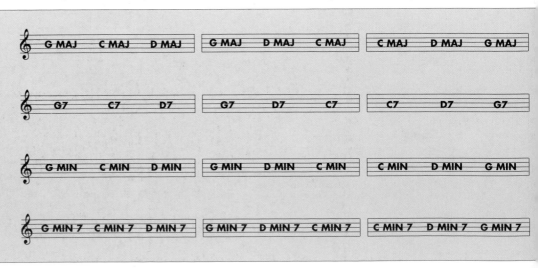

TRANSPOSING G, C, AND D

When similar types of standard voicing are used to play a three-chord sequence, the pattern of movements is very easy to remember visually on the fingerboard. A fixed series of the three chords – G, C, and D major – can be transposed to other keys by shifting the entire system of shapes to different fret positions. For example, G, C, and D major are raised a semitone to the key of A♭ by moving the entire progression up by one fret. Moving up the fingerboard one fret at a time transposes the sequence in ascending semitones. Moving down the fingerboard from the G position on the 3rd fret transposes the sequence in descending semitones to F♯/G♭, F, and finally E on the open-string position.

ROCK CHORDS

The movement of chords using **I-IV-V** in a blues twelve-bar format is one of the most widely used basic structures in rock music. The three chords can be played as a series of sustained open-string chords or fretted shapes. Major chords are often reduced from a triad with a third to a chord that consists of just roots and fifths – the third is not played. The chords, in a **I-IV-V** sequence in G, are sometimes written as G5, C5, and D5. The root and the fifth for each major chord can be played on the 5th and 6th strings. An additional octave root can be included on the 4th or the 3rd string. Other voicings can be constructed with roots and fifths.

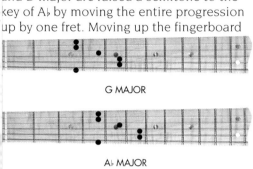

G MAJOR

C MAJOR

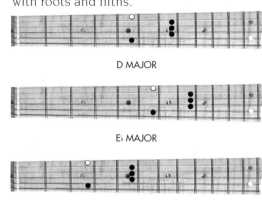

D MAJOR

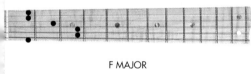

A♭ MAJOR

D♭ MAJOR

E♭ MAJOR

F MAJOR

B♭ MAJOR

C MAJOR

G–C–D ON THE 6TH STRING

The sequence of chords G-C-D can be played by moving a single chord shape up and down the fingerboard. First play a G major chord on the 3rd fret, then move the shape up to the 8th fret to a C major chord, and then on to the 10th fret to make a D major chord.

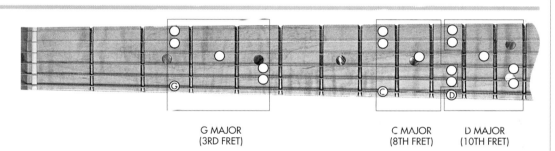

G MAJOR
(3RD FRET)

C MAJOR
(8TH FRET)

D MAJOR
(10TH FRET)

G–C–D ON THE 5TH STRING

The sequence G-C-D can also be played moving a shape based on a 5th-string root up and down the fingerboard. Starting with the G major chord on the 10th fret, the shape can be moved down to the 3rd fret, where it becomes C major, and back up to the 5th fret, to become D major.

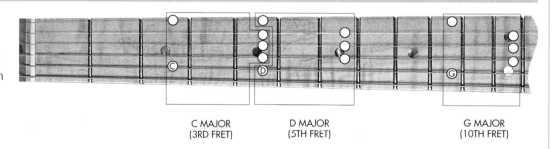

C MAJOR
(3RD FRET)

D MAJOR
(5TH FRET)

G MAJOR
(10TH FRET)

PLAYING 5TH-STRING SEVENTHS

The chord sequence **II-V-I** in C major can be played using seventh shapes along the 5th string. Beginning with D minor 7 (**II**) on the 5th fret, the barre shape is moved up to the 10th fret and modified to a G dominant seventh (**V**). On the 3rd fret, the chord is modified to C major 7 (**I**).

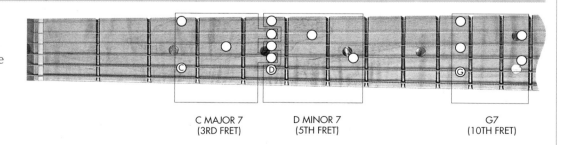

C MAJOR 7
(3RD FRET)

D MINOR 7
(5TH FRET)

G7
(10TH FRET)

Mixolydian major V

The G major dominant chord uses all of the scalar additions of the Mixolydian mode. The seventh (F), ninth (A), and fourth/eleventh (C) are all additions to the dominant chord. The note C acts as a suspended fourth when the third is left out. The note E is referred to as a thirteenth when the chord contains either a seventh or added scale notes. When E is added to the basic triad, it is referred to as a sixth.

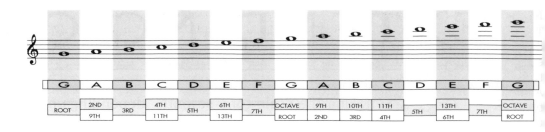

| ROOT | 2ND | 3RD | 4TH | 5TH | 6TH | 7TH | OCTAVE | 9TH | 10TH | 11TH | 5TH | 13TH | 7TH | OCTAVE |
| 9TH | | 11TH | | 13TH | | ROOT | 2ND | 3RD | 4TH | | 6TH | | ROOT |

Aeolian minor VI

The A minor chord uses all of the scalar additions of the minor scale/Aeolian mode. It can be extended using the seventh (G), the ninth (B), and the eleventh (D) notes. The sixth, or thirteenth, is the note F – when used with certain voicings this addition can produce a dissonant sound. It is most commonly used as a flat sixth addition to the chord.

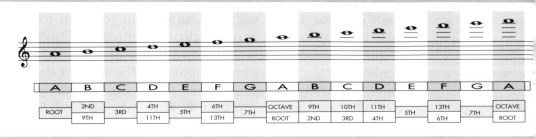

Locrian diminished VII

The B diminished chord can be extended to a minor seventh flat five with the addition of the seventh (A). The fourth/eleventh (E) is often added, but the ninth (C) sounds dissonant above the root. The note G is the sixth/thirteenth. It is often treated as the root note of a related G dominant inversion.

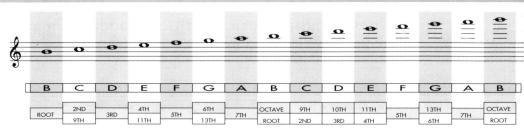

PLAYING MODAL ARPEGGIOS

Play the seven modal arpeggios from the root note of each degree of the major scale. The C modal arpeggios below are placed at their lowest pitch on the guitar, using the 1st string for higher notes. Starting with C on the 3rd fret of the 5th string, play the arpeggio as a series of ascending thirds, with E on the 4th string, G on the open 3rd string, B and D on the 2nd string, and F, A, and C on the 1st string. Listen to each note and pick out weak or dissonant-sounding scale notes in each arpeggio. Play all the arpeggios and compare them with the modal scales in the key of C major. The D arpeggio starts from the 4th string, and the arpeggios from E, F, G, A, and B have been moved down to start on the 6th and 5th strings. When a series of thirds is played over two octaves with every element of the modal scale, the sound and character of the notes can be heard in relation to the root as a series of harmonies.

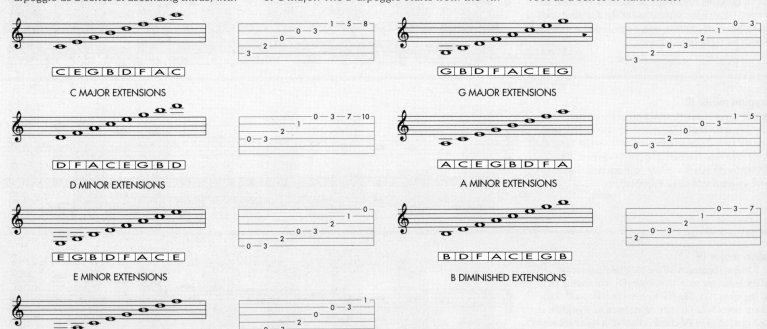

C MAJOR EXTENSIONS

D MINOR EXTENSIONS

E MINOR EXTENSIONS

F MAJOR EXTENSIONS

G MAJOR EXTENSIONS

A MINOR EXTENSIONS

B DIMINISHED EXTENSIONS

MAJOR KEY CHORD CHART

The chords on the major scale are shown below with their constituent notes. On each degree of the scale there are various types of extended chord in frequent use. Abbreviations are used for writing chord types down as symbols: **M** or **MAJ** can be used to represent *major*, and **m** or **MIN** – *minor*. The letter name, triad abbreviation, or other term also has a number for the chord addition. For example, **GM7** indicates a G major triad with the addition of a seventh. The notes that make up the chord between the root and the upper extension are put together to give the chord the structure it requires. Different voicings can be used. A particular chord voicing does not always contain all of the elements that make up the full structure: when it is extended to ninths, elevenths, and thirteenths, elements of the chord are often left out. For example, the full extension of a G dominant thirteenth chord contains the seven notes G, B, D, F, A, C, and E. With only six strings on the guitar, one or more notes have to be omitted in order to play a practical voicing.

Reference chart

The seven chord notes, running from the root to the thirteenth/sixth in each chord, are written from left to right. The seven chord roots built on each of the modal degrees are shown in the first column, and their structure as a series of thirds is written alongside on each line.

		1	3	5	7	9/2	11/4	13/6
I	MAJOR/IONIAN	C	E	G	B	D	F	A
II	DORIAN	D	F	A	C	E	G	B
III	PHRYGIAN	E	G	B	D	F	A	C
IV	LYDIAN	F	A	C	E	G	B	D
V	MIXOLYDIAN	G	B	D	F	A	C	E
VI	MINOR/AEOLIAN	A	C	E	G	B	D	F
VII	LOCRIAN	B	D	F	A	C	E	G

Chords in C major

The main chord types in frequent use are shown in the chart on the right. Sixths, sevenths, ninths, elevenths, and thirteenths, and combinations of sixths and ninths, occur as the main chord types in a major key. There are many other combinations of intervals; they are used in jazz, classical composition, and some types of ethnic music.

		4TH	6TH	7TH	9TH	11TH	13TH	6/9	OTHER TYPES
C	MAJOR	C SUS4	C 6	C M7	C M9			C 6/9	C 6/7 C ADD F C 6/9M7
D	MINOR		D m6	D m7	D m9	D m11	D m13	D m6/9	
E	MINOR			E m7		E m11			E PHRYGIAN CHORDS
F	MAJOR		F 6	F M7	F M9	F M7♯11		F 6/9	F 6/7 F M9♯11 F 6/9M7
G	MAJOR	G SUS4	G 6	G 7	G 9	G 11	G13	G 6/9	
A	MINOR			A m7	A m9	A m11			A AEOLIAN CHORDS
B	DIMINISHED			B m7♭5		B m11♭5			B LOCRIAN CHORDS

Transposing modal chords

The major system of modal chords is built in each major key with the same type of structure and additions. For example, in the key of G major the scale G-A-B-C-D-E-F♯ is used as the basis for the I-VII series of chords. All the chord types are built from these root notes and are developed with the same rules as the C major scale.

		4TH	6TH	7TH	9TH	11TH	13TH	6/9	OTHER TYPES
G	MAJOR	G SUS4	G 6	G M7	G M9			G 6/9	G 6/7 G ADD C G 6/9M7
A	MINOR		A m6	A m7	A m9	A m11	A m13	A m6/9	
B	MINOR			B m7		B m11			B PHRYGIAN CHORDS
C	MAJOR		C 6	C M7	C M9	C M7♯11		C 6/9	C 6/7 C M9♯11 C 6/9M7
D	MAJOR	D SUS4	D 6	D 7	D 9	D 11	D 13	D 6/9	
E	MINOR			E m7	E m9	E m11			E AEOLIAN CHORDS
F♯	DIMINISHED			F♯ m7♭5		F♯m11♭5			F♯ LOCRIAN CHORDS

CHORD CONSTRUCTION

ALTERED DOMINANT AND SEVENTH CHORDS

Dominant extensions
The diagram below shows a series of notes in relation to the note G, on the fifth degree (V) of the C major scale. The notes beneath the staff are from the scale of C major. Those above the staff are other notes that may also be used in combination with the dominant chord.

Dominant chords may be used in many different ways: they act as the **V** chord in major and minor harmony, and as an altered form to replace basic chords in blues, jazz, and many other types of music. The flexibility of the dominant chord can lead to a wide range of additions that use all the notes available from the root, with the exception of the major seventh. This type of harmonic structure has a great number of possibilities for voicing; many of the most unusual chord types are dominant sevenths with added notes.

Additions
In the C major scale, the notes added to the G major triad are the seventh, ninth, eleventh, and thirteenth notes of the G Mixolydian mode (see p. 88). The other notes are approached as fifths, ninths, elevenths, and thirteenths, with adjustments made using flats and sharps.

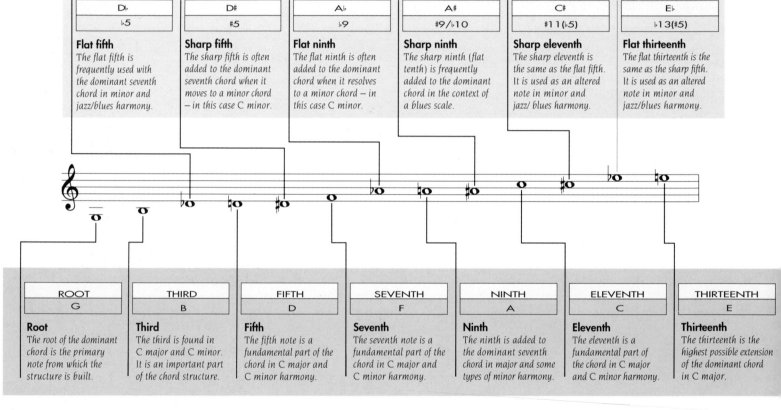

Db	D#	Ab	A#	C#	Eb
b5	#5	b9	#9/b10	#11(b5)	b13(#5)

Flat fifth
The flat fifth is frequently used with the dominant seventh chord in minor and jazz/blues harmony.

Sharp fifth
The sharp fifth is often added to the dominant seventh chord when it moves to a minor chord — in this case C minor.

Flat ninth
The flat ninth is often added to the dominant chord when it resolves to a minor chord — in this case C minor.

Sharp ninth
The sharp ninth (flat tenth) is frequently added to the dominant chord in the context of a blues scale.

Sharp eleventh
The sharp eleventh is the same as the flat fifth. It is used as an altered note in minor and jazz/blues harmony.

Flat thirteenth
The flat thirteenth is the same as the sharp fifth. It is used as an altered note in minor and jazz/blues harmony.

ROOT	THIRD	FIFTH	SEVENTH	NINTH	ELEVENTH	THIRTEENTH
G	B	D	F	A	C	E

Root
The root of the dominant chord is the primary note from which the structure is built.

Third
The third is found in C major and C minor. It is an important part of the chord structure.

Fifth
The fifth note is a fundamental part of the chord in C major and C minor harmony.

Seventh
The seventh note is a fundamental part of the chord in C major and C minor harmony.

Ninth
The ninth is added to the dominant seventh chord in major and some types of minor harmony.

Eleventh
The eleventh is a fundamental part of the chord in C major and C minor harmony.

Thirteenth
The thirteenth is the highest possible extension of the dominant chord in C major.

Chord tone scale
All the notes can be placed in a one octave chromatic scale. Only F# is missing. Compare the altered notes: they have different names according to position.

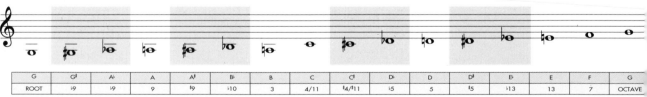

G	G#	Ab	A	A#	Bb	B	C	C#	Db	D	D#	Eb	E	F	G
ROOT	b9	b9	9	#9	b10	3	4/11	#4/#11	b5	5	#5	b13	13	7	OCTAVE

ARPEGGIO EXERCISE

Play the ascending thirds from the root note (G), using the chord additions in C major: G-B-D-F-A-C-E. Add the altered tones by playing the arpeggio slowly and hearing them in relation to the standard fifth, ninth, eleventh, and thirteenth. Dominant chords often consist of standard and altered notes.

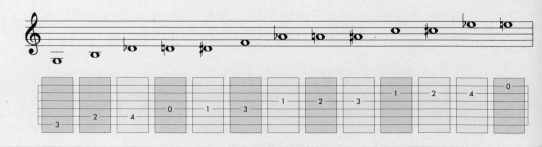

SEVENTHS

Ten different seventh chords can be built from any root by using three superimposed notes. Most chords are based on thirds over a root note; in seventh chords, the first third to be placed over the root is either a minor third or a major third. This note can be combined with additional thirds, or major seconds, to form triads. In relation to the root, the perfect fifth is raised by a semitone to form an augmented fifth (*sharp five*), or lowered by a semitone to form a diminished fifth (*flat five*). These combinations can form one major triad, one augmented triad, one major triad with a diminished fifth, one

minor triad, or one diminished triad. A third is added above the fifth, to create three different types of seventh interval from the root: minor seventh, major seventh, and diminished seventh. The addition of the seventh results in a total of ten different types of seventh chord (including unusual variations). When different chord types are built from one root note, for example C, their combinations of intervals can be compared. Only one chord in the C series is built exclusively using the notes of C major – the other chords are related to various different keys and scales. Build up the chords in stages from the C root on the 3rd fret of the 5th string. Each seventh

chord can be viewed as a series of building blocks, from the root to the third, third to fifth, and fifth to seventh. The sound and structure of each chord varies. Although they are named as a series of thirds with altered notes from the root, the gaps between the four notes in a seventh chord, in each stage from the root to the seventh, sometimes use other intervals in addition to the standard major and minor thirds. The possible intervals are shown below by a series of color-coded squares: red indicates a major second interval; blue, a minor third; yellow, a major third; and white, a perfect fourth.

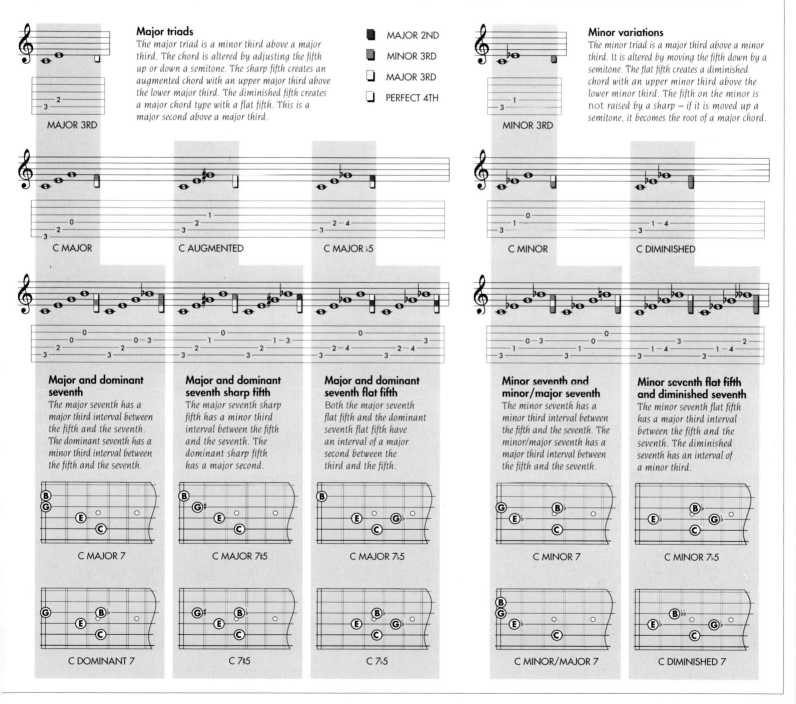

Major triads
The major triad is a minor third above a major third. The chord is altered by adjusting the fifth up or down a semitone. The sharp fifth creates an augmented chord with an upper major third above the lower major third. The diminished fifth creates a major chord type with a flat fifth. This is a major second above a major third.

MAJOR 3RD

■ MAJOR 2ND
▪ MINOR 3RD
□ MAJOR 3RD
□ PERFECT 4TH

Minor variations
The minor triad is a major third above a minor third. It is altered by moving the fifth down by a semitone. The flat fifth creates a diminished chord with an upper minor third above the lower minor third. The fifth on the minor is not raised by a sharp – if it is moved up a semitone, it becomes the root of a major chord.

MINOR 3RD

C MAJOR   C AUGMENTED   C MAJOR ♭5   C MINOR   C DIMINISHED

Major and dominant seventh
The major seventh has a major third interval between the fifth and the seventh. The dominant seventh has a minor third interval between the fifth and the seventh.

Major and dominant seventh sharp fifth
The major seventh sharp fifth has a minor third interval between the fifth and the seventh. The dominant sharp fifth has a major second.

Major and dominant seventh flat fifth
Both the major seventh flat fifth and the dominant seventh flat fifth have an interval of a major second between the third and the fifth.

Minor seventh and minor/major seventh
The minor seventh has a minor third interval between the fifth and the seventh. The minor/major seventh has a major third interval between the fifth and the seventh.

Minor seventh flat fifth and diminished seventh
The minor seventh flat fifth has a major third interval between the fifth and the seventh. The diminished seventh has an interval of a minor third.

C MAJOR 7   C MAJOR 7♯5   C MAJOR 7♭5   C MINOR 7   C MINOR 7♭5

C DOMINANT 7   C 7♯5   C 7♭5   C MINOR/MAJOR 7   C DIMINISHED 7

CHORD FINDER

A DICTIONARY OF CHORD TYPES

Fingerboard symbols
On the fingerboard diagrams throughout the chord finder, numbers inside circles show which left-hand fingers are used. Circles over the nut indicate that open strings should be played. A circle on the fretboard, with no number, shows that the note is optional. A white bar connecting strings represents a barre or a half-barre. The **X** symbol shows that a string is not played.

O ver the following eight pages is an extensive range of chords built from fifth-, sixth-, and fourth-string roots. Altogether, there are 89 chord shapes with roots placed on the 3rd fret. Each shape may be moved up or down the fingerboard to any of the twelve fret positions, providing over a thousand different chords. It is important to practice chords so that adjacent strings that are *not* part of the harmony are not accidentally played. To begin with, accuracy may be difficult to achieve on some of the shapes. However, a controlled technique for playing chords will become second nature with constant practice.

Finding a chord
To find a chord type, first select a string position. For example, in order to play a B7♭9, go to the 5th-string chords based on C roots. Look through the chords until you come to C7♭9 on page 96. If this shape is then moved down one fret to the B root on the 2nd fret, B7♭9 is formed. Some chord types are voiced more easily using certain strings.

ROOTS ON THE 5TH STRING
Using chords with the roots based on the 3rd fret of the 5th string gives all the chord types a C root. From this point, they can be compared harmonically, and the constituent notes can be memorized in relation to a C root. The chords that are rooted on the 5th string work well for sequences and are particularly effective when combined with those that are based on a 6th-string root. Chords with a 5th-string root often have adjacent outer or inner strings that are not played. The player should prevent these unused strings from ringing by letting the sides of the fingers rest naturally against them. This type of chord is generally played without a full barre.

Chord notes
The intervals shown on the fingerboard are named from the root (in this case, C). The same pattern can run from any fret position on the 5th string. The twelve chromatic semitones can be used as a root for any chord.

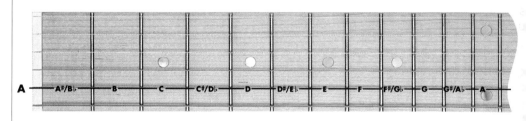

MAJ 3	11/4	♯11/♯4/♭5	5	♯5/♭6/♭13	13/6	MIN 7
MAJ 7	ROOT	♭9	9	♯9/♭10	MAJ 3	11/4
5	♯5/♭6	6/13	MIN 7	MAJ 7	ROOT	♭9
2/9	♯9/MIN 3	MAJ 3	4/11	♯4/♯11/♭5	5	♯5/♭6
	ROOT	♭9		2/9	♯9/MIN 3

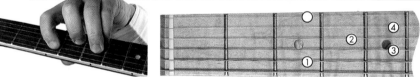

A — A♯/B♭ — B — C — C♯/D♭ — D — D♯/E♭ — E — F — F♯/G♭ — G — G♯/A♭ — A

C MAJOR 7TH (C△7) This uses C (root), G (perfect fifth), B (major seventh), and E (major third). Play the 5th, 4th, 3rd, and 2nd strings.

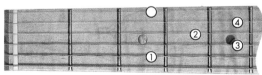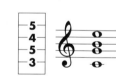

5
4
5
3

C DOMINANT 7TH (C7) This uses C (root), G (perfect fifth), B♭ (minor seventh), and E (major third). The strings used are the 5th to the 2nd.

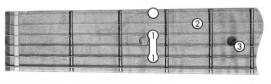

5
3
5
3

C MINOR 7TH (C-7) Play C (root), G (perfect fifth), B♭ (minor seventh), and E♭ (minor third) on the 5th, 4th, 3rd, and 2nd strings.

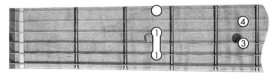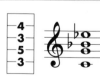

4
3
5
3

C MINOR 7TH FLAT 5TH (C-7♭5) The notes played are C (root), G♭ (diminished fifth), B♭ (minor seventh), and E♭ (minor third).

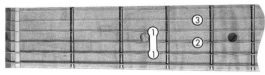

4
3
4
3

C DIMINISHED 7TH (C°7) The notes used are C (root), G♭ (diminished fifth), B♭♭/A (diminished seventh/major sixth), and E♭ (minor third).

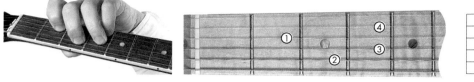

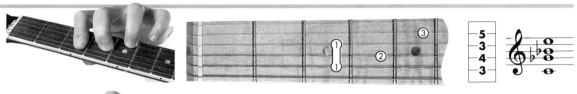

C DOMINANT 7TH FLAT 5TH (C7♭5) The notes used are C (root), G♭ (diminished fifth), B♭ (minor seventh), and E (major third).

C DOMINANT 7TH SHARP 5TH (C7♯5) This chord uses C (root), G♯ (augmented fifth), B♭ (minor seventh), and E (major third).

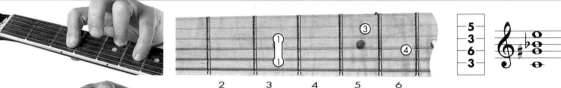

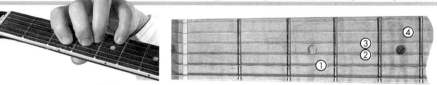

C MAJOR 7TH SHARP 11TH (C△♯11) The chord uses the notes C (root), F♯ (augmented 4th/11th), B (major seventh), and E (major third).

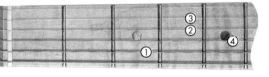

C MINOR/MAJOR 7TH (C-△7) Play C (root), G (perfect fifth), B (major seventh), and E♭ (minor third) using the 5th to the 2nd strings.

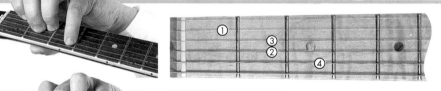

C MAJOR 6TH (C6) This chord uses C (root), E (major third), A (major sixth), and C (octave root). Play all the strings from the 5th to the 2nd.

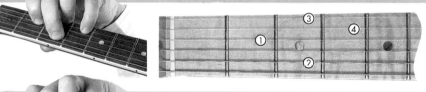

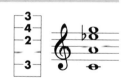

C MINOR 6TH (C-6) The notes are C (root), A (major sixth), E♭ (minor third), and G (perfect fifth). Play the 5th, 3rd, 2nd, and 1st strings.

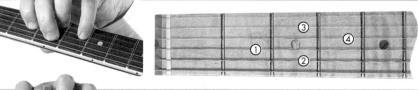

C MAJOR 9TH (C△9) Play the notes C (root), E (major third), B (major seventh), and D (major ninth). The 5th to the 2nd strings are used.

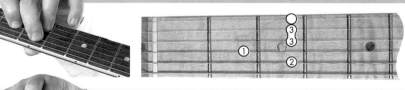

C DOMINANT 9TH (C9) Play C (root), E (major third), B♭ (minor seventh), and D (major ninth) using the 5th to the 2nd strings.

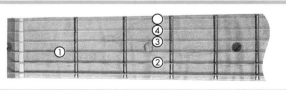

C MINOR 9TH (C-9) The chord is formed using the notes C (root), E♭ (minor third), B♭ (minor seventh), and D (major ninth).

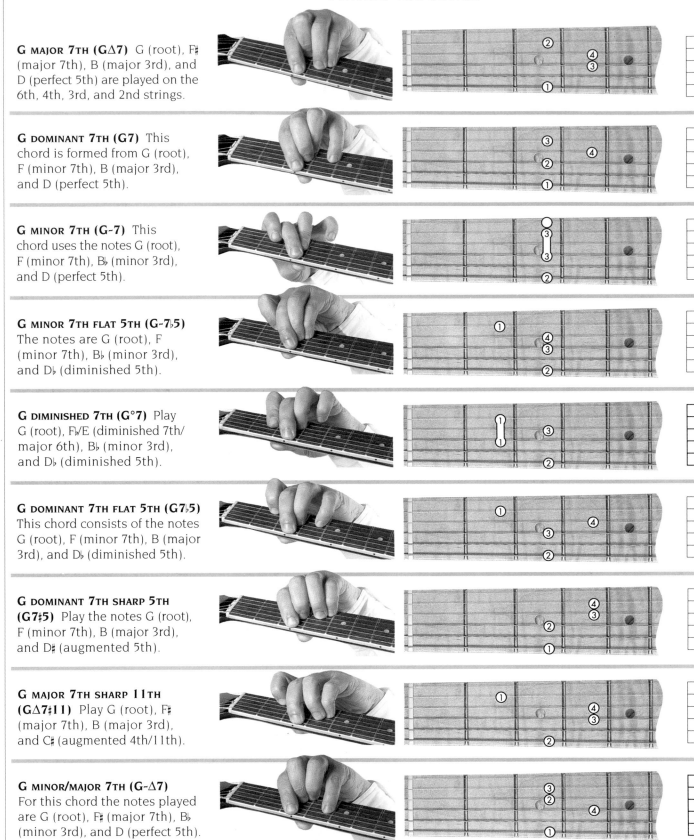

G MAJOR 7TH (GΔ7) G (root), F♯ (major 7th), B (major 3rd), and D (perfect 5th) are played on the 6th, 4th, 3rd, and 2nd strings.

G DOMINANT 7TH (G7) This chord is formed from G (root), F (minor 7th), B (major 3rd), and D (perfect 5th).

G MINOR 7TH (G-7) This chord uses the notes G (root), F (minor 7th), B♭ (minor 3rd), and D (perfect 5th).

G MINOR 7TH FLAT 5TH (G-7♭5) The notes are G (root), F (minor 7th), B♭ (minor 3rd), and D♭ (diminished 5th).

G DIMINISHED 7TH (G°7) Play G (root), F♭/E (diminished 7th/major 6th), B♭ (minor 3rd), and D♭ (diminished 5th).

G DOMINANT 7TH FLAT 5TH (G7♭5) This chord consists of the notes G (root), F (minor 7th), B (major 3rd), and D♭ (diminished 5th).

G DOMINANT 7TH SHARP 5TH (G7♯5) Play the notes G (root), F (minor 7th), B (major 3rd), and D♯ (augmented 5th).

G MAJOR 7TH SHARP 11TH (GΔ7♯11) Play G (root), F♯ (major 7th), B (major 3rd), and C♯ (augmented 4th/11th).

G MINOR/MAJOR 7TH (G-Δ7) For this chord the notes played are G (root), F♯ (major 7th), B♭ (minor 3rd), and D (perfect 5th).

G MAJOR 6TH (G6) This chord consists of the notes G (root), E (major 6th), B (major 3rd), and D (perfect 5th).

G MINOR 6TH (G-6) This chord consists of the notes G (root), E (major 6th), B♭ (minor 3rd), and D (perfect 5th).

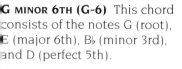  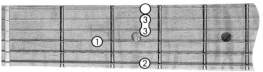 

G MAJOR 9TH (G△9) Play this chord using the notes G (root), F♯ (major 7th), A (major 9th), and D (perfect 5th).

 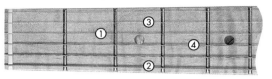 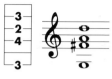

G DOMINANT 9TH (G9) Play G (root), B (major 3rd), F (minor 7th), A (major 9th), and D (perfect 5th) on the bottom five strings.

 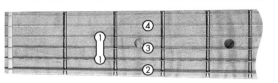 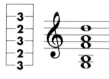

G MINOR 9TH (G-9) The notes used are G (root), F (minor 7th), B♭ (minor 3rd), D (perfect 5th), and A (major 9th).

 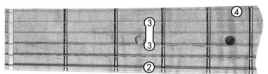 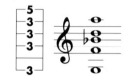

G SUSPENDED 4TH (G SUS 4) G (root), D (perfect 5th), G (root), C (perfect 4th/11th), D perfect 5th), and G (root) are used.

 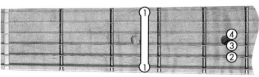 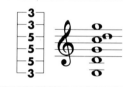

G DOMINANT 11TH (G11) Play G (root), F (minor 7th), A (major 9th), and C (11th) on the 6th, 4th, 3rd, and 2nd strings.

 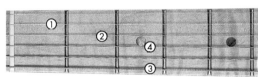 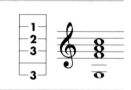

OTHER 6TH-STRING CHORDS

Chords played with 6th-string roots have a different balance than those with roots on the 5th string. Other types of voicing are often used for easily playable and balanced added-note chords. This is partly due to the order of intervals running across the fingerboard from a bottom-string root. Some chord voicings that are moved across from the 5th string are impossible to play, or sound indistinct, in a low register. Positioning the root on the 6th string enables the guitarist to play a wide range of close harmonies and altered dominant chords.

G MAJOR 6/9 (G 6/9) For this chord, play G, B, E, A, and D. The G on the 1st string is optional.

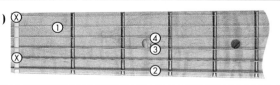

G 6/9 MAJOR 7 (G6/9△7) To play this chord, sound G, B, E, A, D, and F♯. All strings are used.

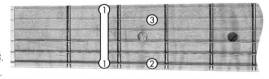

G MINOR 11TH (G-11) Play the notes G, F, B♭, and C. The 1st and 5th strings are not used.

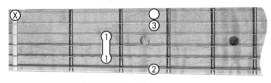

G DOMINANT 13 (G13) In this chord the notes are G, F, B, and E. The A on the 1st string is optional.

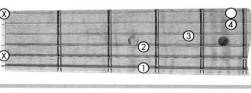

G MINOR 13TH (G-13) The chord uses the notes G, F, B♭, and E. The A on the 1st string is optional.

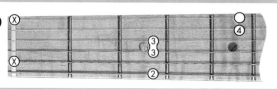

G DOMINANT 7TH SHARP 9TH (G7♯9) The notes are G, B, F, A♯, and D. The 1st string is not played.

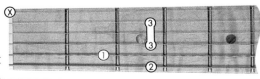

G MINOR 6/9 (G-6/9)
This chord is played with the notes G, E, B♭, D, and A. The 5th string is not used.

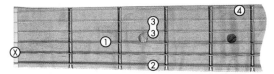

G MAJOR 7 SHARP 5TH (GΔ7♯5) Sound the notes G, F♯, B, and D♯. The 1st and 5th strings are not used.

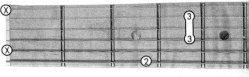

G MINOR FLAT 6TH (G-♭6) G, E♭, B♭, and D are played here. The G on the 1st string is optional.

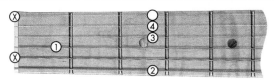

G MINOR/MAJOR 9TH (G-Δ9) The chord is formed from G, F♯, B♭, D, and A. The 5th string is not played.

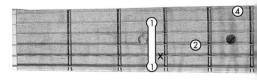

G DOMINANT 7 SHARP 5TH SHARP 9TH (G7♯5♯9) Sound G, F, B, D♯, and A♯. Use all the strings except for the 5th.

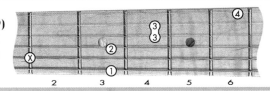

G DOMINANT 7 SHARP 5TH FLAT 9TH (G7♯5♭9) Play G, F, B, D♯, and A♭. The 5th string is not used in this chord.

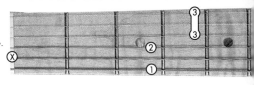

G DOMINANT 13 FLAT 9TH (G13♭9) This chord uses G, F, B, E, and A♭. The 5th string is not played.

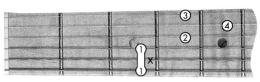

G DOMINANT 7 FLAT 9TH (G7♭9) To form the chord play G, F, A♭, and D. The 1st and 5th strings are not used.

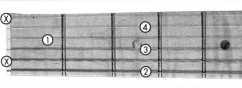

G DOMINANT 9 FLAT 5TH (G9♭5) The chord notes are G, F, A, and D♭. The 1st and 5th strings are not played.

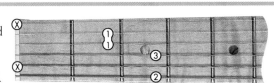

G DOMINANT 13 SHARP 9TH (G13♯9) The notes are G, B, F, A♯, and E. A on the 1st string is optional.

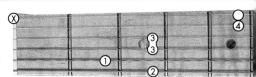

FOURTH-STRING ROOTS

On the four upper strings of the guitar the range of chordal possibilities is more limited. Eleventh and thirteenth chords can be constructed, but with only four voices; they lack some of the important notes that give certain chords their harmonic character. The upper-string chords are ideal for supporting melody. Their bright, clear sound, good separation, and high register also make them useful for chord fills in group playing.

UNDERSTANDING CHORD SHAPES

To develop an understanding of chord types and voicings, it is useful to play all of the shapes on a C fret. With 4th-string root chords added, each shape and voicing on the 6th, 5th, and 4th strings should be compared by moving the 4th-string shapes up to C on the 10th fret, and the 6th-string shapes up to C on the 8th fret. You will notice that although a number of chords

Chord notes
The intervals shown on the fingerboard are named from the root (in this case, F). The same pattern can run from any fret position on the 4th string. Any of the twelve chromatic semitones can be used as a root for any chord.

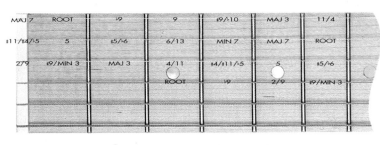

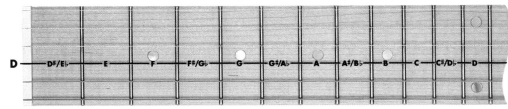

contain the same order of notes, because of the string-tuning intervals across the fretboard they have very different shapes. Moving a voicing across the fingerboard on the same fret is also a useful exercise; for example, try moving G on the 3rd fret of the 6th string to C on the 5th string, and then to F on the 4th string.

F MAJOR 7TH (FΔ) In this chord the notes are F, C, E, and A. The voicing order is root, perfect 5th, major 7th, and major 3rd.

F **DOMINANT 7TH (F7)** The chord is formed from F (root), C (perfect 5th), E♭ (minor 7th), and A (major 3rd).

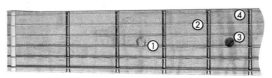

F **MINOR 7TH (F-7)** This chord uses the notes F (root), C (perfect 5th), E♭ (minor 7th), and A♭ (minor 3rd).

F **MINOR 7 FLAT 5TH (F-7♭5)** This chord consists of the notes F (root), C♭/B (dim. 5th), E♭ (minor 7th), and A♭ (minor 3rd).

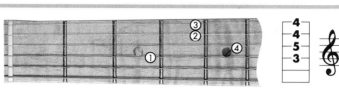

F **DIMINISHED 7TH (F°7)** F (root), C♭/B (diminished 5th), E♭♭/D (diminished 7th/major 6th), and A♭ (minor 3rd). are used.

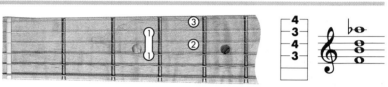

F **SUSPENDED 4TH (F SUS 4)** Sound F, C, F, and B♭. The 5th and 6th strings are not played.

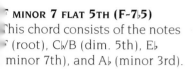

F **DOMINANT 7 FLAT 5TH (F7♭5)** Play F, B, E♭, and A. All strings from the 4th to the 1st are used.

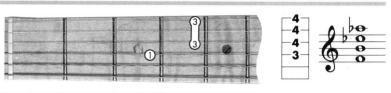

F **DOMINANT 7 SHARP 5TH (F7♯5)** The chord notes are F, C♯, E♭, and A. The 5th and 6th strings are not used.

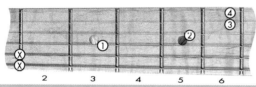

F **MAJOR 7 SHARP 11TH (F△7♯11)** The chord contains F, B, E, and A. Use the 4th to the 1st strings.

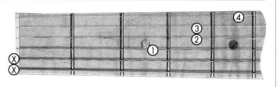

F **MIN/MAJ 7TH (F-△7)** The notes are F, C, E, and A♭. The bottom two strings are not played.

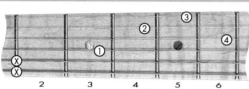

F **MAJOR 6TH (F6)** For this chord use F, C, D, and A. The bottom two strings are not played.

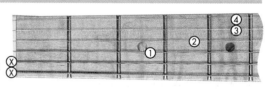

F **MINOR 6TH (F-6)** To sound F-6, play F, C, D, and A♭. The bottom two strings are not used.

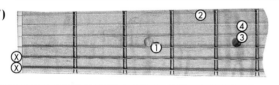

F **MAJOR 9TH (F△9)** The chord consists of the notes F, A, E, and G. Use only the 1st to 4th strings.

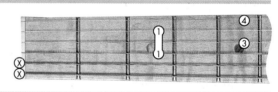

F **DOMINANT 9TH (F9)** The chord notes are F, A, E♭, and G. Use all strings except the 5th and 6th.

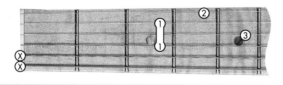

F **MINOR 9TH (F-9)** To form F-9, play F, A♭, E♭, and G. All except the 5th and 6th strings are used.

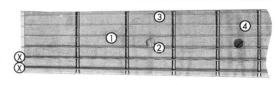

F **DOMINANT 7 SHARP 9TH (F7♯9)** The chord is formed from F, A, E♭, and G♯. The 1st to 4th strings are used.

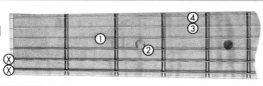

F **DOMINANT 7 FLAT 9TH (F7♭9)** The notes are F, A, E♭, and G♭. The 5th and 6th strings are not played.

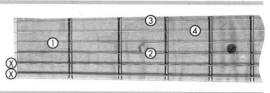

PLAYING MAJOR SCALES

LEARNING TO PLAY THE MAJOR SCALE IN EVERY KEY

Keynotes
The position of each scale below is determined by the lowest **keynote** on the fingerboard. The keynotes run from the first note in E major on the open 6th string to the first note in E♭ major on the 1st fret of the 4th string. The keynotes for E major, F major, F♯/G♭ major, G major, and A♭ major start on the 6th string. A major, B♭ major, B major, C major, and D♭ major start on the 5th string, and D major and E♭ major start on the 4th string.

The capability of playing in all twelve major scales is vital to mastering the guitar. Music is very often transposed from one key to another, altering the pitch or changing its mood and color. The position and structure of different scales must be memorized in order to play them comfortably. Music also modulates between keys. This involves moving from the scale position in one key to that in another while using the same area of the fingerboard. Mastering the major keys is a skill that can be easily developed. Start by fingering the basic one-octave positions for each key, and compare them with their closely related scales. With practice, the range of each scale can gradually be extended to cover the entire fingerboard in stages.

Patterns
The pitch position of each scale in relation to the open strings creates a series of different **patterns**. C major consists of a particular pattern of open-string and fretted notes. When G major is played, it starts a fourth below C major: the series of intervals is the same, but the pattern changes at the top of the scale because of the position of fretted and open-string notes.

C major

This position uses the open strings and the first three frets on the fingerboard. The C major scale starts on the note C on the 3rd fret of the 5th string. This is the lowest keynote for C. The scale ascends with D, E, and F on the 4th string; G and A on the 3rd string; and B and C on the 2nd string.

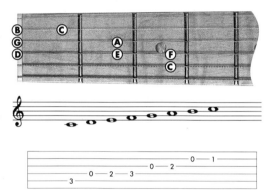

G major (1 sharp)

This position uses the open strings and the first four frets on the fingerboard. The G major scale starts on the note G on the 3rd fret of the 6th string. This is the lowest keynote for G. The scale ascends on the 5th string using A, B, and C; continues on the 4th string with D, E and F♯; and ends with the open G.

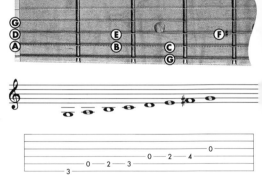

D major (2 sharps)

This position uses the open strings and the first four frets on the fingerboard. The D major scale starts on the note D on the open 4th string. This is the lowest keynote for D. The scale ascends on the 4th string with E and F♯; on the 3rd string with G and A; and on the 2nd string with B, C♯, and D.

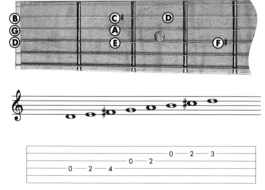

A major (3 sharps)

This position uses the open strings and the first four frets on the fingerboard. The A major scale starts on the open 5th string. This is the lowest keynote for A in standard tuning. The scale ascends with B and C♯ on the 5th string; D, E, and F♯ on the 4th string; and G♯ and A on the 3rd string.

E major (4 sharps)

This position uses the open strings and the first four frets on the fingerboard. The E major scale starts on the note E on the open 6th string. This is the lowest keynote for E. The scale ascends with F♯ and G♯ on the 6th string; A, B, and C♯ on the 5th string; and D♯ and E on the 4th string.

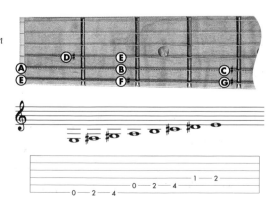

B major (5 sharps)

This position uses an open string and the first four frets on the fingerboard. The B major scale starts on the note B on the 2nd fret of the 5th string. This is the lowest keynote for B. The scale ascends with C♯ on the 5th string; D♯, E, and F♯ on the 4th string; G♯ and A♯ on the 3rd string; and open B.

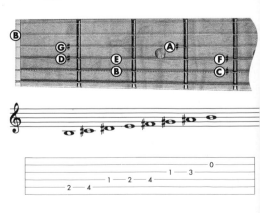

ENHARMONIC SCALES

Three major scales consist of the same notes played at the same pitch and in the same sequence, but with a different set of note names. They are F#/G♭, C#/D♭, and B/C♭.

For example, the notes in the key of F# are F#, G#, A#, B, C#, D#, E#, and F#. The notes in the key of G♭ are G♭, A♭, B♭, C♭, D♭, E♭, F, and G♭. In both series of major scales the notes are identical. The term *enharmonic* is used to describe the same notes, scales, or chords with different names. In practice, however, the keys of C♭ and C# are rarely used.

F# major (6 sharps)

The F# major scale does not use open strings. It starts with the F# on the 2nd fret of the 6th string. This is the lowest keynote for F# in standard tuning. The scale ascends with G# on the 6th string; A#, B, and C# on the 5th string; and D#, E#, and F# on the 4th string. E# is the same as F.

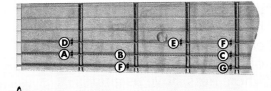

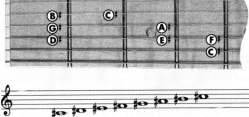

C# major (7 sharps)

This position uses the first four frets on the fingerboard. It does not use open strings. The C# major scale starts on the note C# on the 4th fret of the 5th string. This is the lowest keynote for C# in standard tuning. The scale ascends with D#, E#, and F# on the 4th string; G# and A# on the 3rd string; and B# and C# on the 2nd string.

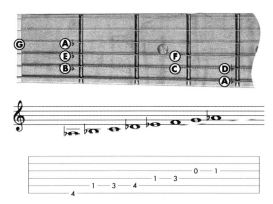

G♭ major (6 flats)

This position uses the first four frets on the fingerboard. The G♭ major scale starts with the note G♭ on the 2nd fret of the 6th string. This is the lowest keynote for G♭ in standard tuning. The scale ascends with A♭ on the 6th string; B♭, C♭, and D♭ on the 5th string; and E♭, F, and G♭ on the 4th string. C♭ is the same as B.

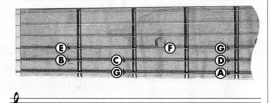

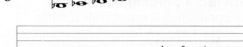
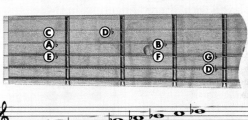

D♭ major (5 flats)

This position uses the first four frets on the fingerboard. It does not use any open-string notes. The D♭ major scale begins with the note D♭ played on the 4th fret of the 5th string. This is the lowest possible keynote for D♭ using standard tuning. The scale ascends from the 4th string with the notes E♭ and G♭. A♭ and B♭ are played on the 3rd string, and C and D♭ are played on the 2nd string.

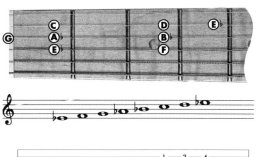

A♭ major (4 flats)

This position uses the first four frets on the fingerboard, and one open string. The A♭ major scale starts with A♭ on the 4th fret of the 6th string. This is the lowest keynote for A♭ in standard tuning. The scale ascends with B♭, C, and D♭ on the 5th string; E♭ and F on the 4th string; and open G and A♭ on the 3rd string.

E♭ major (3 flats)

This position uses one open string and the first four frets on the fingerboard. The E♭ major scale starts on the note E♭ on the 1st fret of the 4th string. This is the lowest keynote for E♭ in standard tuning. The scale ascends with F on the 4th string; open G, A♭, and B♭ on the 3rd string; and C, D, and E♭ on the 2nd string.

B♭ major (2 flats)

This position uses open strings and the first three frets on the fingerboard. The B♭ major scale starts on the note B♭ on the 1st fret of the 5th string. This is the lowest keynote for B♭. The scale ascends with C on the 5th string; open D, E♭, and F on the 4th string; and open G, A, and B♭ on the 3rd string.

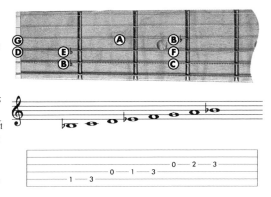

F major (1 flat)

This position uses the open strings and the first three frets on the fingerboard. The F major scale starts on the note F on the 1st fret of the 6th string. This is the lowest keynote for F. The scale ascends with G on the 6th string; open A, B♭, and C on the 5th string; and open D, E, and F on the 4th string.

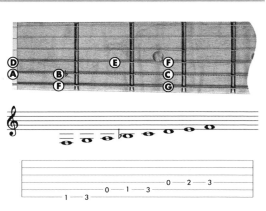

FINGERING ON THE 6TH STRING

C major standard position from the 6th string
Unlike the examples shown on the previous page, this two-octave C major scale pattern starts on the 8th fret of the 6th string. A standard one-octave position is extended across all six of the strings, forming two octaves. Play both octaves across the fingerboard, ensuring that you do not move the thumb position.

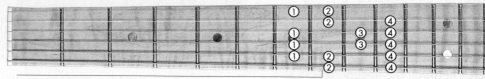

Second finger This C major scale starts with the second finger playing the 8th fret of the 6th string.

C major starting with the fourth finger
This two-octave pattern also starts on the 8th fret of the 6th string. However, in this example, the pattern should be played starting with the fourth finger. The scale is extended across all six of the strings using a block of five frets. This pattern should be played without moving the thumb position.

Fourth finger This C major scale starts with the fourth finger playing the 8th fret of the 6th string.

C major 6th-string pattern with stretch fingering
This pattern starts on the 8th fret of the 6th string. Both octaves are played with three notes on each string, using stretch fingering. As the left hand moves up, the thumb should be kept in approximately the same area. The first finger must be moved up accurately to each consecutive string position.

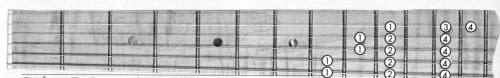

First finger This C major scale starts with the first finger on the 8th fret of the 6th string.

C MAJOR FINGERING IN CONTEXT

The three main two-octave C major fingerings (black circles) are shown in the context of the surrounding C major notes (white circles). The patterns should be played, comparing the points at which they overlap or diverge. An extended fingering area combining all the patterns should be memorized.

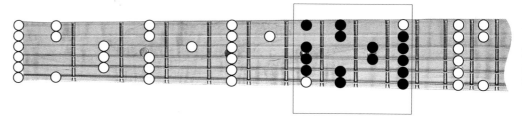

C MAJOR SCALE NOTES

Further comparisons
The fourth-finger and stretch patterns are shown in relation to other C major scale notes. Try extending each double-octave pattern using the notes shown in white circles.

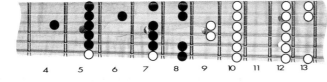

C MAJOR SCALE NOTES

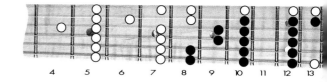

C MAJOR SCALE NOTES

TRANSPOSING A TWO-OCTAVE PATTERN

The patterns above can be shifted up and down the fingerboard to play a two-octave major scale in any key. Fixed-shape transposition is easily achieved by moving the pattern to a fret, using any 6th or 5th string keynote. In this way, when a C major pattern starting on the 8th fret is moved down one fret, to B on the 7th fret, the notes drop by a semitone, and the new major scale of B is played with the same pattern but starts from the new keynote. If the C major pattern on the 8th fret is moved up by one fret, to D♭ on the 9th fret, the notes move up by a semitone, and the new major scale of D♭ has the same pattern but starts from the new keynote. Try moving the positions around the cycle of twelve keys.

Fingering block
The outlined area shows a standard two-octave major scale fingering pattern as a block that can be moved up and down the fingerboard to be played in any key. The F♯/G♭ major scale is shown starting from the 2nd fret, and the C major scale from the 8th fret.

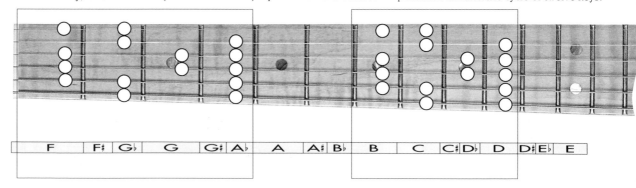

| | F | F♯ | G♭ | G | G♯ | A♭ | A | A♯ | B♭ | B | C | C♯ | D♭ | D | D♯ | E♭ | E |

FULL MAJOR SCALE

PLAYING THE FULL SCALE POSITIONS

Each scale in every key is made of seven notes. These notes are played on every string, forming a pattern along the fingerboard. Major scale patterns surround each keynote, and the order of intervals can be seen as a series connecting every octave scale. Mastering these scale positions is an important skill for musicians in all areas. It is essential for jazz soloing and for developing the ability to improvise over chord changes and harmonies in other styles. The scales are shown in a sequence following the cycle of keys in fifths. The first scale is C major, which uses the notes C, D, E, F, G, A, and B. The keynotes – C, in the first instance – are indicated by black circles.

Above the 12th fret
Each open-string note is repeated an octave higher on the 12th fret. Therefore, the pattern of notes and chords for each key runs up from the 12th fret in the same sequence as the open-string position. The diagrams below show the fingerboard to the 15th fret. Some guitars have twenty-four frets that allow the pattern to be repeated.

C MAJOR
The scale uses the notes C, D, E, F, G, A, and B. The pattern from the open string to the 11th fret repeats from the 12th fret. The keynotes (C) are all marked as black dots.

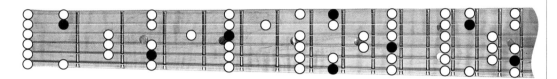

G MAJOR
The scale uses the notes G, A, B, C, D, E, and F♯. The pattern from the open string to the 11th fret repeats from the 12th fret. The keynotes (G) are marked as black dots.

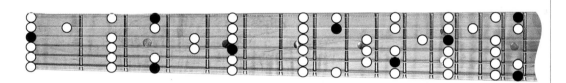

D MAJOR
The scale uses the notes D, E, F♯, G, A, B, and C♯. The pattern from the open string to the 11th fret repeats from the 12th fret. The keynotes (D) are marked as black dots.

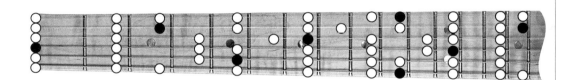

A MAJOR
The scale uses the notes A, B, C♯, D, E, F♯, and G♯. The pattern from the open string to the 11th fret repeats from the 12th fret. The keynotes (A) are marked as black dots.

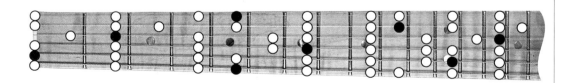

E MAJOR
The scale uses the notes E, F♯, G♯, A, B, C♯, and D♯. The pattern from the open string to the 11th fret repeats from the 12th fret. The keynotes (E) are marked as black dots.

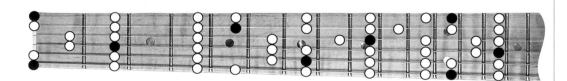

B MAJOR
The scale uses the notes B, C♯, D♯, E, F♯, G♯, and A♯. The pattern from the open string to the 11th fret repeats from the 12th fret. The keynotes (B) are marked as black dots.

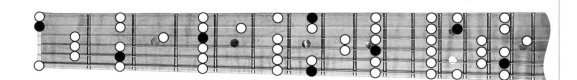

SCALE-TONE CHORDS

STANDARD EXTENSIONS IN EACH KEY

Chord harmonies
The structure and shape of every major key is the same in relation to the note that is used as the keynote, i.e., the first note of the scale. Each major scale has a fixed system of chord harmonies. In the chart below, the chord types on each degree line up vertically. Five chord extensions – sixths, sevenths, ninths, elevenths, and thirteenths – are highlighted across the page by different-colored bands.

The twelve keys each contain an extensive series of chord types. The basic system of chords in a particular key is created using the notes of the scale. In all keys, the seven scale notes are used to form the roots of the chord types. The chords in each key are assigned Roman numerals: **I** is the first note of the scale, **II** the second, **III** the third, **IV** the fourth, **V** the fifth, **VI** the sixth, and **VII** is the seventh. This system is repeated at every level in lower and higher octaves. The triads on the root notes are all extended. Their use and level of development depend on the style and form of the music and on the requirement for certain types of harmonic color.

Comparing keys
The system below has up to five different chord types on each degree. Compare chords and their relationships in one key by transposing them to all the other keys, and reduce chords to triads. One chord type on a root also occurs in different keys. For example, D minor 7 is a **II** chord in C, a **VI** chord in F, and a **III** chord in B♭.

C MAJOR The major scale notes C, D, E, F, G, A, B, and C are written as the roots for each group of **I** to **VII** chords.

	I	II	III	IV	V	VI	VII	I
SIXTH	C MAJ 6	D MIN 6		F MAJ 6	G MAJ 6			C MAJ 6
SEVENTH	C MAJ 7	D MIN 7	E MIN 7	F MAJ 7	G 7	A MIN 7	B MIN 7♭5	C MAJ 7
NINTH	C MAJ 9	D MIN 9		F MAJ 9	G9	A MIN 9		C MAJ 9
ELEVENTH		D MIN 11	E MIN 11	F MAJ 7♯11	G11	A MIN 11	B MIN 11♭5	
THIRTEENTH		D MIN 13			G13			

G MAJOR The major scale notes G, A ,B, C, D, E, F♯, and G are written as roots for each group of **I** to **VII** chords.

	I	II	III	IV	V	VI	VII	I
SIXTH	G MAJ 6	A MIN 6		C MAJ 6	D MAJ 6			G MAJ 6
SEVENTH	G MAJ 7	A MIN 7	B MIN 7	C MAJ 7	D 7	E MIN 7	F♯ MIN 7♭5	G MAJ 7
NINTH	G MAJ 9	A MIN 9		C MAJ 9	D9	E MIN 9		G MAJ 9
ELEVENTH		A MIN 11	B MIN 11	C MAJ 7♯11	D11	E MIN 11	F♯ MIN 11♭5	
THIRTEENTH		A MIN 13			D13			

D MAJOR The major scale notes D, E, F♯, G, A, B, C♯, and D are written as roots for each group of **I** to **VII** chords.

	I	II	III	IV	V	VI	VII	I
SIXTH	D MAJ 6	E MIN 6		G MAJ 6	A MAJ 6			D MAJ 6
SEVENTH	D MAJ 7	E MIN 7	F♯ MIN 7	G MAJ 7	A 7	B MIN 7	C♯ MIN 7♭5	D MAJ 7
NINTH	D MAJ 9	E MIN 9		G MAJ 9	A9	B MIN 9		D MAJ 9
ELEVENTH		E MIN 11	F♯ MIN 11	G MAJ 7♯11	A11	B MIN 11	C♯ MIN 11♭5	
THIRTEENTH		E MIN 13			A13			

A MAJOR The major scale notes A, B, C♯, D, E, F♯, G♯, and A are written as roots for each group of **I** to **VII** chords.

	I	II	III	IV	V	VI	VII	I
SIXTH	A MAJ 6	B MIN 6		D MAJ 6	E MAJ 6			A MAJ 6
SEVENTH	A MAJ 7	B MIN 7	C♯ MIN 7	D MAJ 7	E 7	F♯ MIN 7	G♯ MIN 7♭5	A MAJ 7
NINTH	A MAJ 9	B MIN 9		D MAJ 9	E9	F♯ MIN 9		A MAJ 9
ELEVENTH		B MIN 11	C♯ MIN 11	D MAJ 7♯11	E11	F♯ MIN 11	G♯ MIN 11♭5	
THIRTEENTH		B MIN 13			E13			

E MAJOR The major scale notes E, F♯, G♯, A, B, C♯, D♯, and E are written as roots for each group of **I** to **VII** chords.

	I	II	III	IV	V	VI	VII	I
SIXTH	E MAJ 6	F♯ MIN 6		A MAJ 6	B MAJ 6			E MAJ 6
SEVENTH	E MAJ 7	F♯ MIN 7	G♯ MIN 7	A MAJ 7	B 7	C♯ MIN 7	D♯ MIN 7♭5	E MAJ 7
NINTH	E MAJ 9	F♯ MIN 9		A MAJ 9	B9	C♯ MIN 9		E MAJ 9
ELEVENTH		F♯ MIN 11	G♯ MIN 11	A MAJ 7♯11	B11	C♯ MIN 11	D♯ MIN 11♭5	
THIRTEENTH		F♯ MIN 13			B13			

B MAJOR The major scale notes B, C♯, D♯, E, F♯, G♯, A♯, and B are written as roots for each group of **I** to **VII** chords.

	I	II	III	IV	V	VI	VII	I
SIXTH	B MAJ 6	C♯ MIN 6		E MAJ 6	F♯ MAJ 6			B MAJ 6
SEVENTH	B MAJ 7	C♯ MIN 7	D♯ MIN 7	E MAJ 7	F♯ 7	G♯ MIN 7	A♯ MIN 7♭5	B MAJ 7
NINTH	B MAJ 9	C♯ MIN 9		E MAJ 9	F♯9	G♯ MIN 9		B MAJ 9
ELEVENTH		C♯ MIN 11	D♯ MIN 11	E MAJ 7♯11	F♯11	G♯ MIN 11	A♯ MIN 11♭5	
THIRTEENTH		C♯ MIN 13			F♯13			

ENHARMONIC CHORDS

Chords are generally written with a root letter relating to a key. The overlap of the F♯ and G♭ major scales results in the same chord given two different letter names. These identical but differently named chords are known as *enharmonics*. For example, F♯ major 7 is identical to G♭ major 7. The way the chord is named is largely dependent on context.

In a harmonic modulation from a flat key, G♭ would be the more appropriate chord name. If a piece of music using this chord is related to a sharp key, F♯ would be used. The labeling of *enharmonically* identical chords can depend on the role of the guitar with other instruments. In music with frequent modulations, different letter names for chords are often written in a

manner that can appear arbitrary. Music in chord symbol form can, therefore, be written in two ways. For example, A minor 7, A♭ minor 7, G minor 7, G♭ 7, and F major 7 can also be written as A minor 7, G♯ minor 7, G minor 7, F♯ 7, and F major 7, respectively. The ability to understand this ambiguous labeling is very important in reading music.

F♯ major

The major scale notes F♯, G♯, A♯, B, C♯, D♯, E♯, and F♯ are written for the roots in each group of the chords I to VII. E♯ is the same as F.

	I	II	III	IV	V	VI	VII	I
SIXTH	F♯ MAJ 6	G♯ MIN 6		B MAJ 6	C♯ MAJ 6			F♯ MAJ 6
SEVENTH	F♯ MAJ 7	G♯ MIN 7	A♯ MIN 7	B MAJ 7	C♯ 7	D♯ MIN 7	E♯ MIN 7♭5	F♯ MAJ 7
NINTH	F♯ MAJ 9	G♯ MIN 9		B MAJ 9	C♯ 9	D♯ MIN 9		F♯ MAJ 9
ELEVENTH		G♯ MIN 11	A♯ MIN 11	B MAJ 7♯11	C♯ 11	D♯ MIN 11	E♯ MIN 11♭5	
THIRTEENTH		G♯ MIN 13			C♯ 13			

G♭ major

The major scale notes G♭, A♭, B♭, C♭, D♭, E♭, F, and G♭ are written for the roots in each group of the chords I to VII. C♭ is the same as B.

	I	II	III	IV	V	VI	VII	I
SIXTH	G♭ MAJ 6	A♭ MIN 6		C♭ MAJ 6	D♭ MAJ 6			G♭ MAJ 6
SEVENTH	G♭ MAJ 7	A♭ MIN 7	B♭ MIN 7	C♭ MAJ 7	D♭ 7	E♭ MIN 7	F MIN 7♭5	G♭ MAJ 7
NINTH	G♭ MAJ 9	A♭ MIN 9		C♭ MAJ 9	D♭ 9	E♭ MIN 9		G♭ MAJ 9
ELEVENTH		A♭ MIN 11	B♭ MIN 11	C♭ MAJ 7♯11	D♭ 11	E♭ MIN 11	F MIN 11♭5	
THIRTEENTH		A♭ MIN 13			D♭ 13			

D♭ MAJOR

The major scale notes D♭, E♭, F, G♭, A♭, B♭, C, and D♭ are written as roots for each group of I to VII chords.

	I	II	III	IV	V	VI	VII	I
SIXTH	D♭ MAJ 6	E♭ MIN 6		G♭ MAJ 6	A♭ MAJ 6			D♭ MAJ 6
SEVENTH	D♭ MAJ 7	E♭ MIN 7	F MIN 7	G♭ MAJ 7	A♭ 7	B♭ MIN 7	C MIN 7♭5	D♭ MAJ 7
NINTH	D♭ MAJ 9	E♭ MIN 9		G♭ MAJ 9	A♭ 9	B♭ MIN 9		D♭ MAJ 9
ELEVENTH		E♭ MIN 11	F MIN 11	G♭ MAJ 7♯11	A♭ 11	B♭ MIN 11	C MIN 11♭5	
THIRTEENTH		E♭ MIN 13			A♭ 13			

A♭ MAJOR

The major scale notes A♭, B♭, C, D♭, E♭, F, G, and A♭ are written as roots for each group of I to VII chords.

	I	II	III	IV	V	VI	VII	I
SIXTH	A♭ MAJ 6	B♭ MIN 6		D♭ MAJ 6	E♭ MAJ 6			A♭ MAJ 6
SEVENTH	A♭ MAJ 7	B♭ MIN 7	C MIN 7	D♭ MAJ 7	E♭ 7	F MIN 7	G MIN 7♭5	A♭ MAJ 7
NINTH	A♭ MAJ 9	B♭ MIN 9		D♭ MAJ 9	E♭ 9	F MIN 9		A♭ MAJ 9
ELEVENTH		B♭ MIN 11	C MIN 11	D♭ MAJ 7♯11	E♭ 11	F MIN 11	G MIN 11♭5	
THIRTEENTH		B♭ MIN 13			E♭ 13			

E♭ MAJOR

The major scale notes E♭, F, G♭, A♭, B♭, C, D, and E♭ are written as roots for each group of I to VII chords.

	I	II	III	IV	V	VI	VII	I
SIXTH	E♭ MAJ 6	F MIN 6		A♭ MAJ 6	B♭ MAJ 6			E♭ MAJ 6
SEVENTH	E♭ MAJ 7	F MIN 7	G MIN 7	A♭ MAJ 7	B♭ 7	C MIN 7	D MIN 7♭5	E♭ MAJ 7
NINTH	E♭ MAJ 9	F MIN 9		A♭ MAJ 9	B♭ 9	C MIN 9		E♭ MAJ 9
ELEVENTH		F MIN 11	G MIN 11	A♭ MAJ 7♯11	B♭ 11	C MIN 11	D MIN 11♭5	
THIRTEENTH		F MIN 13			B♭ 13			

B♭ MAJOR

The major scale notes B♭, C, D, E♭, F, G, A, and B♭ are written as roots for each group of I to VII chords.

	I	II	III	IV	V	VI	VII	I
SIXTH	B♭ MAJ 6	C MIN 6		E♭ MAJ 6	F MAJ 6			B♭ MAJ 6
SEVENTH	B♭ MAJ 7	C MIN 7	D MIN 7	E♭ MAJ 7	F 7	G MIN 7	A MIN 7♭5	B♭ MAJ 7
NINTH	B♭ MAJ 9	C MIN 9		E♭ MAJ 9	F 9	G MIN 9		B♭ MAJ 9
ELEVENTH		C MIN 11	D MIN 11	E♭ MAJ 7♯11	F 11	G MIN 11	A MIN 11♭5	
THIRTEENTH		C MIN 13			F 13			

F MAJOR

The major scale notes F, G, A, B♭, C, D, E, and F are written as roots for each group of I to VII chords.

	I	II	III	IV	V	VI	VII	I
SIXTH	F MAJ 6	G MIN 6		B♭ MAJ 6	C MAJ 6			F MAJ 6
SEVENTH	F MAJ 7	G MIN 7	A MIN 7	B♭ MAJ 7	C 7	D MIN 7	E MIN 7♭5	F MAJ 7
NINTH	F MAJ 9	G MIN 9		B♭ MAJ 9	C 9	D MIN 9		F MAJ 9
ELEVENTH		G MIN 11	A MIN 11	B♭ MAJ 7♯11	C 11	D MIN 11	E MIN 11♭5	
THIRTEENTH		G MIN 13			C 13			

HARMONIC RESOLUTION

THE V–I MOVEMENT AND ITS VARIATIONS

Transposition
The resolutions in this section should be played in every key. Take any I chord and count five steps up the scale to the V chord, and play it as a dominant seventh.

The movement from a dominant (**V**) to a tonic (**I**) chord is an important part of chordal harmony. It is a central mechanism in jazz music. Although **V-I** is a resolution with a full close sound used for endings, it is also treated as part of a flowing movement of chordal harmony. It is frequently preceded by a **II** chord of the related key.

Using the cycle of fourths
From a dominant chord, resolve to a I chord using the cycle of fourths. Convert this I chord to a dominant seventh, and resolve this to the next chord a fourth away.

THE LEADING NOTE

The seventh note of the C major scale, the *leading note* B, tends to resolve naturally to C (the tonic). B is the third of the dominant (**V**) chord, and the movement from B to C can be heard in the **V-I** resolution, when the third of the dominant chord of G major resolves to the root note of the tonic, C major. The fourth (F) has a strong tendency to resolve harmonically. When included as a seventh within the dominant chord, it moves to E, the third of the scale and the tonic chord.

Leading note (B)
The movement B to C can be heard using a two-note V chord. With G and B this resolves C major. The bass moves up a fourth – G to C.

Fourth note (F)
F, the fourth note, often falls to E. Play C major with F, and move F down to E. As the seventh in the G dominant seventh chord, it falls in V-I.

Tritone
The combination of F and B sets up a strong tension that needs to resolve. The notes have three tones between them, referred to as a "tritone."

Resolutions
The tritone interval is the same when F is placed above B. Each note must still move by a semitone for resolution.

Intervals
F above B has a tritone interval of a diminished fifth. F below B is an augmented fourth tritone.

Resolving both tritones
When F is below B, the two notes resolve to a C major chord. With F above B, the same movement can lead to a G♭/F♯ chord. The resolution to this chord can be used with F below B, and the movement is similar with F over B, resolving to C.

Tritone resolving to G♭/F♯
The tritone, as two notes resolving in different directions, can lead to a movement to either C or G♭/F♯. Compare these movements to the major chords above.

DOMINANT SEVENTH RESOLUTIONS

The tritone is now played in a number of different settings, where it is used within dominant chords as an important part of the structural resolution. The notes B and F are the third and the seventh of the G dominant seventh chord. As a tritone, these notes can be used to resolve the G dominant seventh chord to a C or a G♭ (F♯) chord, a semitone below. G♭ major is normally preceded by a **V** dominant in its own key. The **V** chord in G♭ major is D♭ major, or D♭ dominant seventh. The D♭ dominant seventh contains the notes F and B (C♭) as a third and seventh. Therefore, the D♭ dominant seventh chord resolves to G♭. With this tritone, it can also resolve down a semitone to a C chord. In everyday use, this overlap of dominant chordal harmony is used to vary the approach to a tonic **I** chord.

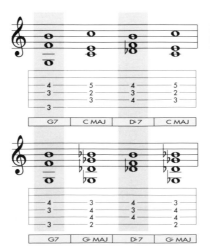

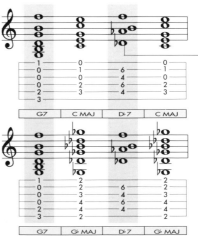

Note names C♭ has been written as B natural for convenience.

Flat five harmony
When G is replaced by D♭, the roots are a flatted fifth apart. Compare the movements of G7 to C or G♭ major, and D♭7 to C or G♭ major.

Full voicings
With full voicings, movements from altered flat five chords must be made carefully. Play the V-I resolutions above. Compare D♭7 to C major, and G7 to G♭ major.

THE FLAT FIVE CHORD

The dominant seventh chord can be modified by moving the fifth note down a semitone. The chord G 7♭5 (G dominant seventh flat five) consists of G (root), B (third), D♭ (flat five), and an F (seventh). D♭ 7♭5 consists of D♭, F, G, and B(C♭). Both chords share these four notes and, under certain conditions, are interchangeable. The flat five is also written as a sharp eleven (G7#11).

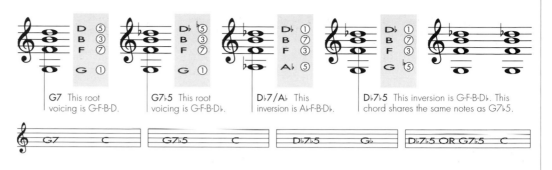

G7 This root voicing is G-F-B-D.

G7♭5 This root voicing is G-F-B-D♭.

D♭7/A♭ This inversion is A♭-F-B-D♭.

D♭7♭5 This inversion is G-F-B-D♭. This chord shares the same notes as G7♭5.

THE II-V-I MOVEMENT

The movement from V to I is preceded by the II chord creating an extended approach with many variations. In C major this basic chord movement is D minor, G major, and C major. The II chord is sometimes an inversion of IV or V before it moves towards C. The V-I movement is developed using all of the scale note extensions of the V chord, and all those of the I chord except F. The added II chord uses all of its extensions.

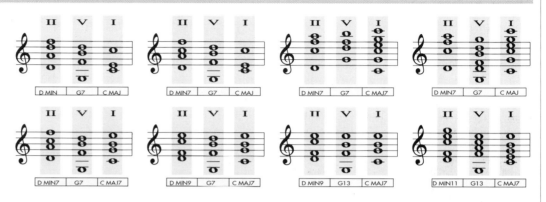

II-♭V-I

A II-V-I movement is often played with a flat five (♭V). The root drops in semitones from D to D♭ to C. This creates a chromatic effect. These chord voicings sometimes descend against fixed upper notes.

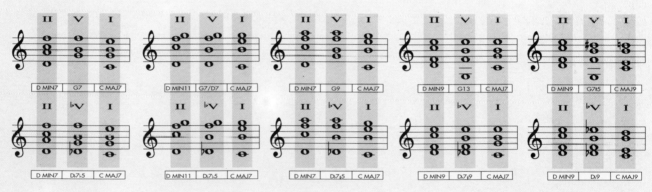

INVERSIONS

Any chord can be inverted by taking the constituent notes and using an alternative bass note. If C major has the third (E) in the bass, and the other notes above, the voicing is termed a first inversion (shown as C/E). If the voicing has G in the bass, it is a second inversion (C/G).

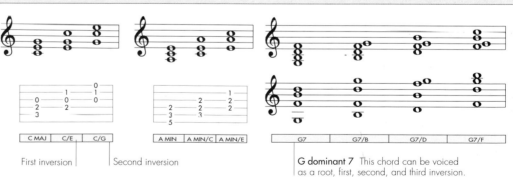

First inversion   Second inversion

G dominant 7 This chord can be voiced as a root, first, second, and third inversion.

INVERSIONS IN RESOLUTIONS

Inversions are often used on the guitar for chord movements. They often use shared pivotal notes. Play G to C in the first example as a chord change using the same bass note. The second example uses a first inversion of G. The third example uses a second inversion. The fourth example uses a second inversion to resolve G to a first inversion of C.

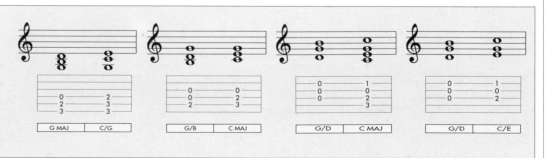

THE MINOR SYSTEM

UNDERSTANDING MINOR SCALES

Intervals
The natural Aeolian minor scale has the following intervals from the root: major second, minor third, perfect fourth, perfect fifth, minor sixth, and minor seventh. The harmonic minor has a major seventh from the root which acts as the leading note in the scale. In comparison with the major scale, the harmonic minor has a minor 3rd and a minor 6th.

After the major scale, the most important scale system is the minor scale. This is based on the Aeolian minor mode on the sixth degree of the major scale. On every major scale, a minor scale may be played from the sixth note. In the key of C major, the scale begins on A. The resulting minor scale, which uses the notes A-B-C-D-E-F-G, is known as the *natural minor*. A sharp may be added to this scale to raise the seventh degree a semitone: the series of notes becomes A-B-C-D-E-F-G♯. This closely related scale is referred to as the *harmonic minor*. The addition of G♯ allows the minor scale to be used with harmonic resolutions that move to the tonic on the first note, A.

The relative minor
All major scales have a relative minor key with a scale and a group of chords based around a minor keynote. The notes and chords are assigned Roman numerals (I–VII) in relation to the minor keynote. There are three different types of relative minor scale: they are the natural Aeolian minor, the harmonic minor, and the melodic minor.

A minor Aeolian scale
This is the natural minor scale. It starts on A and uses the notes of the C major scale starting from the sixth degree.

A minor harmonic scale
This scale starts on A and uses the notes of the C major scale except G natural, which is raised a semitone to G♯.

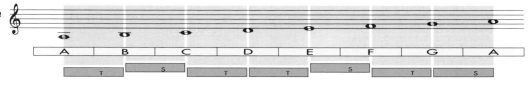

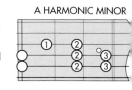

A NATURAL MINOR (AEOLIAN)

A HARMONIC MINOR

MINOR TRIADS

Natural minor triads from A are the same as those in C major, but they start from a different point. The harmonic minor triads are altered by the inclusion of G♯.

| A MIN | B DIM | C MAJ | D MIN | E MIN | F MAJ | G MAJ | A MIN |

| A MIN | B DIM | C AUG | D MIN | E MAJ | F MAJ | G♯ DIM | A MIN |

Natural minor triads
The series of C triads on the left starts on the note A, which is a sixth above, or a third below, C.

Harmonic minor triads
By repeating the series with the addition of G♯, the third, fifth, and seventh triads are altered.

Harmonic minor arpeggios
Play through the triads of the harmonic minor system, noting the G sharps, and compare with the natural minor system.

Hearing the change
Play through the series of arpeggios, paying special attention to the sound of G♯ on the third, fifth, and seventh arpeggios.

Adding a seventh
The harmonic minor series of triads can be extended with the addition of a seventh to each triad. This process is similar to the addition of sevenths to the major scale triads. The extra note is an interval of a third above the fifth on each triad. Adding a G♯ generates unusual harmonies on the I, III, and VII degrees.

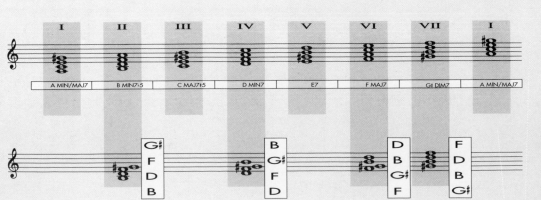

| I | II | III | IV | V | VI | VII | I |

| A MIN/MAJ7 | B MIN7♭5 | C MAJ7♯5 | D MIN7 | E7 | F MAJ7 | G♯ DIM7 | A MIN/MAJ7 |

Diminished chords
The diminished seventh chord on the seventh note of the scale has minor third intervals between the root, third, fifth, seventh, and octave root. Using this structure, any note can be used as the root of a chord. Diminished sevenths with roots of B, D, F, and G♯ (shown on the bottom line) all have the same notes and are inversions of each other.

HARMONIC MINOR CHORDS

The harmonic minor system of chords can be extended to a series of sixths, sevenths, diminished sevenths, ninths, and other types. Some of these minor chords sound unusual and have limited applications. They appear in sections of minor harmony, and are used to contrast major and minor chordal movements.

	SIXTH	SEVENTH	DIMINISHED	NINTH	OTHER TYPES	
A		A MIN/MAJ7		A MIN/MAJ9	A MIN/MAJ11	
B		B MIN7♭5	B DIM7		B MIN11♭5	
C		C MAJ7♯5			C MAJ9♯5	C6♯5
D	D MIN6	D MIN7	D DIM7	D MIN9	D MIN7♭5	D MIN11♭5
E		E7		E7♭9	E7♯5	E7♯5♭9	E7
F	F6	F MAJ7	F DIM7		F MIN/MAJ7	F MAJ7♯11
G♯		G♯ DIM7	G♯ DIM7		G♯DIM7 ADD E	

NATURAL AND HARMONIC MINORS

As an exercise in understanding the differences between natural and harmonic minor chords, play the series of seventh chords shown on the right. Compare the sound and structure of the chords when they are played as a sequence. The first chord is a minor chord with a major seventh. This is used in combination with a standard minor seventh in some progressions. The third chord sounds unusual and consequently is often avoided. The fifth chord is a dominant seventh. It acts as a **V** chord and resolves to A minor 7 as a **V-I**. The minor **I** chord needs to use G♯ for resolution. The B minor 7♭5 is used in the scale as a **II** chord. This chord precedes **V** in a minor **II-V-I** sequence.

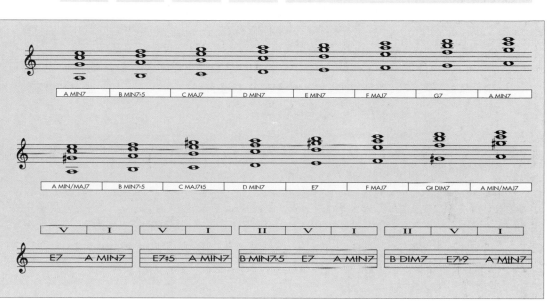

THE MELODIC MINOR SCALE

The melodic minor is the natural minor with the sixth and seventh notes raised a semitone. The diagrams below show three scales with an A keynote. The A harmonic minor scale has a distinctive sound, with a minor third interval between the sixth note (F) and the seventh note (G♯). This is very effective for certain types of music and can impart an ethnic folk sound to minor passages. The melodic minor is a harmonic minor scale with a raised sixth degree, F♯, restoring a smooth movement of tone and semitone intervals. In short passages or in certain other contexts, the melodic minor can sound too close to the A major scale.

To keep a minor effect, the melodic minor is often played as a natural minor when descending. Compare the scales below. The melodic minor can be played in association with the harmonic minor and the ascending natural minor. The ascending melodic minor shares six notes with A major, but they are not closely related harmonically.

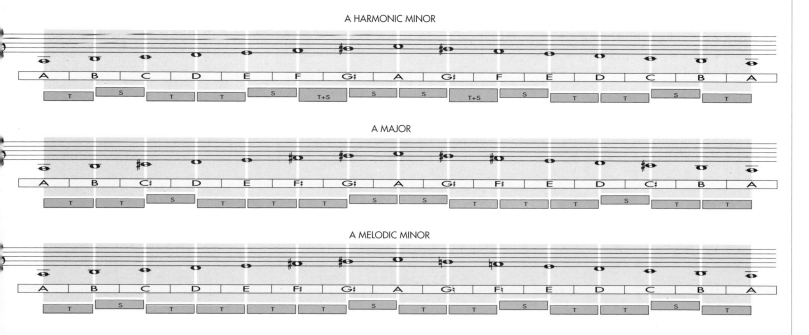

MELODIC AND FIXED MELODIC SCALES

The melodic minor scale has a different series of notes depending on the direction in which it is being played. In the key of A minor, the notes A ,B, C, D, E, F♯, G♯, and A are played when ascending, and A, G, F, E, D, C, B, and A are played when descending. A fixed melodic minor scale, retaining the F♯ and G♯ in its descending form, is often used. The fixed melodic minor in A uses these raised notes for all types of movement. It has the character of an altered scale and, with its subsidiary modal scales from each point, is frequently used in ethnic folk, jazz, and classical music.

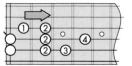

Melodic minor (up)
The melodic minor scale in the key of A incorporates the notes F♯ and G♯ as it moves up the scale.

Melodic minor (down)
The melodic minor scale in A uses the notes F and G with different fingering as it moves down.

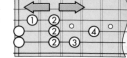

Fixed melodic minor
The fixed melodic scale in the key of A uses the notes F♯ and G♯ as it moves in either direction.

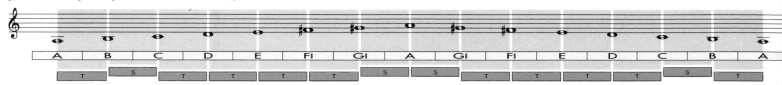

MELODIC MINOR CHORDS

When the melodic minor is used for building harmony, the addition of F♯ creates a new series of chords. Compare the triads and sevenths from the note A with the harmonic minor chords. There are three new triads and four new melodic minor seventh types. The melodic minor chords, with the inclusion of F♯, are further removed from C major harmony.

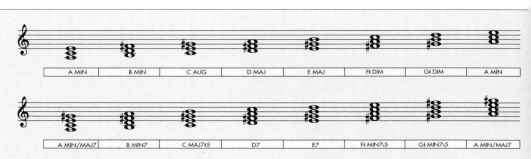

A MIN	B MIN	C AUG	D MAJ	E MAJ	F♯ DIM	G♯ DIM	A MIN

| A MIN/MAJ7 | B MIN7 | C MAJ7♯5 | D7 | E7 | F♯ MIN7♭5 | G♯ MIN7♭5 | A MIN/MAJ7 |

MAJOR/RELATIVE MINOR SCALE CHART

The major scale is the starting point for the minor system: each of the major scales has its own relative minor scale. The movement from major to minor is a shift in tonal center. For example, in the second column below, the G major scale is played from E to E. The note E acts as the new tonal center for the key of E minor. The minor key has a scale that is modified with the addition of a raised seventh to create harmonic sequences with resolutions to a tonal center.

The melodic minor has a raised sixth as well as a seventh for ascending melodic movement, and the natural (Aeolian) scale for descending movement. The major/relative minor keys shown across the chart below are C major/A minor, G major/E minor, D major/B minor, A major/F♯ minor, E major/C♯ minor, B major/G♯ minor, G♭ major/E♭ minor, D♭ major/B♭ minor, A♭ major/F minor, E♭ major/C minor, B♭ major/G minor, and F major/D minor. The enharmonic equivalents for G♭ are not shown on the chart.

The major scale (*below, first row*)
The major scale has the following series of intervals: tone (major 2nd), tone, semitone (minor 2nd), tone, tone, tone, and semitone. There are seven modes in each major scale: Ionian, Dorian, Phrygian, Lydian, Mixolydian, Aeolian, and Locrian. The Ionian scale is the major scale – its first note is the major keynote. The Aeolian scale is the natural minor – its first note is the minor keynote. The major scales below follow the cycle of fifths in the keys of C, G, D, A, E, B, G♭ (F♯), D♭, A♭, E♭, B♭, and F.

C MAJOR/A MINOR	G MAJOR/E MINOR	D MAJOR/B MINOR	A MAJOR/F♯ MINOR	E MAJOR/C♯ MINOR	B MAJOR/G♯ MINOR

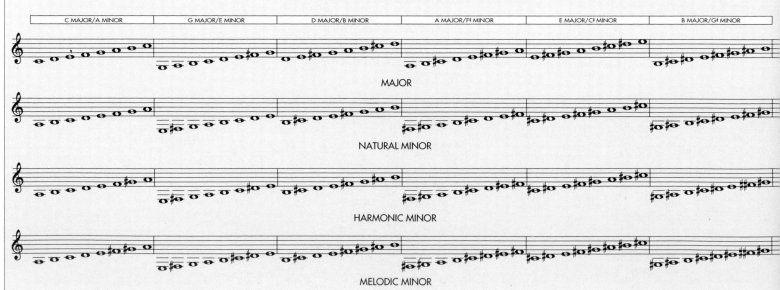

MAJOR

NATURAL MINOR

HARMONIC MINOR

MELODIC MINOR

MELODIC MINOR CHORDS

The melodic system can be extended. It is often used for minor harmony and altered modal scales in jazz, and for compositional structures in other areas of music. Certain chords are used in substitution: they are replaced by a voicing using another root note. For example, D7#11 and G#7#11 may sometimes be interchangeable.

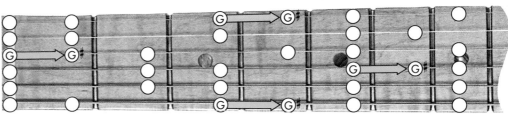

	TRIAD	SIXTH	SEVENTH	NINTH	ELEVENTH	OTHER TYPES		
A	A MIN	A MIN6	A MIN/MAJ7	A MIN/MAJ9	A MIN/MAJ11			
B	B MIN	B MIN6	B MIN7		B MIN11			
C	C AUG		C MAJ7#5	C MAJ9#5	C MAJ7#5#11			
D	D MAJ	D6	D7	D9	D7#11	D13#11		
E	E MAJ		E7	E9	E11	E7#5	E9#5	E13#5
F#	F# DIM		F# MIN7♭5	F# MIN9♭5	F# MIN11♭5			
G#	G# DIM		G# MIN7♭5		G#7#11	G#7#5		

COMPARING MINOR SCALES

The various forms of the minor scale as a relative system to the major scale are compared on the right. The chart shows the fingerboard from the nut up to the 7th fret. The circles mark the position of the notes in the A minor natural scale, running from open E on the 6th string to B on the 1st string. These are the same as the notes of the C major scale. The shifted circles shown with an arrow indicate that the notes G and F are raised by a semitone to G# and F#. The exercises should be played through the position in C major/A minor, A harmonic minor, A melodic minor, and A fixed melodic minor.

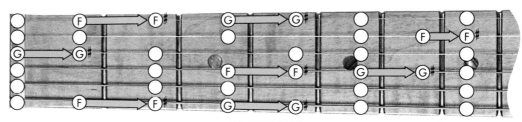

HARMONIC MINOR

MELODIC MINOR

The natural minor scale (below, second row)
This is the Aeolian mode of the major scale, which starts on the sixth (submediant) degree. The natural minor scale has the following series of intervals: tone (major 2nd), semitone (minor 2nd), tone, tone, semitone, tone, and tone. The minor scales shown start a minor third below the major scale. Following each major scale, find the relative minor keynote by counting three notes down, or six notes up, from the keynote of the major scale. For example, F major to D minor is F-E-D descending, or F-G-A-B♭-C-D ascending.

The harmonic minor scale (below, third row)
This is an altered Aeolian mode of the major scale, starting on the sixth (submediant) degree. It differs from the natural minor because it has a raised seventh. To raise natural notes, a sharp is used; with flats, a natural is used. The harmonic minor scale has the following series of intervals: tone (major 2nd), semitone (minor 2nd), tone, tone, semitone, tone+semitone (minor third), and semitone. The minor scales follow a cycle of fifths from left to right. The harmonic minor scale begins on the same note as the natural Aeolian minor.

The melodic minor (below, fourth row)
This is based on the Aeolian mode of the major scale, starting on the sixth degree. It has sixths and sevenths raised by sharps. Flats are raised by naturals. The melodic minor scale has the following series of intervals: tone (major 2nd), semitone (minor 2nd), tone, tone, tone, tone, and semitone. In its descending form, the intervals from the keynote are: tone, tone, semitone, tone, tone, semitone, and tone. The fixed melodic keeps the ascending series of notes in the descending scale.

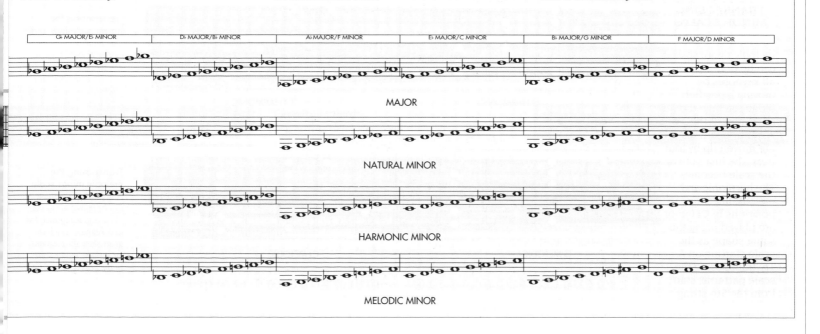

| G♭ MAJOR/E♭ MINOR | D♭ MAJOR/B♭ MINOR | A♭ MAJOR/F MINOR | E♭ MAJOR/C MINOR | B♭ MAJOR/G MINOR | F MAJOR/D MINOR |

MAJOR

NATURAL MINOR

HARMONIC MINOR

MELODIC MINOR

TECHNIQUES AND EFFECTS

PLAYING TECHNIQUES TO INCREASE THE RANGE OF SOUNDS AND TEXTURES

Hammering and pulling-off
The use of hammering-on and pulling-off (see p. 56) is an extremely important technique in guitar playing. It allows music to be played with a flowing quality, and nuances in control and phrasing which cannot be achieved by picking every note out individually.

The guitar has a rich and varied range of tonal colors and sounds. These can be brought out by using a number of techniques involving alterations to notes, such as string-bending, and the use of tremolo arms, slides, hammering-on, and pull-offs. Trills, mordants, and other ornaments can also be used to embellish the sound of simple melodies. Scales can be played utilizing all the textures: vibrato, staccato, and varying degrees of muting and sustain.

Sliding
Practice sliding up and down the fingerboard as a way of moving from one position to another. Try to play a scale on one string with each finger in turn, sliding from note to note. This exercise will help to increase control and develop flexibility in left-hand movements.

THE SLIDE

To achieve this effect, one finger is used to slide notes in pitch up and down the fingerboard. Strike the note F, and then slide with the first finger up to the note G on the 3rd fret *without* releasing the pressure. This makes the note ascend in pitch. This process can also be used to descend from G to F by striking G and sliding down to F.

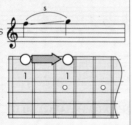

SLIDE WITH STRUCK NOTE

Strike the note F on the 1st fret of the 1st string. Slide the finger up to G on the 3rd fret, and strike the note. Reverse these movements to play a descending slide: play the note G, then slide the finger down to F and strike the note. Try another slide, ascending and descending over a single fret from F to F♯. Extend it to a minor third, using G♯ on the 4th fret.

SLIDING UP TO A NOTE

This variation on the slide is produced by playing a note only after sliding the finger up from any fret position below it. Try sliding up to the note A on the 5th fret by placing the first finger on the 4th fret *without* playing the note, and sliding the finger up to the 5th fret and playing the note. Repeat this exercise for all of the lower fret positions.

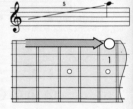

SLIDE WITH TRAIL-OFF

Strike a note and slide up or down three or four of frets, releasing the pressure at any time. This technique gives the effect of a note moving quickly up or down in pitch and then fading away. Extend the slide over a greater number of frets, and again release the pressure on the string at any point so that the sound dies away.

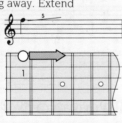

GLISSANDO AND PORTAMENTO

These techniques are based on the slide. *Glissando* is a type of movement that allows every note to be heard in an ascending or descending slide. This is often referred to as *portamento* on a guitar. The first and last notes are both struck. Passages of sliding notes may also be controlled in a way that emphasises certain points.

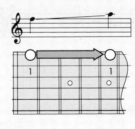

HAMMERING-ON

The finger movements for this technique are the same as those for the *ligado* (see p. 56). Play F on the 1st fret with the first finger. While this note is ringing, place the third finger on the 3rd fret. As the third finger hits the 3rd fret, the *hammering* action causes G to sound. More than one note can be played by hammering.

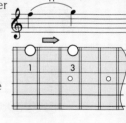

PULLING-OFF

This is a descending legado. A note is struck and one or more subsequent lower notes are then sounded by pulling-off the fretted fingers. Place the first finger on the 1st fret and the third finger on the 3rd fret. Play G on the 3rd fret, then take away the third finger, pulling the string down. This will sound F on the 1st fret.

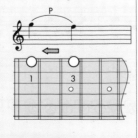

HAMMERING A NOTE

Notes can be played on the guitar without strumming or picking with the right hand. When any left-hand fingers are placed on a fret, the movement of the finger pressing the note against the fingerboard causes the note to ring. If this movement is made with more attack, notes can be sounded clearly. Try playing G and then pulling-off to sound open E.

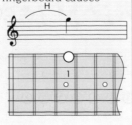

THE TRILL

A trill is a very fast alternating movement between notes fretted by the fingers of the left hand. In essence it is a type of fast hammering technique combined with pull-offs. Play the note F then hammer G. Use a pull-off from G to sound F again. Play these notes as one rapid movement. Try playing a downward trill from G to E.

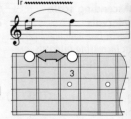

BENDING

Strike the note A on the 5th fret of the 1st string, and bend the string up as it rings to raise the pitch of the note. This technique is used to raise the pitch from microtonal nuances through to intervals as large as a third in blues playing. Try bending the note A one semitone to B♭.

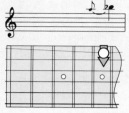

PRE-BEND AND RELEASE

Hold down the note A on the 5th fret, then bend it up to a B♭ position *without* playing it. Hold it in position and strike the note. While it is ringing, pull the string back to its fret position, keeping the finger pressure on. This requires practice. The string must be bent to positions where it is effective.

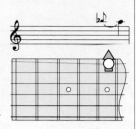

ACCIACCATURA AND APPOGGIATURA

The *acciaccatura* (or crushed note) is played very quickly just before a principal note. Play the note F *very* quickly just before playing G. The *appoggiatura* is also placed just before a principal note. It has half the time value of the note that it precedes.

MUTED NOTES

The letter **X** written at the end of a stem is a direction to play the strings percussively. Lay the left hand lightly across the strings in order to mute them and play the notes; this produces a deadened sound. The palm of the right hand can also be used to muffle fretted notes to the point where they lose tonal quality.

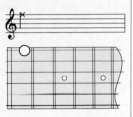

TREMOLO PICKING

When a note is written with one or more small bars placed across the stem, the player is directed to repeat the note rapidly and continuously for the duration of its time value. Two bars indicate very fast movement. Try this technique, using either fast flatpicking or right-hand **I** and **M** fingering.

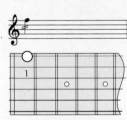

MORDANTS

The two kinds of *mordants* are used as abbreviations for embellishments. The *upper mordant* represents an instruction to play the note itself, a note above it, and then the original note again as one single rapid movement. The *lower mordant* is a direction to play the note itself, a note below it, and then the original note again as one rapid movement.

VIBRATO TECHNIQUE

Hold E on the 5th fret of the 2nd string, rocking the tip of the finger rapidly from *side to side* within a small area behind the fret. This movement produces a minor pitch variation and causes the note to sustain longer. Thumb pressure must be released to allow the finger to move freely. Alternatively, move the finger *up and down* behind the fret. Both methods give a full and attractive tone to the notes on the fingerboard.

USING A TREMOLO ARM

Tremolo arm technique on the electric guitar is an important part of modern playing. A variety of effects can be created by pushing the arm down or pulling it up. Downward pressure lowers the pitch of single notes and chords, and pulling the arm up raises the pitch. Compare bending a note on a fret with the use of the tremolo arm. Hold E on the 12th fret of the 1st string, and bend it up to F natural. Now release the bend and then hold the E again, and with the second and third fingers pull the tremolo arm up to sound F.

Move up to F, then let the arm down to lower the pitch to E. Further movement of the tremolo arm in either direction can be used to adjust the pitch range through a wide series of intervals. Play a phrase, and, on the last note, pull the tremolo arm up or push down to sound a further note in the series. Try pulling the arm up very quickly to create textural variations with the note. Play a note with the tremolo arm pressed down, and let it return to a normal position. This gives a "scooped" effect to the note.

HARMONICS

Open-string *natural harmonics* occur over most frets. Three can be played by touching a string lightly over the 5th, 7th, and 12th frets (the 12th fret produces an octave harmonic). A note held on any fret has *artificial harmonics* between the fret and the bridge. Play F♯ on the 2nd fret, and place the finger lightly over the 14th fret. This point gives the octave harmonic. Play by touching the harmonic over the fret with the 1st finger and plucking the string with the thumb or the second or third finger. This can be played with a flatpick held between the thumb and the second finger.

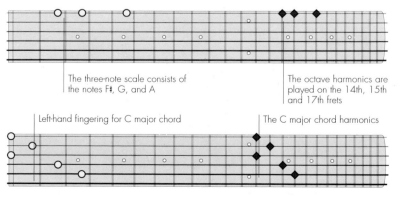

The three-note scale consists of the notes F♯, G, and A

The octave harmonics are played on the 14th, 15th and 17th frets

Left-hand fingering for C major chord

The C major chord harmonics

Variations

A diamond in place of a dot on a staff directs the player to use a harmonic. A series of variations on the different harmonics on a string are often played by brushing the side of the thumb and the flatpick across the strings, covering a wide string area from the fingerboard to the bridge. This is most effective on an electric guitar.

CHORD/SCALE RELATIONSHIPS

PLAYING ARPEGGIOS AND SCALES WITH CHORDS

Modulation
This system of modal seventh chords should be converted to all keys. Write out a major scale and the series of seventh chords, then play each chord with its arpeggios and scales.

To understand how scales and arpeggios relate to chords when soloing, it is important to look thoroughly at the major scale system. Chords must be extended beyond the triads to establish a harmonic framework, otherwise there is a tendency to perceive pentatonic scales against basic major, minor, and dominant chords.

Chord types
Five chord types from the major scale are represented below as a basis for chord improvisation. **I**, **IV**, and **V** are major chords, **II** is a minor, and **VII** is a diminished chord.

SCALES, ARPEGGIOS, AND CHORDS IN C MAJOR

The chords in the C major scale are shown with added sevenths. There are two major sevenths, one dominant seventh, three minor sevenths, and one minor seventh with a flatted fifth. The complete series is C major 7, D minor 7, E minor 7, F major 7, G7, A minor 7, and B minor 7♭5. Play each chord followed by the full arpeggio. The upper extensions are further notes of the C major scale in thirds above the seventh of every chord. A strict application of C major extensions to each of the sevenths creates harmonic tension with certain chords.

CHORD SCALES

The full arpeggio on each chord uses all seven notes of the scale from the root. They can be played as a modal scale on each chord. By playing each mode against the chord, all the notes can be heard in context. Play each scale from the root over the seventh chords. Most of the notes work except for the note F against C major 7, A minor 7, and E minor 7, and C over B minor 7♭5, and E minor 7.

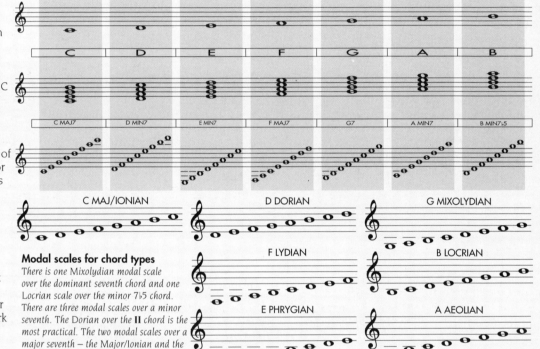

Modal scales for chord types
There is one Mixolydian modal scale over the dominant seventh chord and one Locrian scale over the minor 7♭5 chord. There are three modal scales over a minor seventh. The Dorian over the II chord is the most practical. The two modal scales over a major seventh – the Major/Ionian and the Lydian scales – have a different character.

Chord arpeggios
Play a two-octave arpeggio using all the notes of the chord in one position. Compare the shape of each arpeggio when played in the sequence F-C-G-D-B.

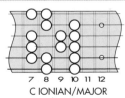
C

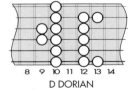
D

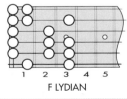
F

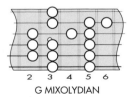
G

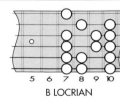
B

Two-octave modal scales
Play a two-octave scale in the same position as the arpeggios. Emphasize the notes of the arpeggio. Compare the pattern with the two-octave scale.

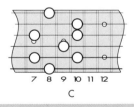
C IONIAN/MAJOR

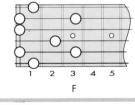
D DORIAN

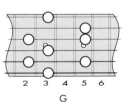
F LYDIAN

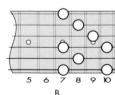
G MIXOLYDIAN

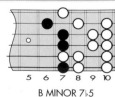
B LOCRIAN

Chord/scale patterns
Play the chords (shown in black) that are derived from the scales. Each chord can be played in the same position as the scale and arpeggio on the fingerboard.

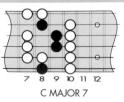
C MAJOR 7

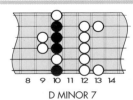
D MINOR 7

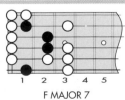
F MAJOR 7

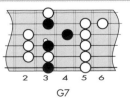
G7

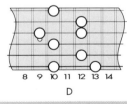
B MINOR 7♭5

MODAL CHORDS

Play the modal scale against each of the seventh chords in C major. Look at the position of the chord and the mode in the two-octave C major scales shown on the right. Each principal note of a mode acts as a pivotal note and the root of the modal chord. Although each chord is composed of the first, third, fifth, and seventh degrees of each scale, adding further notes creates different harmonic effects. On the major seventh **I**, all the notes work in relation to the root, except for the perfect fourth/eleventh. On the major chord **IV**, the augmented fourth – which is usually written as a flat five or sharp eleven – can be used with the chord. With the minor seventh chord **II**, all the notes work. In contrast, with the minor chord **III**, the minor second and minor sixth clash. The minor seventh chord **VI** has a major second in relation to the root that works with the chord, but also a minor sixth that tends to clash. All the intervals from the **V** chord work. In certain conditions, the fourth/eleventh clashes. The same goes for the **VII** chord, with the exception of the minor second, C♮. These *clash-tones* can be used as passing notes, but if they are stressed against the chord they sound weak or highly dissonant.

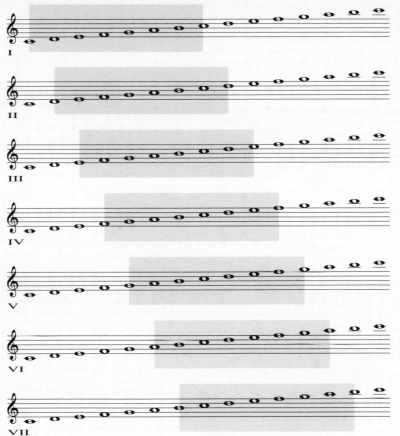

Major/Ionian
The major 7th **I** chord uses C, E, G, and B from this scale as the root, third, fifth, and seventh.

Dorian
The minor seventh **II** chord uses D, F, A, and C from this scale as the root, third, fifth, and seventh.

Phrygian
The minor seventh **III** chord uses E, G, B, and D from this scale as the root, third, fifth, and seventh.

Lydian
The major seventh **IV** chord uses F, A, C, and E from this scale as the root, third, fifth, and seventh.

Mixolydian
The dominant seventh **V** chord uses G, B, D, and F from this scale as the root, third, fifth, and seventh.

Aeolian
The minor seventh **VI** chord uses A, C, E, and G from this scale as the root, third, fifth, and seventh.

Locrian
The minor seventh flat five **VII** chord uses B, D, F, and A from this scale as the root, third, fifth, and seventh.

THE ROOT AND KEY CENTER

When a succession of chords is written down as symbols in a chord sequence, it is important to be able to look at each chord type and relate it to a scale and key center. Five of the chord structures that are found on the major modal system form the basis for most types of chord symbol. The major chord, which has 6th, 7th, and 9th additions, can be treated as either the **I** or the **IV** chord of a major key. As a major/Ionian **I** chord, the root is the keynote of the related major scale; thus C major 7 is found in C major. As a Lydian **IV** major chord with 6th, 7th, 9th, and ♯11 additions, the root is four notes away from the key center – C major 7(♯11) is in G major. When a standard minor chord with 6th(13th), 7th, 9th, or 11th additions is played, it is usually treated as a **II** chord of the major key a tone below. This is because every note of the Dorian scale is effective as a minor chord extension. Therefore C minor 7 is found in B♭ major. The minor chord with 7th, 9th, and 11th additions also occurs as an Aeolian **VI** chord; C minor 7 can be approached as a chord in E♭ major. The major chord in the form of a Mixolydian dominant with 7th, 9th, 11th(4th), and 13th additions occurs as a **V** chord on the major scale. The root is five notes above the key center; C7 is in F major. The Locrian minor seventh flat five chord with an eleventh addition occurs only as a **VII** on the major scale. C minor 7♭5 is in D♭ major. The root is a semitone below the key center.

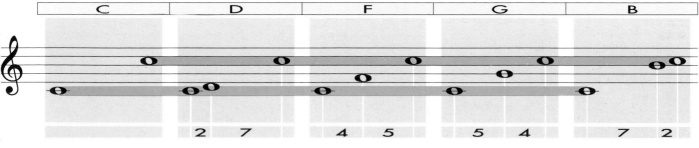

The major as a I chord The major **I** chord is built from the first degree of the major scale. When a major seventh occurs, or when it is extended using major/Ionian notes, it is on the major keynote of its own scale.

The minor as a II chord The minor **II** chord is built from the second degree of the major scale. When a minor seventh and its standard extensions occur, it is one tone (major second) above or seven below a major keynote.

The major as a IV chord The major **IV** chord is built from the fourth degree of the major scale. When a major seventh or Lydian extension occurs, it is four notes (a fourth) above or five notes (a fifth) below a major keynote.

The major as a V chord The major **V** chord is built from the fifth degree of the major scale. When a dominant seventh or an extension occurs, it is five notes above or four notes below a major keynote.

The diminished as a VII chord The diminished **VII** chord is built from the seventh degree of the major scale. When a minor seventh flat five or an extension occurs, it is seven notes above or one semitone below a major keynote.

SCALES WITH SEVENTHS

It is important to compare the use of scales in the major system and the relative minor systems. When a series of seventh chords is written out on the major system and the relative harmonic and melodic minor scales, there are a number of points where materials can overlap. There is also a wide variation in the application of major and relative minor scales against chords. This is linked to their function and position within chord sequences. The major and minor scale systems provide a basis for melody and improvisation. Their modal scales cover most of the harmony written as chord symbols.

THE MAJOR SYSTEM

When each chord is played as a seventh, it relates to other keys aside from C major. The **I** chord is also the **IV** chord of G major. **II** is the **VI** chord of F major. **III** is also the **II** chord of D major and the **VI** chord of G major. **IV** is the **I** chord in F. **VI** is the **II** chord of G major. **VII** is the **II** chord in A harmonic minor.

THE MINOR SYSTEM

I can be played with a melodic minor. **II** can be used with the Locrian mode. **III** can use the melodic minor. **IV** can use the Dorian mode. **V** can use either the Mixolydian or the melodic minor. **VI** can use the Lydian mode. **II**, **IV**, **VI**, and **VII** use the harmonic minor scale as diminished chords. With melodic minor chords, **II** can use the Dorian mode, **IV** can use the Mixolydian and, as a 7♭5, the melodic minor. **V** can use the Mixolydian mode. **VI** can use the Locrian. **VII** as a 7♭5 can use the melodic minor.

MAJOR SYSTEM

Play the seventh chords as a sequence in C using the seven modes. Take each chord and play it on its own out of context. **I**, **III**, and **VI** suggest other modes. **II**, **III**, **IV**, and **VII** can use further modes in certain contexts.

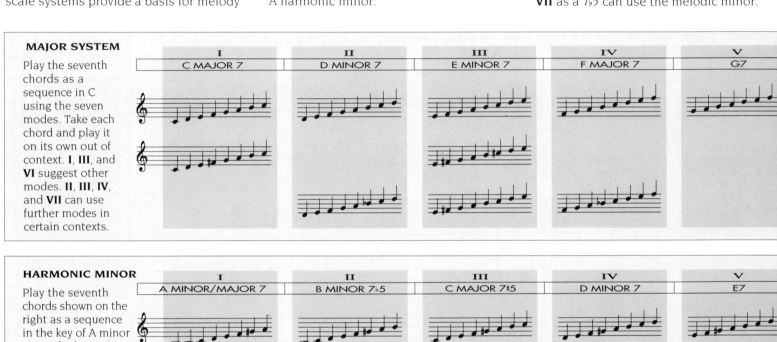

HARMONIC MINOR

Play the seventh chords shown on the right as a sequence in the key of A minor using the harmonic minor modes. With each chord on its own, the related major and melodic minor modes can be used. The **II**, **IV**, **VI**, and **VII** chords can all be played as diminished inversions.

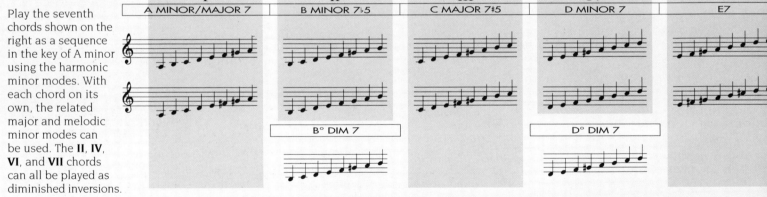

MELODIC MINOR

Play the seventh chords shown on the right as a sequence in the key of A minor using the melodic minor modes. With each chord on its own, other altered modes can be used. **IV** and **VII** as **7♭5** chords are inversions of one another. They use the melodic minor scales.

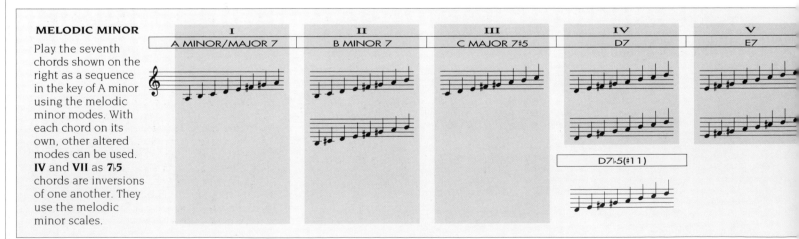

SEVENTH CHORDS ON A C ROOT

If seventh chord types are all written with their primary scale relationships based from a root of C, the scales and modes can be compared. The C chords use different scales in the major and minor key systems. Six of the C chords are written with one alternative scale relationship. Some chords can be used with a large number of scales. The C major chord and the C minor/major chord are the only types that have the root on the keynote. The remaining chords occur on other modal degrees of major and minor scale.

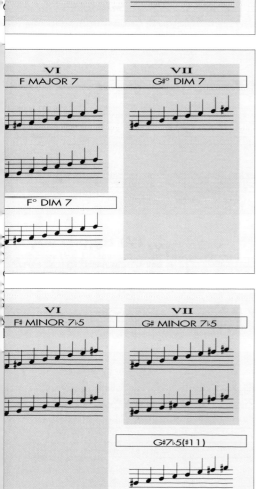

VI	VII
A MINOR 7	B MINOR 7♭5

VI	VII
F MAJOR 7	G#° DIM 7

| F° DIM 7 | |

VI	VII
F# MINOR 7♭5	G# MINOR 7♭5

| G#7♭5(#11) | |

C major 7

This is the **I** chord of the key of C major. C major 7 can also be treated as the **IV** chord when played in the key of G major.

C minor 7

This is the **II** chord of the key of B♭ major. The C minor 7 chord is shown above with the **VI** scale of E♭ major.

C diminished 7

This can also be the **VII** chord of C# harmonic minor. With inversions using the notes F#, A, and D#, it can be related to G, B♭, and E harmonic minor.

C7 flat 5

This can be used as the **IV** chord of G melodic minor. It can also be used as the **VII** chord in the key of C# melodic minor.

C major 7♭5#11

When playing in the key of G major, C major 7♭5#11 is used as the **IV** chord.

C dominant 7

This is the **V** chord in the key of F major. C7 is shown above as the **V** chord of F harmonic minor. It can also be used as the **V** chord of F melodic minor.

C minor 7 flat 5

This is the **VII** chord of D♭ major. It can also be used as the **II** chord when played in the key of B♭ harmonic minor.

C minor/major 7

As the **I** chord in the key of both C harmonic minor and C melodic minor, this chord can be used with either of the two scales.

C7 sharp 5

This can be used as the **V** chord of F harmonic and melodic minor. It can also be used as the **VII** chord in the key of C# melodic minor.

Sequence of seventh chords

Using the C note as a reference point with chords and scale changes, play a sequence of seventh chords on the root C as a chord progression. Play four chords as one chord-type per bar over four bars at a slow tempo. Improvise through the chord changes using the related scales, and compare chord types with keys and modes as they change from bar to bar. As an exercise, play all the seventh chords as each root letter name. Take each chord on a root, and play all the types with each scale and mode.

A MINOR CHORDS (VI)

Chords on the sixth degree of C major use the notes A, B, C, D, E, and G. Common extensions are A minor 7, A minor 9, and A minor 11. They are used in many different types of progression. Altered Aeolian chords can also include the note F.

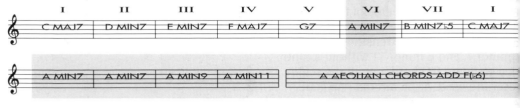

A AEOLIAN

Play the exercises against the standard chords, and the seven-note arpeggio against the A chord and its natural extensions. The F sounds dissonant when stressed on these chords.

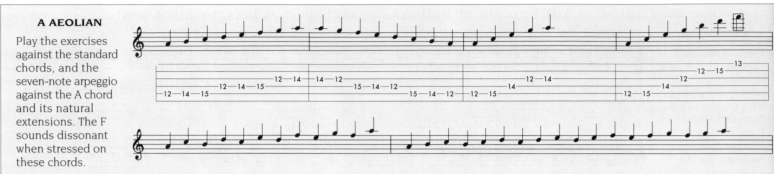

B DIMINISHED CHORDS (VII)

Chords on the seventh degree of the C major scale are formed using the notes B, D, E, F, G, and A. Common extensions are B minor 7♭5, and B minor 11♭5 without a ninth. Altered Locrian voicings can also include the note C.

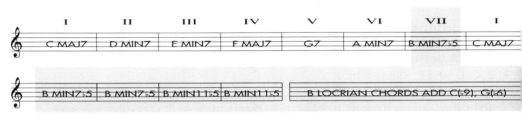

B LOCRIAN

Play the exercise against the standard chords, and the seven-note arpeggio against the B chord and its natural extensions. The note C sounds dissonant when stressed.

PLAYING MODAL SCALES AND CHORDS

Standard chords on each degree vary in their effect as a basis for improvising. For example, the C major I chords create a harmonic structure where the note F becomes dissonant. If each mode is played in the key of C, the F note must be avoided as an accented note over C chords in every position. Therefore, F Lydian as a mode is not practical because it is based around F as a principal note. In other modes F can be used as a passing note. The sound of each mode over a chord is defined by the shape and relation of the principal note to structures and voicings. For example, E Phrygian works well over a D minor 7 chord. The free use of all modes over one chord is best explored with the open-sounding tonal system based around the D minor II harmonies. This group of Dorian chords uses all of the notes of the scale within its chord voicings. There are no clashing notes, and each one of the modes can be used to improvise freely.

Chords on modal degrees

The fingerboard on the right shows seven positions for chords on each modal degree of the scale, running in the key of C major from F on the 1st fret to E on the 12th fret. F major 7, using notes from the Lydian mode, is on the 1st fret. G7, using notes from the Mixolydian mode, is on the 3rd fret. A minor chords on the 5th fret must be voiced using the Aeolian mode. B minor 7 flat 5, using notes from the Locrian mode, is on the 7th fret. C major 7, using notes from the Ionian (major) mode, is on the 8th fret. D minor 7, using notes from the Dorian mode, is on the 10th fret. E minor chords on the 10th fret must be voiced using notes from the Phrygian mode.

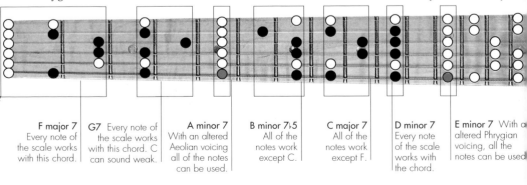

F major 7 Every note of the scale works with this chord. | **G7** Every note of the scale works with this chord. C can sound weak. | **A minor 7** With an altered Aeolian voicing all of the notes can be used. | **B minor 7♭5** All of the notes work except C. | **C major 7** All of the notes work except F. | **D minor 7** Every note of the scale works with the chord. | **E minor 7** With an altered Phrygian voicing, all the notes can be used

MODAL POSITIONS ALONG THE 5TH STRING

Each mode in C should be played as a pattern with a standard fingering (see below, first column). Four of the modes in the second column can be played using stretch fingering, starting with the first finger. Practice the following modes: C Ionian (C major) on the 3rd fret, D Dorian on the 5th fret, E Phrygian on the 7th fret, F Lydian on the 8th fret, G Mixolydian on the 10th fret, and A Aeolian on the 12th fret. To begin with, this last position may be rather difficult to play on a nylon-string acoustic guitar: instead, it can be played from the lower open-string position. Depending on the type of instrument used, B Locrian should be played on either the 2nd or the 14th fret. A series of modal positions can be played easily on most electric guitars from C on the 3rd fret up to an octave repeat of the C position on the 15th fret.

DOUBLE-OCTAVE MODAL POSITIONS

The modal scales can all be played over two octaves across the fingerboard starting on the 6th string. These scales are marked with black dots on the chart below. The modal scales ascending from the 5th string are marked in blue. When a mode is played from the 6th string, it can be fingered easily as a pattern without requiring a shift in position. Modes from the 5th string must be played with a shift in position or stretch fingering if they are to be extended over two octaves. The pattern starting from each string should be combined into one overall fingering position that covers a large area of the fingerboard. On the seven diagrams below, the notes in C that are not part of each fingering pattern are marked with white circles. The position of each mode in relation to the others should be memorized.

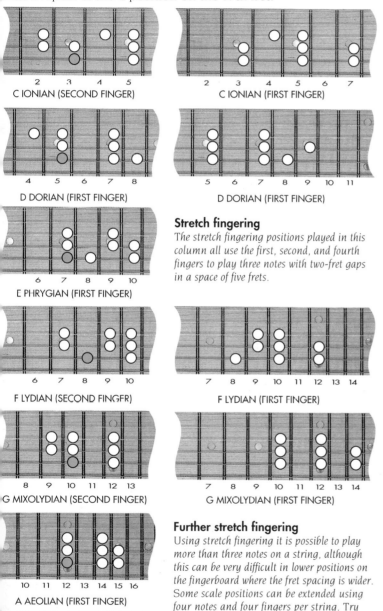

C IONIAN (SECOND FINGER) — 2 3 4 5

C IONIAN (FIRST FINGER) — 2 3 4 5 6 7

D DORIAN (FIRST FINGER) — 4 5 6 7 8

D DORIAN (FIRST FINGER) — 5 6 7 8 9 10 11

Stretch fingering
The stretch fingering positions played in this column all use the first, second, and fourth fingers to play three notes with two-fret gaps in a space of five frets.

E PHRYGIAN (FIRST FINGER) — 6 7 8 9 10

F LYDIAN (SECOND FINGER) — 6 7 8 9 10

F LYDIAN (FIRST FINGER) — 7 8 9 10 11 12 13 14

G MIXOLYDIAN (SECOND FINGER) — 8 9 10 11 12 13

G MIXOLYDIAN (FIRST FINGER) — 7 8 9 10 11 12 13 14

Further stretch fingering
Using stretch fingering it is possible to play more than three notes on a string, although this can be very difficult in lower positions on the fingerboard where the fret spacing is wider. Some scale positions can be extended using four notes and four fingers per string. Try playing part of the A Aeolian scale from the 12th fret, using the first finger to play A, the second to play B, the third to play C, and the fourth to play D. Stretch fingering is used by jazz and rock guitarists.

A AEOLIAN (FIRST FINGER) — 10 11 12 13 14 15 16

B LOCRIAN (FIRST FINGER) — 2 3 4 5

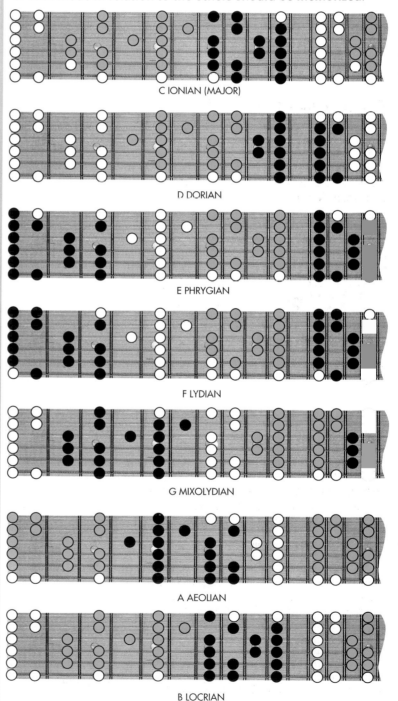

C IONIAN (MAJOR)

D DORIAN

E PHRYGIAN

F LYDIAN

G MIXOLYDIAN

A AEOLIAN

B LOCRIAN

C MAJOR TO G MAJOR AND F MAJOR

There are several approaches to learning the full scale patterns in every key. With a thorough knowledge of the C major pattern over the entire fingerboard, a simple way of learning the patterns of the closely related G major and F major keys is to pick out the one note that differentiates them and adjust the C pattern. The only difference between G major and C major is the note F♯, so every F note is simply moved up by one semitone. In a similar way, C major is converted to F major by picking out every B note and moving it down a semitone to B♭.

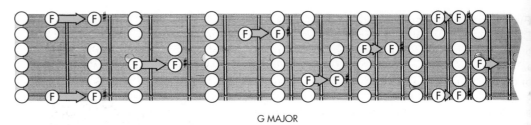

G MAJOR

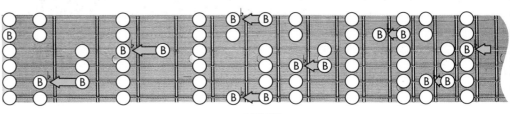

F MAJOR

C MAJOR AND OTHER KEYS

Every key can be cross-referred to C major and memorized as a pattern with a fixed number of variations. There are nine fingerboard diagrams below detailing the position of the C scale in relation to the remaining keys. They show clearly how two keys work as contrasting patterns on the fingerboard. The notes of the C major scale are marked as white circles, and the contrasting key is marked with black circles. Shared notes are black and white.

The relationship between the C major and D major scales can be used to explain the diagram. The two scales share the notes B, D, G, E, and A: the D major scale can be played in relation to C major by moving the notes F and C up a semitone. Study one area of the fingerboard – one octave of the open-string E Phrygian scale pattern in C major, starting on the 6th-string open E. E is shared with the key of D, F is in C only, G is in D and C, A is in C and D, B is in C and D, C is in C only, and D is in C and D. If the

E Phrygian modal scale is played with the notes C and F moved up by a semitone, the scale is converted to E, F♯, G, A, B, C♯, and D. This is a Dorian scale in D. The key center of D is a tone above C, which moves all the modal patterns up by two frets. This can be extended along the fingerboard and repeated for all the other keys in relation to C major. Contrasting scales across the fingerboard is a useful exercise, providing the grounding for soloing and improvising through key changes.

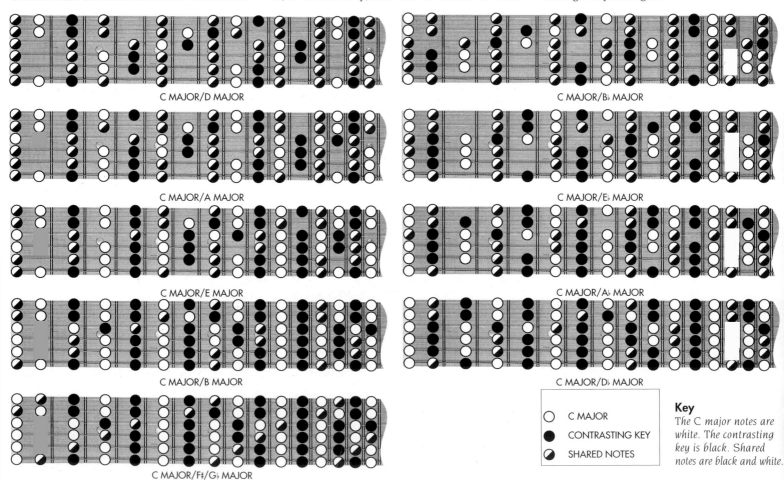

C MAJOR/D MAJOR

C MAJOR/B♭ MAJOR

C MAJOR/A MAJOR

C MAJOR/E♭ MAJOR

C MAJOR/E MAJOR

C MAJOR/A♭ MAJOR

C MAJOR/B MAJOR

C MAJOR/D♭ MAJOR

C MAJOR/F♯/G♭ MAJOR

Key

○ C MAJOR
● CONTRASTING KEY
◑ SHARED NOTES

Key
The C major notes are white. The contrasting key is black. Shared notes are black and white.

FINGERING POSITIONS

One of the simplest ways of learning a full scale position for each of the keys is to take one major scale pattern and memorize it as three modal fingering blocks. There are a number of ways of connecting all the modal patterns in one key across the fingerboard. Shown below is a system where extended double-octave major/Ionian, Phrygian, and Aeolian scales are played as three positions that cover the entire fingerboard. These positions cover every note and repeat in the higher octave positions above the 12th fret. As soon as the patterns have been mastered in C major, the next step is to move them as a visual block up and down the fingerboard. All the keys can be played by moving the extended patterns. For example, Db major is simply C moved up a semitone, and B major is C moved down a semitone.

Three blocks

The major scale fingering pattern is extended over two octaves. The Aeolian pattern is also extended and overlaps. The Phrygian pattern covers the scale notes above the major.

- ● PHRYGIAN
- ◐ AEOLIAN
- ◒ OVERLAP
- ○ MAJOR

DUPLICATION

This is an example of a movement from one key to another. Notes are duplicated in other positions. C is played from the 3rd fret of the 5th string, ascending to G. It moves to the key of Ab major, starting on the 6th fret of the 4th string. The same series can be played starting with the note C on the 8th fret of the 6th string, moving to Ab on the 5th string. These two positions have the same set of notes.

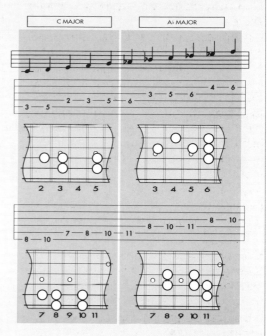

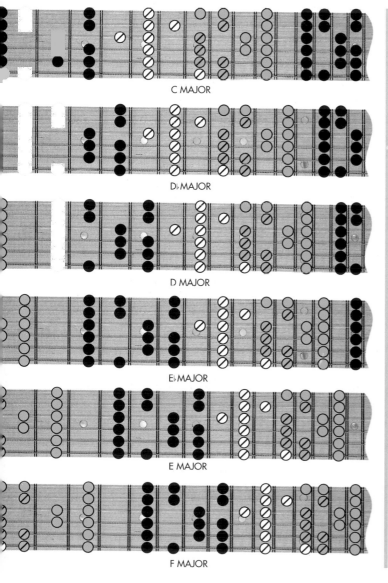

C MAJOR

Db MAJOR

D MAJOR

Eb MAJOR

E MAJOR

F MAJOR

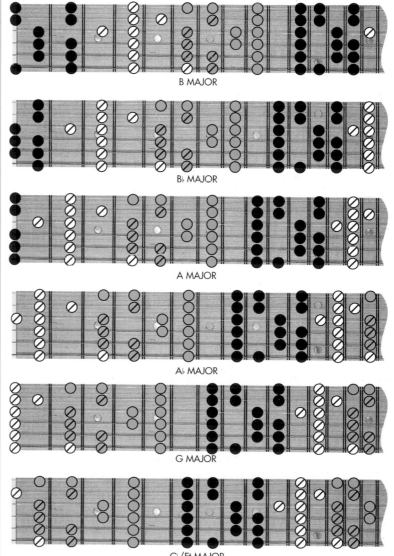

B MAJOR

Bb MAJOR

A MAJOR

Ab MAJOR

G MAJOR

Gb/F# MAJOR

THE PENTATONIC SCALE

LEARNING PENTATONIC SCALE TECHNIQUES AND POSITIONS

Extended patterns
The A pentatonic is shown in the box below from the open 5th string and, using the same notes, from the 6th string, where it can be extended more easily. These positions can be played in an upper octave from the 12th and 17th frets on an electric guitar.

The standard pentatonic scale consists of five notes within an octave. The minor pentatonic scale (see p. 74) occurs frequently as one of the primary scales in all types of music. Minor pentatonic scales are formed from major seconds and minor thirds. This type of scale is one of the most important forms after the major and minor scales. Mastery of the minor pentatonic is vital for the development of skills in composition, improvisation, and playing melodies.

The full pattern
The two main pentatonic positions can cover notes outside a two-octave scale. In A minor, the open 5th-string pattern uses the two notes below on the 6th string; the other fingering has an extra top note. Additional notes can be played by stretching, shifting position, and sliding.

Two-octave pentatonic
This scale, running over two octaves, ascends in the sequence A-C-D-E-G-A-C-D-E-G-A.

| A | C | D | E | G | A | C | D | E | G | A |

FINGERING TWO-OCTAVE SCALES

The pentatonic scale from the lowest A note in standard tuning can be played from the open 5th string or, at the same pitch, on the 5th fret of the 6th string. The lower position from the open strings repeats as a pattern starting on the 12th fret, at a higher octave. These three positions must be memorized to cover the scale on the fingerboard. Play each position, and move between them by shifting the overall left-hand position. The patterns do not cover all the pentatonic notes on the fingerboard. The white circles show the notes of the pentatonic scale that are not covered by the notes on the staff.

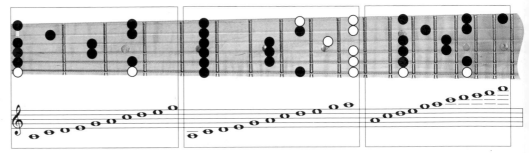

Open position
Play from the open A to the G on the 3rd fret of the 1st string, using standard fingering. Try finishing the two-octave scale by playing G and A on the 1st string with the second and fourth fingers.

Fifth-fret position
Exactly the same notes can be played starting from the 5th fret of the 6th string. The top A on the two-octave scale can be played easily without either changing the fingering pattern or stretching.

Upper-octave position
The pentatonic scale in the upper octave is the same as the open-string pattern. It is played by using the first finger to play the octave equivalents of the open-string notes.

PENTATONIC MODES

The pentatonic scale can be played as a six-note pattern from any of its constituent notes. This creates five different scales, referred to as *modes* of the pentatonic scale. Each scale has its own sound, with the principal note acting as a pivot for the melodic shape and structure. The five scales can be viewed as pentatonic scales in their own right. They often occur as separate scales in folk and ethnic music. The relationship is similar to that between the major scale and modal degrees. The scales below should be played as six-note exercises within the standard pentatonic structure, and extended to two octaves. This will develop the flexibility needed for improvising with the standard pentatonic.

The five scales
Play these five pentatonic scales, based on a 5th-fret position, as a series of separate exercises. When these positions have been thoroughly memorized, move them to the second main pentatonic fingering pattern, which starts on the 5th string. When a pentatonic scale using the notes A-C-D-E-G has been mastered across the entire fingerboard, the five patterns can be played from any position of the scale in every register.

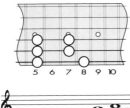

A	C	D	E	G	A
①	④	①	③	①	③
①	③	①	②	①	②

Starting on A Ascend with a minor third, major second, major second, minor third, and major second.

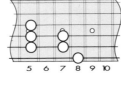

C	D	E	G	A	C
④	①	③	①	③	①
③	①	②	①	②	①

Starting on C Ascend with a major second, major second, minor third, major second, and a minor third.

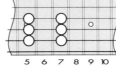
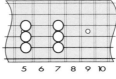

D	E	G	A	C	D
①	③	①	③	①	③
①	②	①	②	①	②

Starting on D Ascend with a major second, minor third, major second, minor third, and a major second.

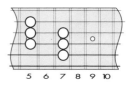

E	G	A	C	D	E
③	①	③	①	③	①
②	①	②	①	②	①

Starting on E Ascend with a minor third, major second, minor third, major second, and a major second.

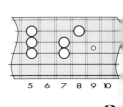

G	A	C	D	E	G
①	③	①	③	①	④
①	②	①	②	①	③

Starting on G Ascend wi a major second, minor th major second, major second, and a minor third

PENTATONIC VARIATION

There are several ways in which a scale can be played across the fingerboard. Standard fingerings using two notes on a string are often combined with stretch fingerings, which enable three notes to be played on a string. Pentatonic scales may be extended beyond two octaves by either stretching or shifting the overall left-hand position, from every note on each string in one position up to higher pentatonic positions and two-octave patterns. The minor pentatonic can be played with two 6th-string patterns beginning on the 1st and 2nd notes of the pentatonic. These start from the 5th and 8th frets. As a standard scale for soloing,

A minor pentatonic is often related to the Dorian mode, and the "major" pentatonic above it is Lydian. Therefore, both are related to G major. It is important to differentiate between the minor and major pentatonic scales in A, which are related to G, and the minor and major seven-note scales in the key of C major.

Minor pentatonic

Play the A minor pentatonic starting with the 4th finger at the 5th fret. This overlaps with the 5th-string pentatonic. Practicing this pattern increases familiarity with the pentatonic and extends fingerboard control.

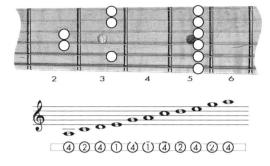

Major pentatonic

This pattern is the second A minor pentatonic mode. It is often used as a "major" approach to its scale. In relation to the first note, it contains a major third and a major sixth. It is used in conjunction with the minor pentatonic to cover the fingerboard.

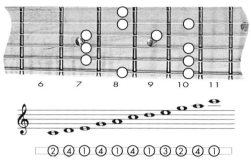

PENTATONIC EXERCISES

These exercises develop skill in playing the scale freely and provide basic grounding and control for melody and improvisation. The first exercise is a series of ascending three-note patterns; this should be extended over two octaves. The second is an ascending four-note pattern. The third combines fourths and thirds, and the final exercise consists of intervals from the root. Move these exercises up to the higher-octave pentatonic, starting on the 12th fret. Try playing descending three- and four-note patterns.

THREE-NOTE PATTERN

FOUR-NOTE PATTERN

FOURTHS AND THIRDS

INTERVALS

Pentatonic to Dorian scale conversion

Five-note pentatonic scales can be converted to seven-note modal scales, related to a major key, by adding a second and a sixth. Natural extensions for the A minor pentatonic are B (the major second) and F♯ (the major sixth).

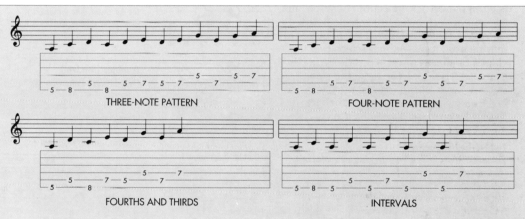

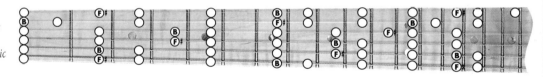

TRANSPOSING THE PENTATONIC

The first note of the minor pentatonic can be thought of as a type of keynote when used within a blues structure. The first chord normally starts on the same note as the minor pentatonic: this note names the key. Blues in the key of A normally uses major chords in conjunction with an adapted A minor pentatonic. A blues sequence starting on A and using minor chords is referred to as *Blues in A minor*. The two main lower positions for pentatonic keynotes are on the 6th and 5th strings. On the right, the C minor pentatonic on the 8th fret of the 6th string is transposed to F♯ on the 2nd fret. C minor pentatonic can also be played from the 3rd fret of the 5th string and moved up to a higher F♯ minor pentatonic on the 9th fret.

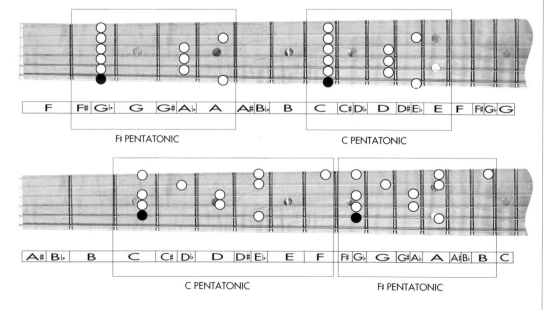

ADVANCED TECHNIQUES

EXTENDING SINGLE-NOTE CONTROL

Transposition
The techniques in this section must be played in all keys. Try tapping along the fingerboard and sweeping on every string. Stretch fingering can be difficult in the lower registers.

Virtuoso electric guitar playing has resulted in innovations and changes in technique. Fast playing and flowing phrases with extended intervals both demand skillful coordination. A modern guitarist will be able to play intervals across the fingerboard, use stretch fingering over all the strings, and fret tapping for higher elements.

String muting
When playing electric guitars at high volume, it is important to mute or damp open strings to stop them ringing. While using certain techniques, place the edge of the right hand on unused strings.

FRET TAPPING

The right hand can play notes by *tapping* the string. Tap G on the 1st string using the third finger of the *left* hand, then pull the finger off, sounding the open E string. Try doing this with the second finger of the *right* hand. Right-hand tapping, combined with left-hand fret positioning, makes it possible to play phrases with any intervals. A three-note movement can be played by tapping the 7th fret with the second finger of the right hand, pulling the note off to sound fretted G, and then pulling-off with the left hand to sound the open E.

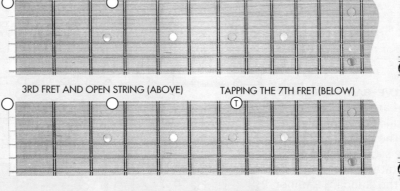

3RD FRET AND OPEN STRING (ABOVE)   TAPPING THE 7TH FRET (BELOW)

Hammer-on G on the 3rd fret and pull-off to the open E.

Tap B on the 7th fret, pull-off to G on the 3rd fret, and pull-off to the open E.

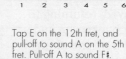

Tap C♯ on the 9th fret, and pull-off to sound A on the 5th fret. Pull-off A to sound F♯.

Tap D on the 10th fret, and pull-off to sound A on the 5th fret. Pull-off A to sound F♯.

Tap E on the 12th fret, and pull-off to sound A on the 5th fret. Pull-off A to sound F♯.

TAPPING ACROSS THE FINGERBOARD

Play an E minor pentatonic scale across the fretboard, using open strings and the 2nd and 3rd frets. Extend the two notes on each string to a three-note motif by playing a high note with the second finger of the right hand. Tap across all the strings, playing (from top to bottom) the 10th, 10th, 9th, 9th, 9th, and 10th frets. Play repeating ascending and descending variations by pulling off to the open string with the left and right hands. Try cyclical phrases, starting with any note. Move up and down using tapping, hammering, and pull-offs.

1ST STRING   2ND STRING   3RD STRING   4TH STRING   5TH STRING   6TH STRING

The right hand
Some players tap with the first finger, while resting the thumb on the neck or the body to give stability. If the second finger is used, it is possible to hold the flatpick between the thumb and first finger and stabilize the tapping finger with the third and fourth fingers.

DIRECTIONAL CONTROL

Notes are played across the fingerboard with controlled directional picking (*sweep picking*), so that strings are played with economic movements. Scales are arranged in fingering patterns so that the flatpick is always on the correct side of the string it has just played for movement to the next string. Play an arpeggio using sweep picking. Release the pressure on the notes as they are played; they should ring as single notes without sustaining together.

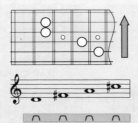

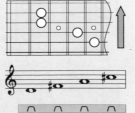

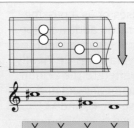

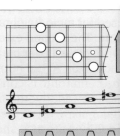

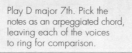

Play D major 7th. Pick the notes as an arpeggiated chord, leaving each of the voices to ring for comparison.

Play D major 7th, picking single arpeggiated scale notes. Release the pressure after each note to stop it ringing.

Play a D major 7th arpeggio with descending scale notes. Start with C♯ on the 2nd string and pick upward.

Play a D major extended arpeggio across five strings as a series of individual notes ascending and descending.

STRETCH FINGERING

Play a G major two-octave scale starting on the 10th fret of the 5th string. Divide the 15-note scale into five groups with three notes on each string. The first note in each group is played with a flatpick downstroke, and the two following notes are hammered. Practice the scale in this form, aiming to create a very even legato effect. Move the first finger quickly and accurately onto the fret positions for each of the strings. Play a descending scale by picking the first note in each group with an upstroke and sounding the two following notes with pull-offs. Play continuous ascending and descending patterns of notes on one string: stretch the fingers to reach extra notes above and below the positions, and move across to all the notes on adjacent strings. Try jumping across adjacent strings to all the other strings. Legato can be played without picking or pull-offs.

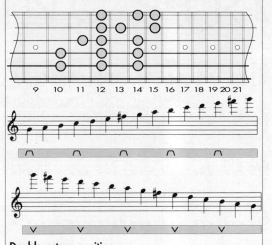

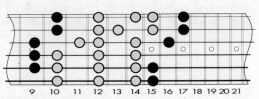

Extending the position
Stretch to include notes outside the standard position. This will allow you to play larger intervals on one string.

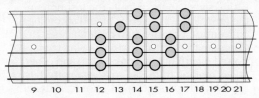

Double-octave position
After playing the double-octave position in G major, starting on the keynote, move to other modal positions using stretch fingering from each string. Memorize the fingering patterns as related blocks, and, when they are familiar, transpose them to other keys.

Dorian with stretch fingering
This Dorian position can be used as a block and as an overlapping position with the the G major scale two frets below. The same notes in each scale are played from different positions. Develop other modal positions in G major.

Rhythmic control
Set a metronome to a slow tempo and build up scale patterns and exercises over four bars using a diatonic turnaround pattern in C major with the roots C, A, D, and G. Build up from one note in the bar to sixteen. Develop speed on these exercises by increasing the tempo. Use standard picking techniques and make up new variations and combinations. Take the scales, pentatonic patterns, and arpeggios up to a higher octave that can be played without running out of upper-register notes on the fingerboard. Experiment with all types of fingerboard positions and left- and right-hand techniques.

SUBDIVISION OF THE BAR

The diagram on the right shows a 4/4 bar as a mathematical chart with all the notes in accurate time relationships. The left-hand side represents the first beat of the bar: each quarter note on the top row sustains for a quarter of the bar. The fifth quarter note represents the beginning of the next bar. Compare these with the quarter-note triplets. The first of the triplet groups starts at the beginning of the bar, and the second starts at the same point as the third quarter-note beat. The first note in each group of eighth-note triplets can be timed in relation to quarter-note and eighth-notes beats.

Quarter notes

Quarter-note triplets

Sixteenth notes

Sixteenth-note triplets

Sixteenth notes

JAZZ PROGRESSIONS

A SERIES OF STANDARD JAZZ SEQUENCES AND BASS LINES

Chord transposition
Certain types of progression can be transposed by converting the main scale-tone chords on each tonal center to Roman numerals.

Learning standard sequences is helpful for improvising within a structure. Standard blues and jazz forms can be memorized for use as structures on which to base further development. They provide ideal frameworks for chord substitution and creative chord thinking.

Blues variations
Play the variations, comparing each sequence with the basic jazz blues structure in the first example. All the sequences shown are in 4/4 time.

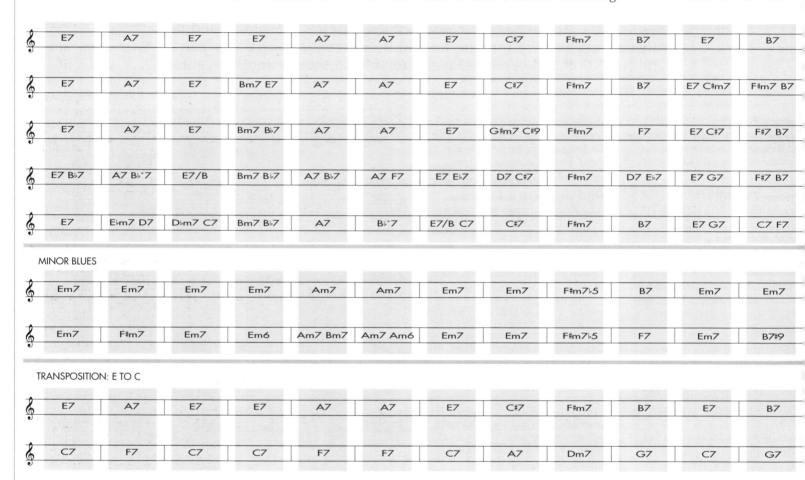

E7	A7	E7	E7	A7	A7	E7	C#7	F#m7	B7	E7	B7
E7	A7	E7	Bm7 E7	A7	A7	E7	C#7	F#m7	B7	E7 C#m7	F#m7 B7
E7	A7	E7	Bm7 B♭7	A7	A7	E7	G#m7 C#9	F#m7	F7	E7 C#7	F#7 B7
E7 B♭7	A7 B♭°7	E7/B	Bm7 B♭7	A7 B♭7	A7 F7	E7 E♭7	D7 C#7	F#m7	D7 E♭7	E7 G7	F#7 B7
E7	E♭m7 D7	D♭m7 C7	Bm7 B♭7	A7	B♭°7	E7/B C7	C#7	F#m7	B7	E7 G7	C7 F7

MINOR BLUES

| Em7 | Em7 | Em7 | Em7 | Am7 | Am7 | Em7 | Em7 | F#m7♭5 | B7 | Em7 | Em7 |
| Em7 | F#m7 | Em7 | Em6 | Am7 Bm7 | Am7 Am6 | Em7 | Em7 | F#m7♭5 | F7 | Em7 | B7#9 |

TRANSPOSITION: E TO C

| E7 | A7 | E7 | E7 | A7 | A7 | E7 | C#7 | F#m7 | B7 | E7 | B7 |
| C7 | F7 | C7 | C7 | F7 | F7 | C7 | A7 | Dm7 | G7 | C7 | G7 |

TURNAROUNDS

The term *turnaround* applies to chordal movements that start from one chord and turn around through a series of variations before returning to the beginning. These are normally based around the use of **V-I** movements at the end of a sequence. Develop a two-bar turnaround in stages. Play the chord sequence C major 7, A minor 7, D minor 7, G7, and C major 7. Convert all the chords to dominant sevenths or ninths. Now link the four chords with a series of bass notes. This creates a bass line with a note on every beat, running C-B♭-A-D♭-D-A♭-G-B. The last note B leads back to C at the beginning of the two-bar sequence. Try flat fifth substitution on the turnaround. Move from C9 to E♭9 (the flat fifth of A7) and from D9 to D♭9 (the flat fifth of G7).

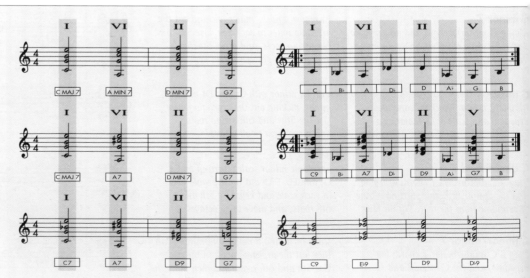

STANDARD JAZZ SEQUENCE

This uses **II-V-I** movements with link chords. The first two bars are **II** and **V** chords, moving to **I** in the third bar and **IV** in the fourth. The fifth bar is a **II** chord of the relative minor; the sixth is the relative minor **V**; the seventh is the relative minor **I**. The chord on the eighth bar acts as a dominant chord. Bars 17 to 24 are the major to minor **II-V-I** chords. Bars 25 to 32 form a cycle leading back to the beginning.

Dm7	G7	CM7	FM7	Bm7♭5	E7	Am7	A7
Dm7	G7	CM7	FM7	Bm7♭5	E7	Am7	Am7
Bm7♭5	E7	Am7	A7	Dm7	G7	CM7	FM7
Bm7♭5	E7	Am7 G#7	Gm7 F#7	FM7	Bm7♭5 E7	Am7	Am7

RHYTHM CHANGES

The sequence shown on the right follows a series of standard rhythm changes. The first four bars are a B♭ turnaround, followed by a **II-V-I** movement in E♭ with a link chord leading back to a turnaround. The middle eight section (bars 17 to 24) is a series of **II-V** movements in the cycle of keys running from G major, C major, F major, and B♭ major. The last section is a repeat of the first eight bars.

B♭7 G7	Cm7 F7	B♭7 G7	Cm7 F7	Fm7 B♭7	E♭ E♭m	B♭7 G7	Cm7 F7
B♭ B°7	Cm7 C#°7	Dm7 G7	Cm7 F7	B♭ B♭/D	E♭ E°	B♭7 G7	Cm7 F7
Am7	D7	Dm7	G7	Gm7	C7	Cm7	F7
B♭ G7	Cm F7	B♭ G7	Cm7 F7	Fm7 B♭7	E♭ E°	B♭	B♭

SIXTEEN-BAR MINOR BLUES STRUCTURE

A minor 7 (**I**) is played for the first four bars. This is raised by a fourth (D minor 7) for two bars. A minor **II-V** chords take the sequence back to four bars of **I**. A movement to the **V** chord takes the sequence back to **I**.

| Am7 | Am7 | Am7 | Am7 | Dm7 | Dm7 | Bm7♭5 | E7 |
| Am7 | Am7 | Am7 | Am7 | CM7 Am7 | FM7 E7 | Am7 | Am7 |

BASS LINES

This is a bass line for the standard sequence shown at the top of the page. Try playing the notes with varying sequences, e.g., start with D and move to E above or drop to E below. After the root has been played at the beginning of the bar, the remaining notes are played as chord harmonies and link notes. Chord notes, the related scale, and notes to lead in from a semitone above or below a root are standard approaches.

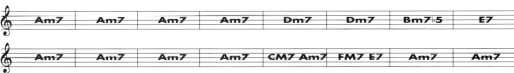

D E F A	G A G B	C G C E	F E D C	B D F A	G# E D B	A B C E	C# B A E
D E F A	G A G B	C G C E	F E D C	B D F A	G# E D B	A B C E	A E C A
F D B G#	E F# G G#	A B C E	B♭ G E C#	D E F A	G F E D	C E A G	F E D C
B F D B	E D C B	A C G# F#	G B♭ F# E	F A C B♭	B F E G#	A B C E	A

CHROMATIC SEVENTHS

Jazz sequences can be filled by using chords chromatically as links. The examples shown on the right are based on a two-bar turnaround. On the last beat of the first bar, C7 is moved to B♭7 as a lead-in chord to A7. This chord movement acts like a bass line moving from B♭ to A. Similarly, A7 is played until the last beat of the bar when D♭7 leads back to D7. D7 is played until the final beat of the bar when A♭7 is used to lead to G7, which is used to return to a C chord.

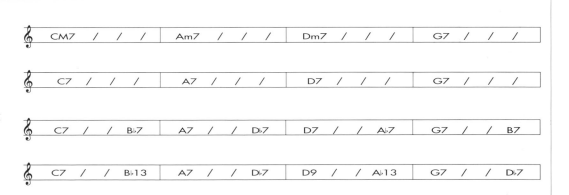

CM7 / / /	Am7 / / /	Dm7 / / /	G7 / / /
C7 / / /	A7 / / /	D7 / / /	G7 / / /
C7 / / B♭7	A7 / / D♭7	D7 / / A♭7	G7 / / B7
C7 / / B♭13	A7 / / D♭7	D9 / / A♭13	G7 / / D♭7

DEVELOPING VOICINGS

USING INVERSIONS AND OTHER CHORD VOICINGS

Chord movements
In order to understand many of the more complex chord types, it is helpful to work within a single key. One approach is to take each of the seven major-scale triads and play through the chord changes using inversions. The next step is to add a seventh to every triad and experiment with the possible voicings. Using a full inverted seventh system, major and minor sixths can be seen as first inversions of minor sevenths and minor sevenths with a flat fifth.

The majority of chords are built by using combinations of thirds. For creating harmony, an approach in which triads are combined with added thirds, suspended fourths, and sixths covers a large part of the most commonly encountered guitar music. Chords may also be voiced with fourths and fifths. These types of harmony are very effective and are commonly found as two- and three-note structures in all types of music, and as extended forms in pop, jazz, and classical music. In addition, there are ways of forming chords and harmony that make use of other interval structures. For instance, when chords are made up from scale notes, each note can be placed in close proximity to the others to form intervals of seconds. Chords with voicings that include seconds, based on modes and scales, are used in folk and jazz.

Chordal transposition
Many of the effective chord voicings in one key cannot be transposed fully to another key. The guitar has a limited octave range, and the open strings are normally tuned to a standard pattern. For example, a piece of music in A major may use close harmony and open-string notes, with the low E string as a pedal note. If the music is transposed to another key, the same types of voicings using open strings may no longer be available.

TRIAD INVERSIONS

Play the seven C triads in root voicings. Take each of the chords and move the root to the top. This leaves the third in the bass, which is the lowest note: this is referred to as a first inversion. Take the third and put it at the top of the chord, leaving the fifth in the bass: this is known as a second inversion. Other positions can be used to place the remaining chord notes above the bass note.

INVERSIONS WITH SEVENTHS

It is possible, in theory, to play all of the seventh chords as inversions. By doing this the player can create a wide range of harmonic effects, which can be used to alter the function of the chords. There are practical limitations, though; the tuning of the guitar simply does not allow some inversions of sevenths to be played easily. Seventh chords have a third inversion where the seventh is placed in the bass. Play the series of seventh chords in C major in root voicings. Try playing all of the chords, first with the third in the bass as a first inversion, then with the fifth used in the bass as a second inversion, and finally with the seventh in the bass as the third inversion. A large number of these chords are highly effective when used in chord sequences, particularly in some areas of modern jazz.

INVERSIONS IN A SEQUENCE

Each of the eight-bar chord sequences shown on the right should be played through as a repeating structure. Try transferring elements from one sequence to another. In the first eight bars, chords are used in root voicings. The second and third sequences have first, second, and third inversions replacing root inversions. All of these generate striking harmonic contrasts in comparison to root voicings. Inversions can be used in conjunction with root voicings to allow more than one version of a chord to be played in a bar.

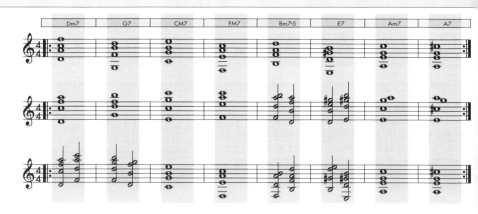

TRIAD RELATIONSHIPS

Take the triads of the C major scale and play them in relation to all the other triads. A given triad can move to six other triads in the scale. In the exercise on the right, the triads on every scale degree have been placed in seven columns. Try all the movements by taking the C major triad and moving it to all the others based on the major scale. This gives C major to D minor, C major to E minor, C major to F major, C major to G major, C major to A minor, and C major to B diminished. Repeat the exercise for the chords on each degree. The lines of chords on the staff across the scale show the chords moving by intervals. On the first line the chords move in scalar steps: C to D minor, D minor to E minor, E minor to F major, F major to G major, G major to A minor, A minor to B diminished, and B diminished to C major. On the second line the scale chords move in thirds. The third line covers fourths, and the fourth line covers fifths. Each movement can be inverted. A move from a triad to a chord a third above is harmonically similar to a move to a sixth below. On the fifth line, the movement to a chord a sixth above has been positioned a third below. The sixth line covers the move in sevenths, which is similar to a second below. Play all the chord movements with full voicings.

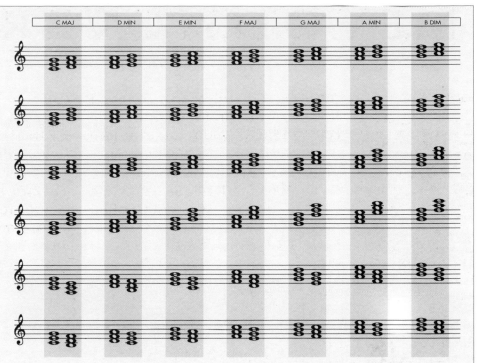

| C MAJ | D MIN | E MIN | F MAJ | G MAJ | A MIN | B DIM |

CHORDS IN FOURTHS AND FIFTHS

Chords can be constructed with superimposed fourths and fifths built from the root. In the first series of chords on the right, four-note fourth voicings move from C to B. The second series shows fourth chords with an extra note, a fourth above the top voice. The third set of chords has the root, an interval of a fifth, and two fourths. Try combining fourths and fifths to build other chord voicings.

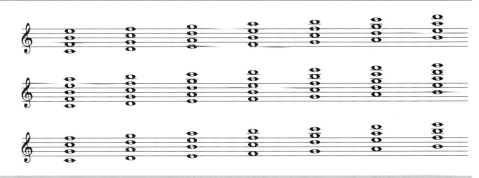

CLOSE VOICINGS AND CLUSTERS

When chords are voiced with constituent notes in relationships using seconds, this produces *close voicings*. The first of the C major chords on the first staff is a C6/9 with an interval of a second between the ninth (D) and the third (E), forming a close voicing. The remaining chords work in a similar way. In the examples on the second staff, combinations of close voicings form *clusters*. The chords are shown as diatonic clusters, which create a particularly unusual harmonic effect.

CLOSE VOICING

CLUSTERS

CHORD SYNONYMS

Certain chord voicings can be labeled in various ways. Common overlaps include voicings and chords over different roots, inversions, or one triad positioned over another.

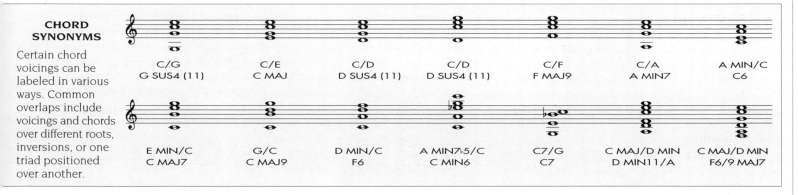

| C/G | C/E | C/D | C/D | C/F | C/A | A MIN/C |
| G SUS4 (11) | C MAJ | D SUS4 (11) | D SUS4 (11) | F MAJ9 | A MIN7 | C6 |

| E MIN/C | G/C | D MIN/C | A MIN7♭5/C | C7/G | C MAJ/D MIN | C MAJ/D MIN |
| C MAJ7 | C MAJ9 | F6 | C MIN6 | C7 | D MIN11/A | F6/9 MAJ7 |

MELODY OVER CHORDS

SCALES AND MELODY USING MODAL CHORDS

Voicings
When all the notes on the scale are played with chord voicings over every root note, inversions are are produced in some instances. Discordant harmonies occur when the top note clashes with the root or with another part of the chord structure. In the chart below, the major scale as a movement over modal chords is not a chord sequence.

Chords as blocks of vertical harmony can be used to play scales and melodies. Using this approach, an effective starting point is to experiment with a full system of harmonized notes in one key. Every major scale note can be placed over chords on each of the scale degrees, either by playing a scale note against each of the seven bass notes, or by playing all seven scale notes against one bass note. Several combinations, however, will give unusual chord voicings. Notes that are not part of the normal harmonic extensions must be voiced carefully so that chords do not sound weak or dissonant.

Two-note chords
Forming two-note chords by supporting a scale with an added interval is a simple way to harmonize notes. In the chart below, the C major scale is played with intervals **above** the scale notes. In addition, scale notes can be harmonized by playing them in pairs with intervals **below**. This technique is used to support melody and build chords with other voicings.

C MAJOR WITH MODAL CHORDS

C to C over C Ionian/major chords
The major scale ascends from C to an octave C, using different chord types in C major with a C root.

C to C over D Dorian chords
The major scale ascends from C to an octave C, using different chord types in C major with a D root.

C to C over E Phrygian chords
The major scale ascends from C to an octave C, using different chord types in C major with an E root.

C to C over F Lydian chords
The major scale ascends from C to an octave C, using different chord types in C major with an F root.

C to C over G Mixolydian chords
The major scale ascends from C to an octave C, using different chord types in C major with a G root.

C to C over A Aeolian chords
The major scale ascends from C to an octave C, using different chord types in C major with an A root.

C to C over B Locrian chords
The major scale ascends from C to an octave C, using different chord types in C major with a B root.

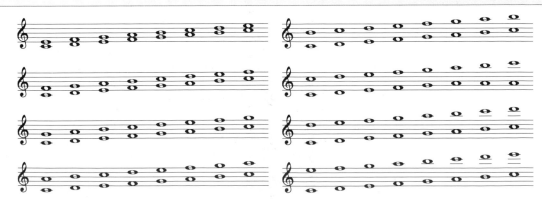

Thirds
Play E to E as thirds above the C major scale.

Fourths
Play F to F as fourths above the C major scale.

Fifths
Play G to G as fifths above the C major scale.

Sixths
Play A to A as sixths above the C major scale.

Sevenths
Play B to B as sevenths above the C major scale.

Octaves
Play C to C as octaves on the C major scale.

Ninths
Play D to D as ninths above the C major scale.

Tenths
Play E to E as tenths above the C major scale.

MELODY USING INTERVALS

The examples shown below are written in the key of C major over a **II-V-I** movement based on D minor, G major, and C major chords. A melody played over chords often uses parts of the voicings. Melody over the chords is also played with scale notes. A combination of these two approaches is one of the simplest ways to play a single-note line over harmony. A scale or melody can also be supported with a series of lower intervals over chordal harmony. The single-note passages can be harmonized with intervals under each of the notes over block chords. Play the third example, which uses thirds: each note of the melody with the **II-V-I** chords is harmonized with thirds, and the entire passage can be played over the chord changes. The note B has been left as a single note. The fourth example uses fourths and takes the same approach. The top two notes in each of the chords are fourths, and the single-note melody between the chords also uses fourths. In the fifth example, each note at the top of the **II-V** chords is shown supported by fifths. In the final example, each of the melody notes is shown with sixths over the top of the **II** and **V** chords and supported by chord root notes.

1. CHORDS WITH MELODY

3. CHORDS WITH MELODY SUPPORTED BY THIRDS

5. CHORDS WITH MELODY SUPPORTED BY FIFTHS

2. CHORDS WITH MELODY

4. CHORDS WITH MELODY SUPPORTED BY FOURTHS

6. CHORDS WITH MELODY SUPPORTED BY SIXTHS

PEDAL NOTE

A pedal note under a series of chords or single notes creates a sense of flowing continuity and sets up a reference point for melodic and harmonic movement. Tune the 6th string down to a low D, and play the melody with block chords. Pick out the top note of each chord, and play the single line over the pedal note.

UPPER NOTE

An upper note is often played through a series of chord changes. The effect of the top note changes as the harmony moves underneath. In the example below, G is the eleventh of the first chord, an upper octave root of the second, the fifth of the third, and the ninth of the last. Play the upper note with the bass movement D-G-C-F.

PEDAL NOTE UNDER II-V-I

When a pedal note is played under a series of chords, the direction of the harmony can be retained, but it changes its character. Play the **II-V-I** in C major with G under each chord. The G under the **II** changes it to an extended G dominant. The second chord is the G dominant with an altered voicing, and the last is the **I** with a fifth in the bass.

INTERNAL VOICES ON A MINOR

Chords often have movement on the middle voices while the top and bass notes are held in position. A scale or melody can be played on these internal voices. In the example below, A is held in the bass and C and E on the top two strings. B-A-G-F#-F-E are played as a descending scale.

C MAJOR ON THE 4TH STRING

Play C major 7, using the 4th string to play a scale or melody. With the little finger, play D on the 12th fret, then C-B-A-G. To stretch to D and C you may need a barre for the chord positions. The scale changes the chord from C major 9 to C major, C major 7, C 6, and a variation of C major.

C MAJOR ON THE 3RD STRING

Play C major 7, using the 3rd string to play a scale or melody. With the little finger play F# on the 11th fret, then F#-E-D-C. To reach F# you may need a barre for the outer chord notes. The scale changes the chord from C major 7 #11 to C major 7, C major 9, and C major 7 with an extra C.

BASS NOTE LINKS

Chords are often connected by playing changes while using a bass note to link movements. Below, descending diatonic notes are used with steps to fill the scale. Play the movement D minor 7-B minor 7♭5-E7#9-A minor 7. The bass note C links D minor 7 and B minor 7♭5, forming the line D-C-B. Play A minor 7, A minor 7 over G, F# minor 7♭5, F major 7, E7#5, and back to A minor 7. In the move from A minor 7 to F#, the A root drops a tone to G, and this leads on to F# minor 7♭5. The bass root moves down a semitone to form F major 7. The bass drops by a semitone, and two middle notes by a tone and a semitone, to form E7#5. A series of chord movements using a descending bass line links two voicings of C major 7 with a cycle using modal chords to approach the **II-V-I**. Play C major 7, C major 7 over B, A minor 7, A minor 7 over G, F major 7, F major 7 over E, D minor 7, G7, and C major 7. This is a **I-VI-IV-II-V-I** with scale links.

SEQUENCE VARIATIONS

USING VOICINGS, SUBSTITUTIONS, AND INVERSIONS

Application
To control chord movements and compose or improvise creatively, it is important to be able to reduce a chord sequence to its basic movements. The sequences shown below move around a major and minor II-V-I. These mechanisms and voicings can be used in a standard jazz sequence. It is useful to write out the chords and locate all the V-I resolutions.

The potential of different chord voicings and movements can be explored by first becoming familiar with a framework of basic chords, and then using this structure as a guide in evaluating the sound and tonal quality of variations. If a chord sequence is played without regard to the melody, the movements of harmony and upper voices can be given free rein. When a piece is played solo, the player can vary the bass line and make substitutions, so moving the sequence away from the original tonal centers. The **V-I** movements below, with approach chords and variations, form useful models for experimentation.

Transposition
Take the chord sequence below in its most basic form as a major II-V-I to a minor II-V-I and transpose it to every key. One of the simplest ways to do this is to locate the major I chord and treat this as a pivotal tonal center for the whole sequence. The minor II-V-I chords can be found on the VII, III, and VI degrees of the major scale.

The major II-V
In this movement, the **II-V** approach to the major chord should be played using triads through to thirteenths with standard and close voicings.

Major II-V variation
The **II** chord may be played as an inversion, and the **V** chord as a flatted fifth.

The major I chord
Major **I** chords may be varied over one or two bars by revoicing them. One of the most common methods is to move a major seventh to a major sixth.

Major I variation
A **IV** chord may follow a **I** chord. These chords may be connected with scale steps.

The minor II V
The minor **II-V** approach to the minor **I** chord should be voiced from triads through to extended chords. The **II** chord may be replaced by a diminished seventh.

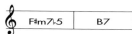

Minor II-V variation
In this movement four diminished chords and a flatted five are used.

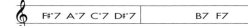

The minor I chord
Minor **I** chords may be varied by moving minor sevenths to minor sixth chords. The minor seventh is converted at the end of the sequence below to a dominant seventh.

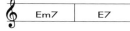

Minor I variation
This moves in steps from the minor **I** to a diminished substitution for **V**.

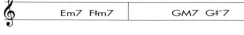

Sequence 1
This is a major II-V-I to a relative minor II-V-I. The minor **I** is converted to a **V7#5** chord, leading back to the beginning.

| Am7 | D9 | GM7 | G6 | F#m7b5 | B7b9 | Em7 | E7#5 |

Sequence 2
Here the major II-V-I supports a high B as the top note. The minor **II-V-I** has higher voicings, with a **V7#5#9** at the end.

| Am9 | D13 | GM7 | G6 | F#m7b5 | B7#5#9 | Em7 | E7#5#9 |

Sequence 3
The major **II-V-I** and the minor **II-V-I** are played with close voicings and open strings, with a **V7#5b9** at the end.

| Am9 | D9 | G6/9M7 | G6/9 | F#m11 | B13 | Em9 | E7#5b9 |

Sequence 4
This is a major **IIbV-I** to a minor **IIbV-I**, with a **V7#5** at the end. The bass line descends in semitones through both progressions.

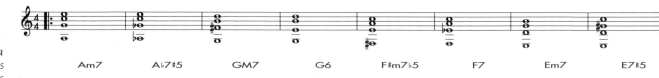

| Am7 | Ab7#5 | GM7 | G6 | F#m7b5 | F7 | Em7 | E7#5 |

Sequence 5

Here the major **II**-♭**V-I** has close voicings. The minor **II**-♭**V-I** has a **V9♭5** chord. The minor **I** chord uses a close voicing and moves to a **V13♭9** at the end.

Am9   A♭9   GM9   G6/9   F♯m11   F9♭5   Em9   E13♭9

Sequence 6

This major **II**-♭**V-I** uses close voicings and moves to a **IV** chord in the fourth bar. After the minor **II-V-I**, the minor **I** moves to a ♭**V13** as a substitution.

Am9   A♭13   G6/9M7   C6/7   F♯m7♭5   B7♯5♭9   Em11   B♭13

Sequence 7

The major **II** and **V** chords use two voicings before moving to **I** and **IV**. The minor **II** ascends with inversions to the **V**, which uses two voicings.

Am7 Am11 D13 D7♭9♯5   G6/9M7   C6/9♯11   F♯m7♭5 Am6   B7♯5 B9   Em11   E13♭9

Sequence 8

II moves to E♭ over D, which then resolves to **I**. The **IV** chord moves to an inversion of the minor **II**. The **V** leads to a series over a pedal note.

Am11   E♭/D   G6/7   C6/9M7   F♯m7♭5/C   B13   Em11 F♯m11/E GM9/E G♯°7/E

Sequence 9

Major **II**-♭**V-I** and minor **II**-♭**V** move to the minor **I** that ascends in steps up to a G♯ diminished seventh voicing, which leads back to the beginning.

Am11   A♭7♭5   GM7   G6   F♯m11   F13   Em7 F♯m7   GM7 G♯°7

Sequence 10

This major **II-V** uses inversions, and the **I** chord moves to **IV** in a step pattern. The minor **II-V** moves to a series of chords over a pedal note.

Am7 C6   F♯m7♭5/C D9   GM9 Am7   Bm7 CM9   F♯m11♭5   B7♯5♯9   Em7 A/E   Bm/E A/E

Sequence 11

A **II** chord here moves to a ♭**V** preceded by its own **II** chord, before resolving to **I** as an inversion. The ♭**V** and the related **II** are used for succeeding resolutions.

Am11   E♭m11 A♭13   Em9   Em7   Cm11   F13   Em7   Fm9 B♭13

Sequence 12

Here a **V** moves to a series of **I** inversions by means of a diminished link chord. The minor **II-V** movement is played as a series of diminished chords.

Am7   D9 E♭°7   GM7/B GM7   GM9 G6/9   F♯°7 A°7   C°7 D♯°7   Em7   Fm7 B♭7

Sequence 13

The major **II-V-I** moves to a minor **II** chord inversion. The **V7♯5** moves to A♭ over B. The **I** is converted to an augmented chord, moving in whole-tone steps.

Am9   D13♭9   G6/7   C6/9M7   F♯m7♭5/C   B7♯5 A♭/B   Em11 E+   F♯+/E G♯+/E

SECOND ARRANGEMENT

This developed arrangement turns the piece into interesting music with a number of harmonic devices and approaches. It moves further away from conventional jazz, using a compositional approach. The function of the chords is not as support for the melody or even as a framework for linear improvisation. There are more adventurous close voicings and flat five (♭V) substitutions and inversions. Step movements, where a chord can move up a related scale or mode, and bass links create variety and interest. Many of the chords are worked out as individual voicings first. Theory, involving systems of organizing chords, compositional thinking, improvisation, inspiration, and even fortuitous accidents, have contributed to playing and writing down this sequence. It stands on its own without the melody.

First eight bars

F minor 7 is converted to a close-voiced F minor 6/9 with the use of an open G string. A13♭5 replaces E♭9. The series of chords from D♭ major 7#11 to C major 9 uses subtle common notes.

Second eight bars

C minor 7 has been converted to an inversion of C minor 11 with a G in the bass. This voicing has been moved as a parallel harmony to F minor 11/C. D9 has been converted to A♭7#9, which leads to E minor 9, a developed inversion of G major 7.

Middle eight bars

A minor 7 moves up to a first inversion C6, which pivots on the C to move to D7/C and then D7♭9. G major moves with a bass link through its related E minor chord to F# minor 7/C#. E major is turned into an ascending modal step movement.

Last 12 bars

A high F minor 9 moves down using a standard B♭ minor 7 to an E♭13♭9. Here, the voice movement resolves the E natural (♭9th) up into an F (6th) in A♭ major 6/7. Five-note chords run from D♭6/7/9 to A♭ major 7, which rests with a four-note voicing.

F MIN6/9   B♭MIN9   A13♭5   A♭6/7/9

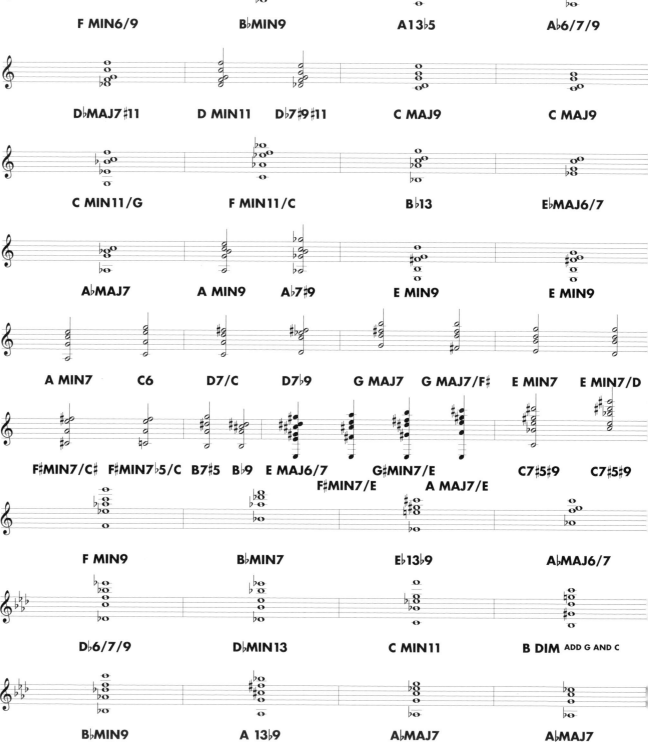

D♭MAJ7#11   D MIN11   D♭7#9#11   C MAJ9   C MAJ9

C MIN11/G   F MIN11/C   B♭13   E♭MAJ6/7

A♭MAJ7   A MIN9   A♭7#9   E MIN9   E MIN9

A MIN7   C6   D7/C   D7♭9   G MAJ7   G MAJ7/F#   E MIN7   E MIN7/D

F#MIN7/C#   F#MIN7♭5/C   B7#5   B♭9   E MAJ6/7   G#MIN7/E   C7#5#9   C7#5#9

F#MIN7/E   A MAJ7/E

F MIN9   B♭MIN7   E♭13♭9   A♭MAJ6/7

D♭6/7/9   D♭MIN13   C MIN11   B DIM ADD G AND C

B♭MIN9   A 13♭9   A♭MAJ7   A♭MAJ7

THIRD ARRANGEMENT

The final fully developed arrangement turns *All The Things You Are* into another harmonic composition, using approaches similar to the last version. This time there are more inversions, inner voice movements, and the use of a pedal tone

G under a long section. Even when fully developing a jazz standard, the harmonic foundation must be accurate. It is still important to think in simple terms about the basic tonal centers or keys and the direction of the harmony. Throughout this arrangement, melodic ideas have

shaped many chord voicings and movements. Play the arrangements in time, but work on developing them in free time, without a fixed beat, as well. Compare chords in all the arrangements with the basic "jazz voicings" under the melody on the first page.

First eight bars

F minor 7 is converted to a close-voiced F minor 9 inversion with the fifth, C in the bass. This moves as a parallel voicing to Bb minor 9/F. Ab major 7 and Db major 7 become inversions with the fifth in the bass. The Ab is used to move into the Db minor 7b5/Ab.

Second eight bars

C minor 7 has been converted to a C minor 9 with the fifth, G in the bass. The G is retained in the bass as a pedal tone for the next chords all the way through until the tension is released on a simple G major 7.

Middle eight bars

The G pedal tone is retained for the A minor and D 11 chords, moving to G major 7. G continues under the F# diminished and F13 chord. The tension is released on the E major, which is played as a low close voicing. A G minor 13 chord and Gb9b5 (bV) lead back to F minor 7.

Last 12 bars

F minor/major 9 moves to F minor 9 with inner voice movement. Bb minor 9 to Bb minor 6/9 and Eb9 to Eb7b9 also use inner voice movement. Db minor 6/9 uses fretted and open B notes. B diminished add G uses two fretted D notes. Bb minor 6/7 uses an open G before going to the Eb13b9 and resolving to Ab major 9.

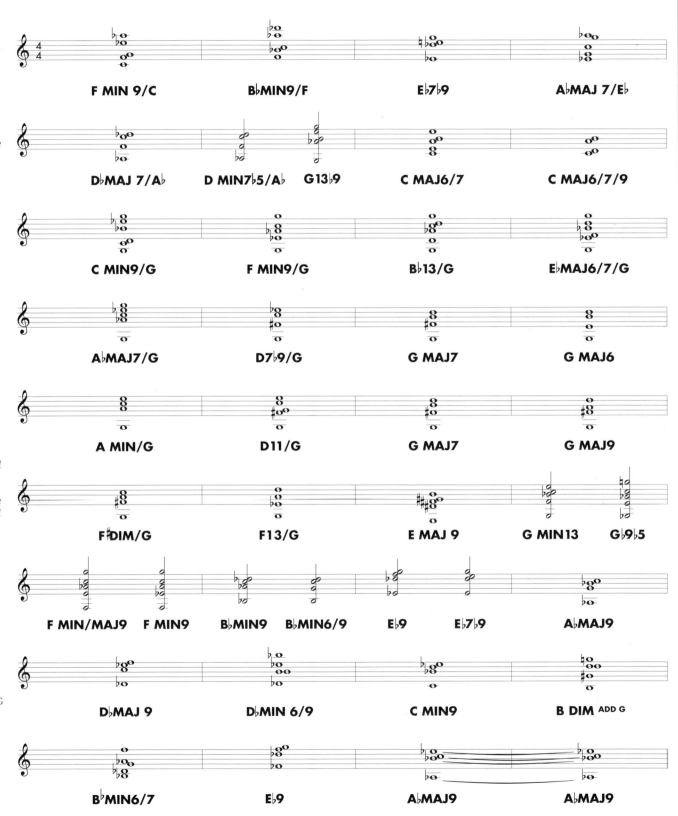

First eight bars:
F MIN 9/C   BbMIN9/F   Eb7b9   AbMAJ 7/Eb
DbMAJ 7/Ab   D MIN7b5/Ab   G13b9   C MAJ6/7   C MAJ6/7/9

Second eight bars:
C MIN9/G   F MIN9/G   Bb13/G   EbMAJ6/7/G
AbMAJ7/G   D7b9/G   G MAJ7   G MAJ6

Middle eight bars:
A MIN/G   D11/G   G MAJ7   G MAJ9
F#DIM/G   F13/G   E MAJ 9   G MIN13   Gb9b5

Last 12 bars:
F MIN/MAJ9   F MIN9   BbMIN9   BbMIN6/9   Eb9   Eb7b9   AbMAJ9
DbMAJ 9   DbMIN 6/9   C MIN9   B DIM ADD G
BbMIN6/7   Eb9   AbMAJ9   AbMAJ9

SOUND AND AMPLIFICATION

For the modern guitarist, amplification, sound processing, and recording are important complementary skills. In fact, to many rock musicians they are as central to their art as playing the guitar itself. With the myriad of valve and solid-state amplification, low-cost digital multiple-effects units, and reasonably priced home-recording equipment, the areas covered in this section of the book are now more accessible than ever before.

GUITAR AMPLIFICATION

AN INTRODUCTION TO AMPLIFYING THE ELECTRIC GUITAR

Choosing a guitar
Because guitars differ in their sonic characteristics, it is important to select a model that suits your musical purposes. If you are interested in only one type of sound, such as chunky rock textures, the task is relatively easy. Many players, though, want versatility. This can be achieved with certain guitars – the super-Strat, the coil-tapped Les Paul, the varitone-equipped Gibson semi, or the PRS. The other solution is to opt for two or more distinct instruments and to use each where appropriate.

The first electric guitars were produced with a single pickup. Height-adjustable polepieces were introduced in the 1940s, enabling players to balance the response for each string. Guitars with two or more pickups also began to appear around this time: the ability to switch between pickups, use combinations to produce different textures, and adjust the volume and tone controls for both lead and rhythm settings increased the versatility of the guitar. During the 1950s, the commercial success of solid-body guitars took place at the same time as the development of improved amplifiers, leading to new types of sound. The spectrum of color produced by the electric guitar was fully utilized with the advent of guitar-based groups playing electric blues and rock music.

Creating a sound
Although there are hundreds of different amplifiers and effects on the market, certain approaches to enhancing guitar signals are used repeatedly. Distortion gives guitar a raunchy or sustaining edge. Reverb adds a subtle sense of space. Echo gives fast, rhythmic repeats or layered effects. Chorus, phasing, and flanging also provide interesting textures. A good amplifier will have powerful tone-shaping capabilities, either via its tone controls or thanks to electronics and speakers with a distinctive "voice."

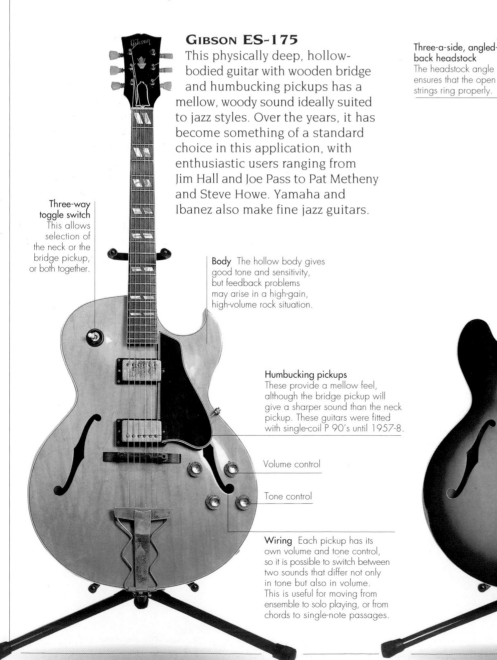

GIBSON ES-175

This physically deep, hollow-bodied guitar with wooden bridge and humbucking pickups has a mellow, woody sound ideally suited to jazz styles. Over the years, it has become something of a standard choice in this application, with enthusiastic users ranging from Jim Hall and Joe Pass to Pat Metheny and Steve Howe. Yamaha and Ibanez also make fine jazz guitars.

Three-way toggle switch
This allows selection of the neck or the bridge pickup, or both together.

Body The hollow body gives good tone and sensitivity, but feedback problems may arise in a high-gain, high-volume rock situation.

Humbucking pickups
These provide a mellow feel, although the bridge pickup will give a sharper sound than the neck pickup. These guitars were fitted with single-coil P 90's until 1957-8.

Volume control

Tone control

Wiring Each pickup has its own volume and tone control, so it is possible to switch between two sounds that differ not only in tone but also in volume. This is useful for moving from ensemble to solo playing, or from chords to single-note passages.

GIBSON ES-335

This famous "semi-solid" combines hollow-body and solid-body attributes. Acoustic cavities and "f"-holes give the sound a woody character, while the solid-center block provides much-enhanced sustain. Famous 335 users include Alvin Lee, Chuck Berry, Larry Carlton, and B.B. King; this very versatile guitar is also popular with pop and funk players.

Three-a-side, angled-back headstock
The headstock angle ensures that the open strings ring properly.

Body The body depth, at around 2 in (5 cm), is modest compared with that of the 175. However, the center block and the overall size make this a relatively heavy instrument.

Pickups High-output, twin-coil humbuckers give a raunchy rock/blues sound with good touch-sensitivity.

Tune-O-Matic Bridge

Stud tailpiece

Wiring The 335 has the standard Gibson layout of two volumes and two tone controls with three-way pickup selector, although some luxury versions (such as the 355 and Lucille) feature stereo wiring and the Varitone six-position tone selector.

A BRIEF HISTORY OF GUITAR AMPLIFIERS

Guitar amplification originally developed in the 1930s and was based on radio and hi-fi technology of the day. However, the first major advances were made in the 1950s and 1960s, with the advent of rock'n'roll in the US, and then the "beat boom" in the UK. Many Fender and Vox models from this era are now valuable vintage items, prized for their tone and quality of distortion, although any raunchy overdrive or biting "edge" was quite unintentional from a design point of view. With the UK heavy rock scene in the later 1960s came the development of the Marshall stack – a powerful amplifier with either one or two 4x12 inch speaker cabinets – where distortion at high volume was purely intentional. The 1970s saw a craze for "hot-rodding," especially in the US, with amp-

techs squeezing more gain and greater distortion from classic Fender and Marshall designs. Randy Smith built "cascaded" gain-stages into his high-power 1x12 in Mesa/Boogie combo; the distorted output from one preamp stage was fed into the next, and so on, to give a very high-sustaining, high-gain distortion. By the end of the decade, all the major manufacturers offered "master volume" models that enabled distorted sounds to be obtained at any volume. Then came channel-switching, with three-channel designs such as the Boogie Mk III or Marshall Anniversary, allowing players to select clean, "crunch," or lead sounds via a footswitch. However big the venue or varied the set, it is now possible to take a small, versatile combo on stage, mike it up, and let the PA provide the "bulk" sound out front, with wedge monitors

filling in the onstage sound. The latest developments include programmable preamps, digital effects, and MIDI control. Running parallel to this high-tech "rack" approach is a renewed interest in the simple, high-quality combos and heads of the past, used with warm-sounding (if technically flawed) analog effects such as tape echo. Similarly, solid-state technology – bi-polar transistors, FETs, ICs, MOSFETs, and so on – was meant to make "old-fashioned" tubes redundant but has not succeeded, even after three decades of innovation. All-solid-state combos such as the Peavey Bandit are light and versatile. Hybrid designs are also enjoying a wave of popularity. However, the top end of the market is still dominated by all-tube designs, including vintage reissues.

GIBSON LES PAUL

This small but heavy, high-quality solid-body guitar is associated with rock playing and tremendous sustain. Though in 1952 Les Paul and Gibson were thinking of a clean, jazz sound rather than the fat, raunchy overload with which Eric Clapton, Jimmy Page, Keith Richards, and Mike Bloomfield made the model popular in the 1960s and 1970s. The first instruments had P90 single-coil pickups, but it is the Sunburst model with PAF humbuckers from 1958–1960 that is the most coveted – and widely copied – variant.

Six-in-line headstock As this is not angled back, a string-tree is used so that open treble strings ring properly.

FENDER STRATOCASTER

The Strat is probably the most familiar of all electric guitars, having been made popular by players from Buddy Holly and Hank Marvin to Jimi Hendrix and Eric Clapton. This solid-body instrument with three single-coil pickups gives a bright and clear sound with plenty of cut and "twang," while the controls are designed to offer plenty of subtle tonal variation. The combined tremolo unit/bridge is standard. It has a bolt-on neck that contributes to the characteristic resonance and tone.

Three-way toggle switch

Pickups These are high-output Patent-Applied-For pickups (PAFs) will easily overload the input stages of a good amp. The dual-coil construction also keeps hum and buzz at bay.

Wiring This model has the standard two volumes and two tones. The neck pickup gives a rich sound, while the bridge pickup provides a fat sound with a biting edge. Selecting both with varied settings produces different types of sounds. Some players wire the pickups out of phase for a nasal midtone, associated with players such as Peter Green.

Volume control

Tone control

Body The Strat is comfort-contoured and lightweight, with an ash or alder body.

Single-coil pickups The low output level makes the Strat sound cleaner than a humbucker-equipped guitar at a given amp setting.

Middle pickup

Tremolo arm

Wiring The standard instrument has a master volume and two tone controls. Many variations are possible with the use of the pickup selector.

FROM JAZZ TO ROCK

CHOOSING A CLEAN OR DISTORTED SOUND

Distortion
If a very high-level signal is fed into an amplifier, for instance when playing a humbucker-equipped guitar, the early preamplifier stages distort to give the sound a fuzzy, sustaining edge. Using the amplifier on full volume pushes the power stage to the limit, producing a different kind of distortion and, in classic valve designs, a loose, warm sound. Overworked speaker cones also contribute to this effect.

Different styles of playing often make widely varying demands on amplifiers, particularly in terms of the distortion and volume level required. The Marshall stack, wah-wah pedal, fuzz box, and tremolo-equipped Fender Stratocaster used by Jimi Hendrix and shown on the facing page are geared to produce extremely high levels of distortion and volume. This equipment would be unfamiliar territory, and perhaps an inappropriate set-up, for most jazz guitarists. These musicians would probably prefer the wide-band, distortion-free amplification given by the set-up shown below, which provides mellow acoustic tones and is also ideal for use in small, intimate settings.

Inside an amplifier
The principal sections inside an amplifier are the preamp, power amp (output stage), and power supply. The pre-amp includes the input, tone circuitry, gain and volume controls, and effects loop. The signal then passes to the output stage, which provides the "magnification" needed to drive one or more speakers. The power supply converts AC power to DC, which is required to run the amplifier.

Gibson ES-175
The volume and tone controls can only subtract from the signals that come from the pickups; they cannot boost the volume, treble, or bass at all. The two tone controls (one for each pickup) work identically, either "rolling off" the treble or passing signals to the amp unhindered. The maple-and-plywood laminated body has tonal clarity and excellent acoustic resonance. This type of guitar is frequently used with the treble rolled off to give a warm, "jazzy" sound. It is one of the few archtop jazz guitars to be used in rock music, in spite of feedback problems.

Selector switch This has a rubber mount to prevent an amplified switching noise being heard from the soundboard when the guitar is used at high volume.

Pickups The ES-175 is fitted with two Gibson humbucking pickups.

Bridge Standard models are fitted with a metal "Tune-o-matic" bridge. This model has been fitted with a wooden bridge.

ARCHTOP AMPLIFICATION
Jazz guitarists often seek harmonic, melodic, and rhythmic inventiveness rather than layered soundscapes or touch-sensitive distortion textures. This combination of a Gibson ES-175 guitar and Polytone amplifier is suited to jazz musicians and has been used by Joe Pass and many other players. The single-channel combo has simple tone controls, with no overdrive or built-in effects. It does, however, feature solid-state amplification, driving a high-quality Eminence 12-inch speaker. The good bass extension and definition are ideal for the 175, with its humbucking pickups.

Polytone Mini-Brute I
The 90-watt model shown on the right dates from 1978. It features both high- and low-sensitivity input sockets, plus treble and bass controls. A sliding tone filter switch is used for "bright," "middle," and "dark" tone selection. The Mini-Brute I has a single volume control: it is not possible to balance gain, channel volume, and master volume as you can with a modern channel-switching amplifier. A kick-proof grille protects the speaker cone.

Sliding tone switch

High- and low-sensitivity inputs

POLYTONE AMPLIFIERS
Polytone amplifiers were developed in the United States in the mid-1970s. During the design stage, several leading jazz guitarists were brought in as consultants. The small portable combo that was created had a clear, balanced solid-state sound; this proved ideal for the amplification of archtop guitars, which are frequently used by jazz players. The particular strengths of these amplifiers have also resulted in their use with the double bass and other acoustic instruments.

GUITAR EFFECTS
Foot-controlled effect units provide the player with sounds outside of the range of a normal guitar and amplifier combination. They put control of tone and distortion at the guitarist's feet so that the sound can be adjusted while both hands are kept on the guitar. Early units included fuzz boxes, which produce instant distortion; treble boosters; volume and tone pedals, first designed for setting the volume or tone while playing but later used for "swell" and "wah-wah" effects; and tape echo, creating single repeats or layered echo. Many floor units are battery-powered but can also accept DC from an adapter; some are also AC-powered. Units such as digital multi-FX may be mounted in a rack with a footswitch, or a MIDI controller may be used as an optional extra. Floor pedals are usually designed to receive guitar-level signals, whereas some rack units need line-level signals from, for example, a combo's FX loop or a stand-alone preamp.

THE MARSHALL STACK

The most effective way to use this Hendrix-style rig is to set all the controls to "10"; the guitarist can then control the distortion, tone, and loudness accurately by using the guitar's volume control and the effects pedals. Turning down the guitar reduces the level of the input signal, resulting in clean sounds. The wah-wah pedal may be used to boost the treble or bass, while the fuzz box provides extra raunch and (by overloading the Marshall's input) helps create smooth lead lines with extra-long sustain. Using the rig at full stretch gives grinding power-amp distortion and howling feedback; in experienced hands, though, the latter may be controlled to harmonize with the music.

Feedback and tremolo

The position of the guitar in relation to the speakers produces different levels of feedback. Tremolo control is also important. Jimi Hendrix was a master in this area, with an impressive repertoire of techniques. Modern tremolo systems such as the Kahler and the Floyd Rose are more acutely responsive than the older Fender unit, suiting fingerboard-tapping, rapid arpeggiating, and sweep-picking techniques.

Rosewood fingerboard

Pickguard This model features a discolored early plastic pickguard.

Connections The guitar lead runs first into the wah-wah pedal, then into the Fuzz Face, which can be adjusted with the rotary controls. The output is finally plugged into the Marshall head.

Standby switch

Marshall head The output is nominally 100 watts, but with modification the head is capable of 150 watts. There is no reverb, channel switching, or master volume control.

Cabinet The top cabinet has a sloping front

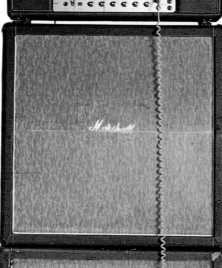

Arbiter Fuzz Face

Vox wah-wah pedal

Hendrix Stratocaster

This is the guitar used by Jimi Hendrix at the Woodstock festival. A stock 1968 model, this has neither special pickups nor customized wiring, but notice that it is reverse-strung, with the low E nearest to the volume control. This is because Hendrix played left-handed but (with Strats, at least) simply used right-handed guitars turned upside-down. Maple-fingerboard Strats like this one have a brighter sound than those for which rosewood is used, but the difference is subtle and Hendrix used both types widely. Some of his instruments were also re-wired and modified extensively.

Maple fingerboard

Strap button Hendrix moved the strap button to the body's lower horn for left-handed playing.

Laminated pickguard

Tremolo unit The arm has been removed from the tremolo unit.

HENDRIX AND EFFECTS

Jimi Hendrix enhanced his music with several different effects. At first he used a fuzz unit, then, when he moved to England, he switched to the Arbiter Fuzz Face, with a Vox wah-wah pedal. In the late 1960s, Hendrix was joined by the engineer and inventor Roger Mayer, who built the Octavia. This unit is a frequency doubler which adds upper frequencies to the guitar signal. The Uni-Vibe is a filtering device that simulates a Leslie rotating speaker. It produces chorus and vibrato effects. One of the combinations used was the wah-wah with a fuzz unit, rewired by Roger Mayer and fed through an Octavia to the Uni-Vibe.

Octavia The design ensures that the unit cannot be accidentally overturned on stage.

Uni-Vibe This unit has a separate floor switch to control the speed.

SPRING REVERB

THE IMPORTANCE OF REVERB TO THE GUITARIST

Small amplifiers
It is tempting to think that a large and heavy combo, or a powerful amp-top plus 4x12, must be better than a small, old-fashioned combo with a modest power rating. Many older models, though, are prized for their distinctive tone, classic good looks, fine buildup quality, and the fact that they can be wound up loud for natural tube distortion and compression at clubs or small gigs.

If electric guitars are played in a large acoustic space such as a hall or room, then the natural reverberation produced will add a satisfying "bloom" to the sound, smoothing out chord-work and helping individual lead-notes to die away gradually. This effect may be simulated within an amplifier by sending the guitar signal down long springs in the reverb section. "Spring reverb," as it was known, became a popular feature in the early 1960s. Fender, for instance, provided it first as a stand-alone unit (shown below), and then as a built-in effect in many of their medium-sized and larger combos.

Speaker size
Although the 12-in speaker is now the standard choice for use with electric guitars, many famous combos have used other sizes. In general, bigger cones handle the bass-end easily, but are not so good at conveying detail and dynamic shading; thus the 4x10-in format may give a punchier sound than 4x12 in, and a 15-in speaker will set off the warmth and depth of a good six-string guitar.

Fender Telecaster
The Fender Telecaster is very much a "guitarists' guitar," chosen for the quality of its sound, a solid "feel," and overall simplicity. It is capable of producing a crisp, clean sound, or a raunchy, thick-textured effect. Many of the finest players have favored this solid-body instrument.

FENDER VIBROLUX
This 2x12 all-tube combo with brown Tolex covering dates from the early 1960s and has two channels – Normal and Bright – though players cannot change channels by footswitching as on a modern amplifier. The "Vibro" prefix indicates that it has built-in vibrato (hence the *speed* and *intensity* controls), but note that this is a rhythmic variation in volume rather than pitch and gives a tremolo effect.

FENDER REVERB UNIT
In 1961, Fender offered spring reverb as a stand-alone unit with its own power-supply, before including the effect in many of its amplifiers the following year. The reverb unit was operated by plugging the guitar into the unit's single input and running a lead from the unit's output to the input on an ordinary amplifier. Signals arrived at the amplifier with reverb superimposed on them, and players were able to alter the proportion of affected to original signal, the depth of the effect, and its tone. The tone-shaping facility, and the sound from the all-tube circuitry, make this unit popular with many players.

Covering White or brown Tolex was used to cover Fender amplifiers in the early 1960s.

Circuitry The Fender reverb featured tube circuitry with its own power supply.

Screening-cans

Swell control This feeds reverb by varying the amount of "swell."

Mix This control mixes the dry and reverb signals.

Output

Tone control

REVERB TRAY
At the heart of this unit is the reverb tray, or *pan*. This sturdy metal tray has a sprung subchassis that carries a delicate spring with a small transducer at each end. The electrical signal taken from the pre-amp is converted by the first transducer to a mechanical vibration, which is fed along the spring and changed back into an electrical signal at the other end. The *return* signal, with heavy reverb, is fed back to the pre-amp, where it is mixed with the *dry* signal sent by a direct route bypassing the reverb tray; *reverb level* alters the proportion. Usually, two or three springs run in parallel to cover bass, midrange, and treble frequencies.

TUBE SOUNDS

THE VINTAGE TUBE SOUND OF THE FENDER BASSMAN

Acombination of the clean, cutting edge and fine tone of the 4x10 Fender Bassman combo, produced in the late 1950s, make it both one of the most widely copied amplifiers of all time and a highly valued item of music memorabilia. The simple, all-tube circuit has no modern extras such as reverb or pull-boosts to dilute signal quality, while the *tube rectifiers* ensure that the amplifier gives rich-sounding compression and distortion when played at high volumes. Eddie Cochran, Buddy Guy, and Freddie King are among the many famous players who regularly used the Bassman.

Tube or solid-state?
Tubes and transistors both amplify guitar signals, but the two technologies produce very different sounds. Solid-state models tend to be small and cheap to produce. They offer wide-band sound at low frequencies but may lack harmonic richness. Tube amps give interesting tones and tasteful overload but are less effective for producing a high-gain sound.

Hybrid amplifiers
There are two types of hybrid amplifier. The first has tubes in the pre-amp, and a solid-state power-stage. The second combines a solid-state front-end with a tube power-stage. Modern rectifiers are usually solid-state. The tube rectifiers on early amplifiers were inefficient but had a distinct "feel." Tubes are often included as an option on certain models.

Different materials
Fender Stratocasters with maple fingerboards have a slightly different sound and feel than those with rosewood fingerboards. The use of ash or maple for the body can also affect the resonance, tone, and bodyweight. In addition, alterations in construction over the years can lead to wide variations between models.

Materials and finish This 1965 model has a rosewood neck with a three-tone sunburst finish. Rosewood was introduced in 1959. Around the same time, three-tone finishes started to replace the two-tone variety.

Pickups Modern Stratocasters are fitted with new pickups, which alter the tone and output considerably.

Bridge cover Many players prefer to remove the "ash tray" bridge cover because it inhibits right-hand damping.

COMBINATIONS
Although the ubiquitous Stratocaster has partnered many amplifiers over the years, the original Fender company always presented certain combinations of guitar and amplifier as natural partners. Many famous recordings have been made with a combination of a 1950s Stratocaster with a Fender Bassman from the same period. This pairing was often used in conjunction with an Echoplex echo unit.

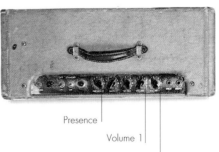

Presence

Volume 1

Volume 2

4X10 FENDER BASSMAN

This example is from 1956 or 1957 and has a standard Fender tweed finish. During this period, the models were fitted with bass and treble controls, but without "middle." They also had two tube rectifiers rather than one. The *presence* control, which was a major contributor to the amplifier's cutting tone, was part of the unit's power-amp circuitry: on many modern amplifiers presence is simply another pre-amp tone control. As a result of their enduring popularity, both the tweed Bassman and the brown Tolex Vibroverb, which was essentially the Vibrolux with built-in reverb, have been reissued by Fender.

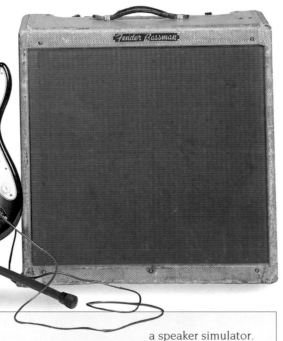

GETTING THE MOST FROM A VINTAGE AMPLIFIER

Vintage amplifiers can sometimes seem unyielding. They often have to be played at full volume to produce the right distortion and compression, while the dry sound and lack of reverb may be unattractive in a confined space. One solution involves using a speaker simulator. These soak up the excess power of the amplifier, turn it into heat, and leave a signal that may be sent directly to a speaker, mixing desk, or tape machine. The major drawback is that old style power-tubes and output transformers are heavily stressed by regular use at full volume. Older speakers should last for a long time.

THE VOX AC30

A CLASSIC COMBO

Class "A"
The Vox AC30 differs from other guitar amplifiers in that it runs its power valves in the old-fashioned and inefficient Class "A" – a mode of operation that yields only 30 watts from the four EL84 valves. However, it produces sonic rewards, with satisfying sustain, dynamic "punch" even in overload, and overtones that enhance the sound of the guitar.

Early recordings by the Beatles, the Rolling Stones, and the Shadows, and most of Queen and Rory Gallagher's music are all enhanced by the sound of the Vox AC30 amplifier. Since its design in 1960, the AC30 has suited a wide range of musical styles, supplying a clean, punchy sound with harmonic richness even at relatively low volumes. As the decade passed by, these attractive qualities were complemented by increasing amounts of raunchy overdrive as the volume was wound up, especially on *Top Boost* models. The original combo was reissued in the early 1990s.

Controls
Combos designed up to the early 1960s almost always had top-mounted, rear-facing control panels. The idea was that the combo would sit at the front of the stage – often doubling as a PA system – and controls could be adjusted from behind. When the "backline" idea came in, control panels were moved to the front of the combos, some angled back for better legibility.

The Fender Stratocaster
One of the great strengths of the tried-and-trusted Fender Stratocaster is that it can serve so many styles superbly. When combined with an AC30 and an early tape-echo unit such as a Watkins Copycat (below) or an Echoplex, it is possible to produce the sort of clean, rich, and powerful sound associated with music by many well-known musicians. By turning up the amplifier, hitting the strings harder, and adding a vintage fuzz box such as the Tone-bender, players can produce a fine blues/rock sound in the style of Jeff Beck or Rory Gallagher.

AC30 SPECIFICATIONS
The all-valve, 30-watt, 2x12 AC30 has three channels – "brilliant," "normal," and "vib-trem" – each with high and low inputs, so a whole band (three guitars, bass, and two microphones) can plug in and play. The Bulldog speakers are famed for their tone and pleasing "break-up" sound, but the earliest models could handle only 15 watts each, so the coils sometimes burned out. The effects channel features both vibrato (pitch modulation) and tremolo (volume modulation).

Alternative combinations
Over the years, the Vox AC30 has been used successfully with many guitars. A combination of a Gretsch guitar and an AC30 can be heard extensively on early recordings by The Rolling Stones.

Handle The Vox AC30 has three carrying handles.

Covering Early Vox amplifiers had a beige cloth finish. Black plastic covering was introduced in the early 1960s.

Vox Teardrop Mk VI
This guitar was produced by Vox to complement their amplifier range. It has a Bigsby-type vibrato unit, three pickups, three controls, and a selector switch.

Level control

Attack control

Casing Die-cast aluminium is used for the unit's casing.

Tone-bender
Produced by Sola Sound at the beginning of the 1960s, the Tone-bender was one of the first commercially produced fuzzboxes to appear. The attack control mixes the fuzz and normal signals, the level control adjusts the output volume, and an on-off footswitch can be used to bypass the effects circuit.

The Watkins Copycat
This echo unit was developed by Charlie Watkins. The guitar signal is recorded onto a continuous loop of tape; the echo is produced by a series of playing heads. Controls adjust the speed and depth of the echo. This unit went through a number of changes throughout the 1960s. Demand for tape echo led to its reintroduction in the early 1990s.

RICKENBACKER 325

A Rickenbacker 325, finished in black, was used by John Lennon in his early Beatles days. Its construction and relatively low-output single-coil pickups gave the guitar a bright, "jangly" sound, with especially good mid-range definition and clear string separation. The Vox AC30 combo responds beautifully to these qualities, giving a crispness that can be heard on many recordings of the Beatles. This type of three-quarter-size Rickenbacker was first produced in 1958. This model has a small, semisolid body made from pieces of routed maple and a narrow 21-fret unbound fingerboard made from African rosewood. The guitar has a short scale length and a metal-plate vibrato. The three "toaster-top" pickups are controlled by a selector switch and two pairs of tone and volume controls with a mixer switch.

Speakers Early Vox AC30s used Celestion G12 Bulldog speakers produced with a blue finish. The silver-gray finish, shown here, was introduced later.

Ventilation grilles Heat is allowed to escape from the valves through a series of ventilation grilles.

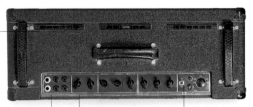

Input channels There are separate input channels for "vibrato" and "normal" channels.

Control panel The controls are segregated into three groups: vibrato, volume, and tone.

On-off switch

AC30 HISTORY

The Vox AC30 grew from the diminutive but highly regarded AC15 combo used by such groups as The Shadows in the late 1950s. The drive for more power in live performances led Dick Denny to develop the AC30, which was effectively two AC15s driving a pair of Celestion 12-inch speakers specially made for Vox. The two-speaker format became very popular during the "beat boom" of the early 1960s and was later applied to the AC15 and the less highly specified AC10.

Neck The unusually small neck is made from maple and shedua laminates.

Control panel The controls are mounted on the top of a two-tier white Plexiglas pickguard.

Modifications

This classic combo has been widely used from the 1960s to the present day. During the 1970s, the design and construction of the AC30 were modified. Solid-state circuitry was used as a replacement for valves, changing the characteristic sound of the original amplifier. In 1990, Vox launched a reissue of the original combo from the 1960s. The AC30 has become a part of the standard equipment used by numerous pop musicians, ranging from bands with a single combo to heavy rock guitarists using a large number for stadium performances.

EFFECTS OVER THE DECADES

Over the years, various effects setups have been de rigueur for the fashionable guitarist. The first popular effect was spring reverb, with or without tape echo; later, fuzzboxes, treble boosters, and the wah-wah pedal became essential equipment for guitarists. By the 1970s such companies as MXR and Electro-

Harmonix were offering vast ranges of battery pedals, including phasers and flangers. Morley produced expensive but sturdy steel-cased pedals. Later in the decade a large range of solid-state analog effects, covering chorus, ADT, flanging, and echo, became available. There were, however, compromises in frequency

response. Stereo rack-mounted digital effects appeared in the 1980s, at first with studio price tags, then in more affordable packages such as the Alesis Quadraverb. The late 1980s saw the widespread use of *multieffects* units, often used with a valve-based guitar preamp for authentic analog distortion.

THE MODERN COMBO

THE VERSATILITY OF THE MESA/BOOGIE

Master volume
In the 1970s, the master volume became a standard feature. This allows distortion in the preamp when the poweramp is at a low volume. Early amplifiers had different channels for tonal emphasis and effects but without a remote switching facility to obtain contrasting sounds. This flexibility is the main reason for multiple channels in modern amplifiers.

When playing music that requires a mix of clean and distorted styles, combo amplifiers like the popular Mesa/Boogie are ideal. Three different sounds – "clean," "crunch," and "high-gain lead" – can be set up and selected by remote switching. When a five- or seven-band graphic equalizer is fitted, the tone can be radically altered without affecting the distortion. The Mesa/Boogie Mk III has a pair of footswitches controlling channel settings: the first can be used to switch from a rhythm to lead sound, the second gives a clean or distorted "crunch" sound used for rhythm playing.

High-gain sounds
Over the past twenty years, rock players have sought more gain from amplifiers. Many now use high-gain lead channels, providing smooth distortion, compression, and endless sustain: ideal for heavy-rock playing. Recent technology makes this easy to provide; the major difficulty is preserving the full-bodied tone of the guitar while avoiding too much background noise.

Gibson ES-335

The Gibson ES-335 remains one of the most popular designs because it can give good results with almost any amplifier. When used in conjunction with a Mesa/Boogie, it can produce a lengthy sustain and a smooth, bluesy overload. Combined with the Fender Twin reverb on the opposite page, the same guitar gives a rich, deep sound with good dynamics but no distortion, on heavily played passages.

MESA/BOOGIE SPECIFICATIONS

The model shown below is an Mk III combo finished in wicker and hardwood. It is an all-valve "overengineered" design that features spring reverb and three channels – "clean rhythm," "fat rhythm," and "high-gain lead" – each with some form of independent control. The single 12 inch speaker is a Black Shadow. Some models also use a heavy-duty Electrovoice with a large magnet assembly that provides great clarity. The combo's "Simul-Class" output stage allows a power choice of either 15 or 60 watts.

Presence control

Solid teak cabinet

Reverb control

Body materials A solid centerblock running through the laminated maple body helps give the guitar greater sustain.

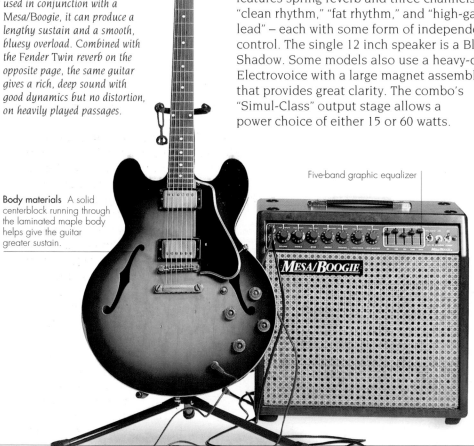

Five-band graphic equalizer

MESA/BOOGIE SOUND

It was the compact (but very heavy and expensive), open-backed Mesa/Boogie combo that made the 1x12 in format acceptable to blues and rock players. The design has not changed fundamentally since the 1970s. The five-band graphic equalizer on this model gives tonal versatility, allowing a reduction of the amplifier's inherent brightness. The sound can be further fine-tuned by swapping the 6L6 power valves for EL34s. A socket on the back panel also allows a line to be run out to a separate 1x12 in speaker cabinet.

FOOTSWITCHES AND EFFECTS

The majority of modern amplification systems are channel-assignable with the switching controlled either by dedicated or MIDI-based footswitches. Some of the early amplifiers had built-in effects such as vibrato and tremolo. Since the 1970s, there has been a trend to provide effects loops – input and output points for external sound processing units – on amplifiers. Chorus and echo work well when linked up in this way, but effects that change signal gain can be extremely noisy – these should be placed between the guitar and amplifier in the normal way. On some recent combos, channels with reverb and graphic-equalization settings can also be controlled by foot switching. A very sophisticated switching system can be seen on page 170.

THE TWIN REVERB

AMPLIFICATION FOR PRODUCING A CLEAN SOUND

Electroacoustic guitars
A relatively new breed of guitar, the electroacoustic is ideal for performing clean, tuneful material on stage. It is usually of acoustic or semi-acoustic construction but includes a Piezo transducer under the bridge saddle and an on-board preamp. The benefits are acoustic sound and good sustain without feedback. The disadvantage is a slightly artificial tone.

Some amplifiers are outstanding when it comes to producing clean sounds but have little to offer when distortion or overdrive is required. The Fender Twin Reverb is one such combo: a 2x12 in valve amplifier that sounds superbly rich and deep with humbuckers and very lively and detailed with single coils, but even at high volumes it will not produce a Marshall or Vox-style overloaded sound. The Roland JC 120 "Jazz Chorus" also excels at producing clean sounds. A high-specification all-transistor amplifier, it is one of the few Japanese combos to rank with the best British and American models.

Other factors affecting sound Two identical guitar-and-amplifier setups can sound very different. Factors affecting the final sound are playing style; string gauge and condition; pickup height; quality of all leads and plugs; condition of preamp, effects, and batteries; quality and condition of valves – new valves are capable of transforming a dull sound.

The changing face of the ES-335
The first Gibson ES-335s were launched in 1958. They featured an unbound fingerboard with dot inlays, PAF pickups, a long pickguard, and clear-topped gold-backed control knobs. The strap buttons were made from cream plastic, and the metal parts were nickel-plated. To begin with, the 335 was available only in a natural or sunburst finish. A very small number of guitars were produced as a special order with a red finish; this was introduced fully in 1960 as a replacement for the natural finish. By the middle of the 1960s, the accumulation of gradual changes had spoiled the original design. The guitar had block inlays on a bound fingerboard, patent number pickups, a trapeze tailpiece, a short pickguard, metal-capped control knobs, and double-ring machine heads. The shape of the body and headstock angle had also been slightly altered. Some of these changes affected the sound of the guitar.

Finish The laminated maple body of this model features a sunburst finish.

Twin Reverb specification
The Twin Reverb, originally produced with 80 watts driving two Jensen 12 in speakers, has a long history of modifications: different types of speaker have been used, and the power output was increased to 100 or even 120 watts. These changes have led to combos from different periods producing very different sounds and tone.

Rear controls The back of the Twin Reverb houses standby and on-off switches, footswitch inputs, and a voltage selector switch for use in other countries.

FENDER TWIN REVERB
This powerful combo has become a standard choice for those seeking clean valve sounds. The *Twin* has two channels and high-quality valve-driven reverb and vibrato effects.

Power output has varied over the years, but between 80 and 100 watts from the four 6L6GC valves is normal. The speakers used are frequently JBLs. From the mid 1960s, throughout the United States, the *Twin* was often bought by studios and clubs as the main high-quality amplifier for recording and performing. Many of the most famous musicians in all areas of popular music have performed using this classic amplifier.

EFFECTS FOR CLEAN PLAYING

Using a volume pedal, or *violining* (rotating the volume control while playing), reverses a note's usual dynamic of a strong transient that dies away quickly; notes or chords seem to appear from nothing to full volume. A compressor provides clean sustain and will balance any differences in note volumes. This is useful for fast passages that mix single notes, string bends, and two- or three-note chords, making compressors popular with country players. Chorus effects also help to give notes body and sustain without distortion. Chorus, compression, and other effects can also be achieved with the use of individual floor units connected by a series of leads.

UPDATED CLASSICS

UPDATING THE ROCK SOUND OF THE MARSHALL STACK

Feedback
One way to alter the guitar's natural dynamic is by increasing gain and physical volume so that, when the guitar is in a certain position relative to the speakers, the notes begin "feeding back." Sustained notes are continually reproduced and eventually grow in volume. Finger vibrato assists this process. Examples of Eric Clapton's skill in using this technique can be heard on the album "Bluesbreakers."

Over the years, certain setups have been considered by rock guitarists to be vital for producing particular sounds. The combination of a Marshall "stack" and a Gibson Les Paul guitar is a good example. The early setup shown below, which is now extremely valuable, features the loud and sweet-sounding 45-watt JTM from the mid-1960s, teamed with a 1959 sunburst Les Paul. The modern-day counterpart, shown opposite, combines a 100-watt, three-channel Marshall Thirtieth-Anniversary head and speaker cabinet, with a 1990 Paul Reed Smith custom 10 Top guitar, a hybrid instrument that combines both Fender and Gibson attributes.

Vintage reissues
A number of early amplifiers, including Marshall, Fender, and Vox, are available as reissues. In most cases the circuitry is similar to the original except that printed circuit boards, rather than expensive hand-wired tag-boards, are used. Famous speakers have also been reissued – some use modern materials, while others sacrifice hardiness and power for complete authenticity.

Gibson Les Paul Standard
Gibson first produced the Les Paul Standard, with a maple top and a sunburst finish, between 1958 and 1960. This superb example from 1959 has a 22-fret fingerboard with crown inlays, two PAF humbucker pickups, and a stud tailpiece with a height-adjustable Tune-o-matic bridge. The pickups are controlled by a three-way selector switch and two pairs of tone and volume controls. The small frets found on 1958 models were enlarged in 1959. In 1960, the depth of the neck was reduced. The specifications of the 1959 Les Paul have made it a much sought-after model.

Selector switch A feature of the Gibson Les Paul is that the pickup selector switch is mounted on the top half of the body away from the tone and volume controls.

Gibson PAF ("patent-applied-for") pickups

Serial number Found behind the headstock, this guitar is number 9 0403

MARSHALL JTM45
The first JTM45 amplifiers were produced in 1962, built by Jim Marshall and Jim Bran in their West London shop.

The amplifier was influenced by the circuitry of the Fender Bassman. An unusual combination of components was assembled, producing a sound unlike that of any other amplifier. Marshall continued to modify and develop the JTM amplifier in stages before it was finally superseded in the late 1960s by the more powerful 100-watt head.

Cabinet This 4x12 slope-fronted speaker cabinet from the late 1960s houses four Celestion G12 speakers

EFFECTS PEDALS

During the 1960s, rock players started to use effects pedals and high volume to produce a new type of electric sound. Some guitarists used a fuzz pedal with overdriven amplifier distortion and feedback, while others used an overdriven sound for sustain without effects. Wah-wah pedals were used at some time by most players. Eric Clapton's Cream recordings featured wah-wah blended with overdrive to produce a searing and expressive sound with a heavy texture. Individual approaches varied from using fuzz with overdrive, for increased sustain, to using a wah-wah pedal with a clean sound at high volumes.

Overdrive and wah-wah
The Colorsound Overdriver unit, produced by Sola Sound, features treble and bass controls as well as a drive control. The wah-wah unit manufactured by Jennings in the late 1960s was called the Cry Baby.

CHOOSING AN AMPLIFIER

Testing an amplifier before purchase is not an everyday occurrence; knowing what to look for makes the task less daunting. A methodical approach can pay dividends when comparing several models. First, if possible, the guitar for which the amplifier is being bought should be used to ensure that the required sound can be obtained from that combination of equipment. The sound from the clean channel, with the channel volume low and master volume high, should be completely clean even when using humbucker pickups. Keeping the master volume low while turning the channel volume up full should give a "crunch" sound that adds edge to chord work. Many players like the option of this sound. If the amplifier has a separate "crunch" channel, the sound should be compared with that of the overdriven clean channel. Easing the guitar's volume down or playing more gently should clean up the sound in both cases. With the lead channel set to a modest gain, the guitar should retain good tone and dynamics; a high gain should produce a compressed and distorted sound with long sustain (possibly endless at full gain). At high levels, background hum and hiss should not be too intrusive and distortion should not have an overly harsh or "papery" edge. Tone controls should remain effective: it should still be possible to achieve a traditional warm rock or a nasal heavy-metal sound. At high volume, the sounds should be powerful while faithfully reproducing the frequency range of the guitar. Avoid amplifiers with clean channels that do not stay clean or that lose definition when used at high volume. On-board effects units, such as reverb, should not cloud the sound on lead settings. Vintage or reissue amplifiers should generate a distinctive sound without the use of full gain. When buying second-hand, amplifiers should be checked for all the above points, but also ensuring that the speakers are original, without misaligned coils, so that they work without buzzing on clean settings.

Paul Reed Smith custom 10 Top

This 1990 PRS guitar is built with a mahogany body and neck, with a two-piece flamed maple top. The 24-fret rosewood fingerboard has ten pearloid inlays with an outline shape of birds in flight. Two humbucker pickups are governed by volume and tone controls, and a five-way selector switch. The PRS has clean sustain, excellent separation, and a wide range of color. This makes it ideal for use with overdriven amplifiers.

Tremolo unit
The PRS features a "locking" tremolo system.

Dedicated footswitch *Modern Marshall amplifiers feature a dedicated footswitch unit to change channels.*

MARSHALL THIRTIETH-ANNIVERSARY HEAD

This three-channel, 100-watt all-valve head is a hybrid of new and old. The "crunch" channel can provide three generations of Marshall sounds, while the lead channel balances gain with such factors as headroom to produce high *perceived* gain, without sacrificing tone or dynamics. The automatic control over damping factor ensures that the clean sounds are well defined, with the sound loosened up for "crunch" and lead selections. An indicator warns of power valve failure, but the amplifier can still be used with reduced power. Other features include half/full power operation, effects loop, low-volume compensation, frequency adjusted recording output, and a MIDI channel control facility. Celestion speakers have been central to the "British sound"; the G12 series has been fitted to most Marshall cabinets for the last thirty years.

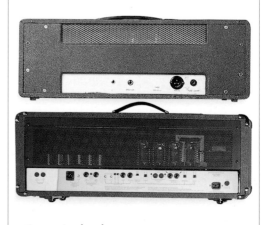

Comparing heads

The 1960s JTM45 (top) and the modern Jubilee head (above) can be compared. The first has simple speaker outputs and a Bakelite socket with a fuse. The modern Marshall head has a switching unit and an effects loop.

RACK-MOUNTED SYSTEMS

THE ULTIMATE SETUP FOR THE MODERN GUITARIST

MIDI

MIDI
"Musical Instrument Digital Interface" is a standardized system that allows communication between the microprocessors built into many types of modern effects units, switching systems, pre-amps, and, occasionally, amplifiers. This allows a guitarist to control programmed and preset changes from a switching system or other source such as a sequencer. It is also commonly used for linking synthesizers, drum machines, and sequencers.

In recent years, portable rack-mounted amplification and sound-processing equipment has become increasingly popular. These systems enable guitarists to obtain a sound with the sort of quality and control normally exclusive to the recording studio. Portable rack-mounted equipment can be assembled with flexibility. Each item is fitted with bolts to the front of a standard 19-inch rack frame. Items such as power supplies and patch bays can be mounted at the back.

Mono or stereo?
To re-create studio sounds and effects in a live performance, many guitarists are now using some form of stereo amplification. These can range from a basic 2x12 stereo combo with a stereo chorus effect to large rack systems incorporating studio-quality signal processors.

STAGE-AND-STUDIO RACK SYSTEM

The system shown over the next four pages was designed and put together by the guitarist Jim Barber for playing both on stage and in the recording studio. It consists of an extensive range of high-quality amplifiers, equalizers, and speaker simulators that have been assembled in such a way that a particular type of guitar can be matched with the right amplifier and routed through specified rack-mounted effects to create a mono or stereo image for stage or recording use.

THE SYSTEM IN ACTION

When playing a solo with the Gibson Les Paul, the guitar is routed through the Marshall 4500 amplifier to give an overdriven sound, a Palmer PDI-03 speaker simulator, and one of the PAST equalizers through to a combination of effects. These may include a stereo delay with panning and additional reverb. The programmable VCA (*Voltage Controlled Amplifier*) and *Hush* noise reduction can also be used to increase the level of the chosen preset and eliminate any unwanted noise. Alternatively, if the Fender XII twelve-string guitar is used, a clear sound for chordal picking is likely to be required. In this case, the guitar can be routed through the clean channel of the CAE preamplifier, and channel one of a Palmer PDI-05 speaker simulator, through to the Eventide harmonizer with added reverb and the TC1210 chorus unit, which will create a wide stereo effect.

Fender XII
This Fender XII twelve-string Stratocaster was made in Japan. It is refinished in a fluorescent yellow and features a simulated mother-of-pearl pickguard.

Jackson Soloist
This early Soloist was built by Grover Jackson for Jeff Beck. It has an unusual pickguard that shows the influence of a Fender Precision bass. It has an orange finish, an ebony fingerboard with dot inlays, three single-coil pickups, and a Floyd Rose tremolo unit.

Gibson Les Paul Custom
This black Les Paul Custom has a Seymour Duncan bridge pickup and a prototype ESP neck pickup. Unusually, a Floyd Rose unit with a locking nut has been specially fitted, making it a powerful and versatile instrument that combines traditional design with modern hardware.

LIVE MONITORING

To give a clear and precise reproduction of the amplification and effects, the rack system shown below uses four Marshall 4x12, 400-watt speaker cabinets fitted with Celestion G12 speakers. An HH V800 transistor power amplifier is used to produce distortion-free power at any level of volume. This enables the player to achieve a specific sound and alter the volume without having to change the characteristics. This approach is especially useful for monitoring a guitar sound in a live situation. Many players have a preference for the warmth of valve-power amplification, but there are inherent problems that result from the alteration of the volume level. Using Celestion G12M 25-watt speakers can also help to produce a vintage sound with more character. They have less definition, though, as well as a tendency to distort. The four cabinets may be positioned and separated as two pairs, to create a wider stereo image, or placed close together.

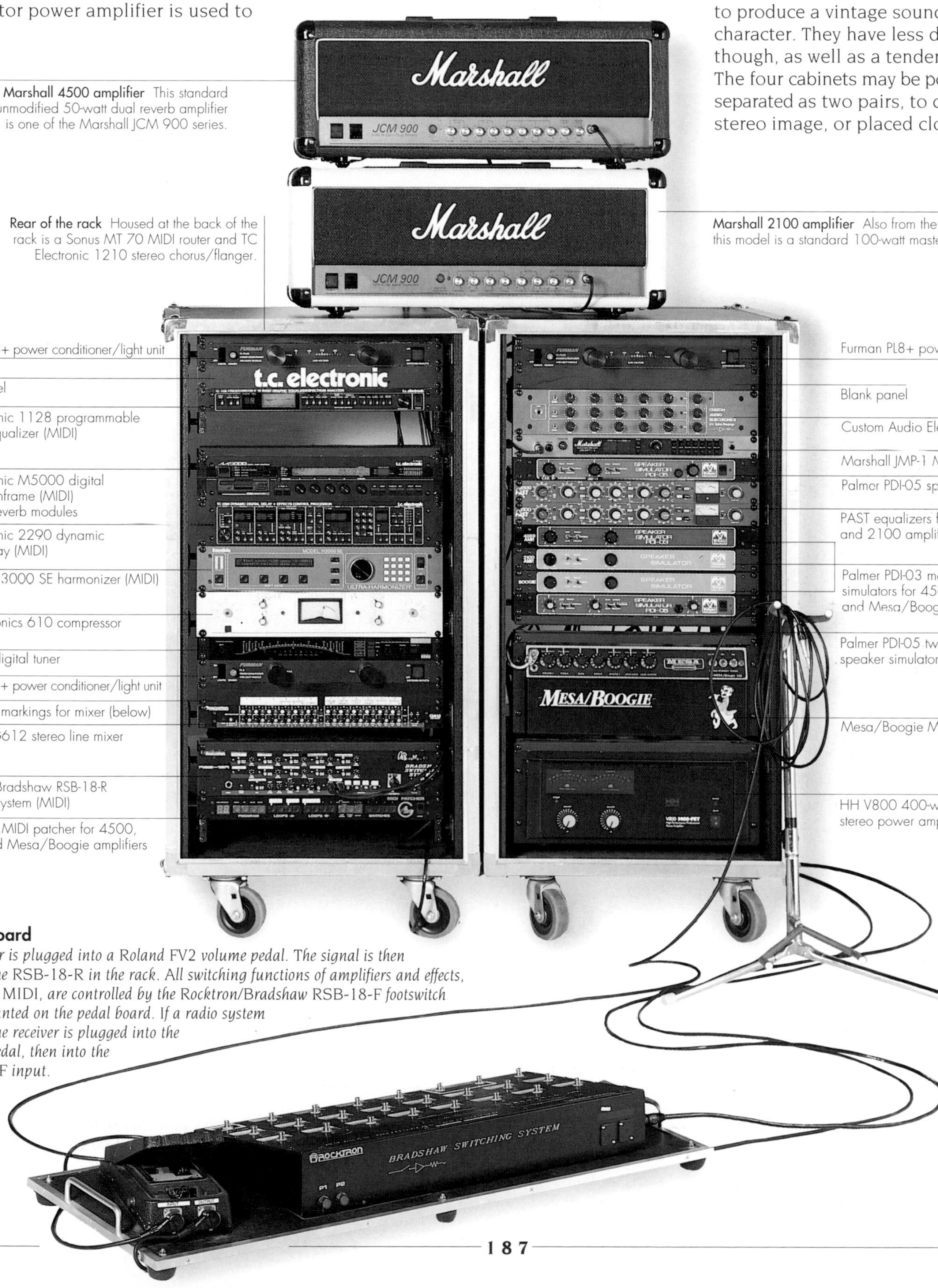

Marshall 4500 amplifier This standard unmodified 50-watt dual reverb amplifier is one of the Marshall JCM 900 series.

Rear of the rack Housed at the back of the rack is a Sonus MT 70 MIDI router and TC Electronic 1210 stereo chorus/flanger.

Marshall 2100 amplifier Also from the JCM 900 series, this model is a standard 100-watt master volume amplifier.

Furman PL8+ power conditioner/light unit

Blank panel

TC Electronic 1128 programmable graphic equalizer (MIDI)

TC Electronic M5000 digital audio mainframe (MIDI) with two reverb modules

TC Electronic 2290 dynamic digital delay (MIDI)

Eventide H3000 SE harmonizer (MIDI)

Spectra Sonics 610 compressor

Korg DT1 digital tuner

Furman PL8+ power conditioner/light unit

Panel with markings for mixer (below)

Rocktron G612 stereo line mixer

Rocktron/Bradshaw RSB-18-R switching system (MIDI)

Valley Arts MIDI patcher for 4500, 2100, and Mesa/Boogie amplifiers

Furman PL8+ power conditioner/light unit

Blank panel

Custom Audio Electronics 3+ preamplifier

Marshall JMP-1 MIDI preamplifier

Palmor PDI-05 speaker simulator

PAST equalizers for 4500 and 2100 amplifiers

Palmer PDI-03 mono speaker simulators for 4500, 2100, and Mesa/Boogie amplifiers

Palmer PDI-05 two-channel speaker simulator for main outputs

Mesa/Boogie Mk11 100-watt amplifier

HH V800 400-watt stereo power amplifier

Pedal board

The guitar is plugged into a Roland FV2 volume pedal. The signal is then fed into the RSB-18-R in the rack. All switching functions of amplifiers and effects, including MIDI, are controlled by the Rocktron/Bradshaw RSB-18-F footswitch unit, mounted on the pedal board. If a radio system is used, the receiver is plugged into the volume pedal, then into the RSB-18-F input.

RACK SYSTEM DIAGRAM

There is considerable variance in the way rack-mounted systems are put together and used. The different approaches are due largely to individual tastes and music styles. The system on the previous page is shown here as a chart, with a detailed description of the components (below). The audio links between the units are shown with arrows depicting the direction of flow. The MIDI links are indicated by a series of dotted lines. This system was designed by Jim Barber to emulate the sounds effected in a recording studio when used in a live situation. A major benefit of using this type of system, with its extensive use of new technology, is that it enables the musician to record an album and then faithfully reproduce on stage the sounds and textures associated with particular tracks.

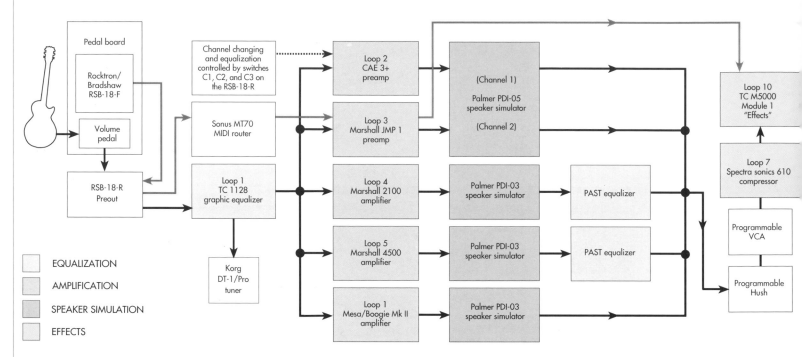

- EQUALIZATION
- AMPLIFICATION
- SPEAKER SIMULATION
- EFFECTS

SWITCHING SYSTEM

The heart of this system is built around the Rocktron/Bradshaw switching system, which controls the signal routing through the different stages of amplification and effect processing. The system consists of ten mono loops (marked as L1–L10) and one stereo loop (L11). A *loop* is simply a circuit comprising a *send* signal fed to the input of an effect (or chain of effects) and a *return* signal from the output of the same effect. There are also twenty-five banks of five presets. These can be used to program twenty-five songs with five variations in each. Using MIDI, this allows different combinations of amplifier and effects in different parts of a song. For example: preset 1 – introduction; 2 – verse; 3 – chorus; 4 – middle-eight; 5 – soloing. The switching system controls all MIDI-compatible units, although there are also four control switches that allow for the bypassing of non-MIDI effects. The guitar is plugged into a volume pedal mounted on the pedal board; the output from this feeds to the RSB-18-R, which is mounted in the rack. The floor unit – RSB-18-F – also connects to the RSB-18-R.

LEVEL MATCHING AND TUNING

The first item in the chain is the TC 1128 programmable graphic equalizer, which is patched into loop 1. The equalizer is on all the time and is used to balance the input levels of any guitars used in the system. In this case, it would be used to match up the levels from the Jackson to the Les Paul, which have considerably different output levels. A signal is also fed to the Korg DT 1 guitar tuner, which is permanently monitoring the guitar signal.

Control cable This links the footswitch to the RSB-18-R rack unit.

Loop selector switch There are ten mono loops. Loop 3 controls the Marshall JMP 1 preamp.

Hush noise reduction switch

Control switch There are four control switches. C4 is set up as a bypass switch to the chorus unit.

Output

Input

Bank selection

Bank presets

Stereo loop Loop 11 controls the stereo reverb.

Volume pedal

Pedal board

The custom-built floor unit consists of an electronic switching system made by Rocktron/Bradshaw with a volume pedal. The switching system uses MIDI to control amplification and effect processing. It features twenty-five groups of "song" presets. Each bank contains five individual presets.

MIDI

MIDI plays an important role in this system. The control computer built into the Rocktron/Bradshaw footswitch controls all MIDI functions through the Sonus MT70 MIDI router. This enables a constant flow of MIDI data preventing MIDI messages from occurring.

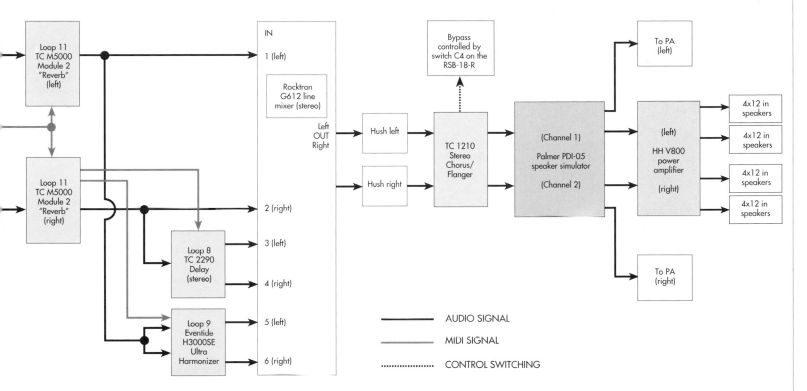

Legend:
- AUDIO SIGNAL
- MIDI SIGNAL
- .... CONTROL SWITCHING

AMPLIFICATION, EQUALIZATION, AND SPEAKER SIMULATION

The signal runs to loop 2, 3, 4, 5, or 6, depending on which is selected. **Loop 2** is a CAE 3+ preamplifier, which goes into channel 1 of a Palmer PDI-05 speaker simulator. The channels of the preamp are switched by control switches **C1** ("crunch"), **C2** ("lead"), and **C3** ("EQ"). **Loop 3** activates the Marshall JMP 1 preamp, which goes into channel 2 of a Palmer PDI 05 speaker simulator. **Loop 4** controls the 100-watt Marshall 2100 amplifier, the output of which goes into a Palmer PDI 03 speaker simulator and then the PAST equalizer. **Loop 5** runs the Marshall 4500 amplifier, which goes into a Palmer PDI 03 speaker simulator and then the PAST equalizer. **Loop 6** controls the Mesa/Boogie Mk II amplifier, which goes into a Palmer PDI-03 speaker simulator.

All these loops pass through a programmable Hush and VCA for noise reduction and level control, which is programmed into their presets. For example, when soloing and driving an amplifier at high volumes, the VCA would be adjusted for greater level, and the Hush would have a more extreme setting to compensate for added noise resulting from changes in volume.

THE SOUND-PROCESSING STAGE

Loop 7 is a Spectra Sonics 610 (mono) compressor. This feeds **loop 10** containing a TC M5000 digital audio mainframe. This is mainly used for room simulation effects. This loop splits into **loop 11**, which is also a TC M5000 and provides stereo reverb. The left output channel of the reverb feeds channel 1 of the Rocktron G612 mixer (panned left) and **loop 9**, which is the Eventide H3000SE Ultra Harmonizer. The stereo outputs of this are fed into channels 5 and 6 of the mixer (panned extreme left and right). The right output channel of the reverb feeds channel 2 on the mixer (panned right) and **loop 8**, a TC 2290 stereo digital delay, whose stereo outputs go into channel 3 (panned left) and channel 4 (panned right) of the mixer.

OUTPUTS

The stereo output from the mixer passes through a secondary Hush in the RSB-18-R rack unit. This signal then passes into the TC 1210 chorus unit. The on-off bypass of the chorus unit can be switched via control switch **C4** on the pedal board. Finally, the stereo signal from the chorus unit goes to the left and right channels of the Palmer PDI-05 speaker simulator.

LIVE USE

In a live situation, the balanced outputs of the PDI-05 speaker simulators are fed directly into the PA system's monitor console and then to the front-of-house console. This eliminates the need for miking up the speaker cabinets. The *thru* signal from the PDI-05 is fed into the HH V800 power amplifier, which is linked up to the Marshall 4x12 speaker cabinets. When used in this way, the amplifier and speakers become the monitor system for the guitar but have no effect on the level or the balanced signal sent to the PA.

STUDIO USE

In a recording studio, the balanced outputs are taken directly to the mixing console, again eliminating the need for miking. If necessary, the *thru* signal from the PDI-05 can be used to feed a valve power amplifier and vintage 4x12 in speakers. This sound can then be mixed with speaker simulators.

RECORDING

RECORDING THE GUITAR IN A STUDIO AND AT HOME

The modern studio
Studios comprise rooms for recording performances, and a separate control room housing the mixing desk and computers. The mixing desk has a number of separate channels, each with various sound-processing functions, so that a combination of tracks, such as rhythm and solo, can be controlled, edited, and assembled in stages.

Before the invention of the tape recorder in the 1930s, sound was recorded by etching a pattern mechanically onto disc: once a recording was made, it could not be altered. The advantage of using a magnetic tape recorder was that tape could be wiped clean and the same section used to record again. The principles of sound-on-sound – recording layers of sound on top of one another – and multi-tracking, where the sounds are recorded as tracks on separate tape channels, were developed in the 1940s. This allowed two or more pieces of music to be recorded onto tape and played back at the same time. So a guitar rhythm track could be recorded and have a melody laid over it. The two tracks could be played back and heard together. These basic principles have been used ever since.

Recording the guitar
The guitar is often recorded at the same time as other instruments. Isolating each sound can be achieved using separating screens or different rooms: players can listen to each other on headphones. A song is often recorded starting with a guide track, which may include a rhythm guitar part. Additional guitar parts are played over this rhythm track, at which point the guide track is sometimes re-recorded or removed.

THE COMPUTER

Today, computers have virtually replaced tape recorders in studios. Normal "analog" sound is converted to a digital code, routed through converters and computers, and stored on hard disks. Computers sit at the heart of the control process and can replace almost any piece of musical equipment, although "outboard" equipment is still used. There are almost unlimited numbers of channels, and computers can give tremendous control when it comes to altering and editing music. Mistakes or unwanted ideas can be cut and stored, and single notes or entire sections can be dropped in or pasted anywhere, using on-screen controls that show the music as graphic wave forms and as scores. It is possible to record and entirely change the character of the sound through on-screen software manipulation.

Mixing desk Modern mixing desks, such as this SSL, have computer-controlled consoles.

The Beatles (*above*)
The Beatles perform their single All You Need Is Love *for a worldwide audience broadcast by the BBC from Abbey Road's Studio 1 in June 1967. With producer George Martin and the studio engineers, the Beatles used innovative recording studio techniques and approaches to, for instance, sound processing, to advantage.*

Real World (*right*)
Real World studios, situated in the rural setting of Box in Wiltshire, were opened in 1987. There are four separate studios, equipped with Otari, Studer, and Mitsubishi tape recorders and three SSL mixing consoles. Part-owner Peter Gabriel, the Happy Mondays, and New Order have all recorded here.

THE MIXING DESK

The signals that make up a piece of music are routed into the separate channels of a mixing desk (or mixing console) to create mono and stereo "images." An example of this process is to make a recording using two microphones positioned (panned) left and right in the stereo "field." In addition to controlling the balance of the recording as a whole, each individual channel of the mixing desk can be used to modify the sound, either in volume or equalization or by adding various types of effect.

CHANNELS

A group of individual channels can be run into a single channel that can then be used to control the group as a whole. For example, a drum kit consisting of twelve individual channels can be sub-mixed into a pair of channels panned left and right. This provides the master volume for an overall stereo drum sound. Grouping can also be used where a guitar sound comes from a number of different sources, e.g., a speaker with three different microphone signals, and one from a speaker simulator. Mixing desks are frequently described by the number of input channels, grouped channels, and output channels on board. For example, a console described as "twenty-four into eight into two" (24-8-2) has twenty-four input channels, eight sub-group channels, and two output channels.

SOUND PROCESSING

The effects units commonly used in the recording studio are similar in principle to dedicated guitar pedals, but are built to a much higher specification. They can be used to process sound in a wide variety of ways, including delay (phasing, chorus, flanging, and echo), adding a digitally generated harmony (harmonizing), and compressing the signal. Sound processing is often connected to the mixing desk using a send and return loop: auxiliary volume controls on each channel of the desk are normally used to control how much of the effect is added to the signal. It is possible to add effects during the recording stage. However, most studio engineers prefer to record a dry signal, adding effects during the final mix-down. Effects are often built into some of the more sophisticated mixing desks.

The Power Station

Started in the late 1970s, the Power Station studio in New York can provide anything up to ninety-six-track recording facilities. It features four separate studios equipped with Studer analog and Sony digital tape recorders and SSL and Neve mixing consoles. A number of the best-known names in rock music have recorded here.

Abbey Road control room

Now one of the world's legendary studios, Abbey Road was officially opened as EMI Recording Studios by Edward Elgar in 1931. This is one of the control rooms where engineers, producers, and musicians listen back to the music through various types of monitoring speakers using an SSL desk and computers. There are four studios and extensive facilities. Abbey Road has been used for recording a vast amount of music in all kinds of fields from film music scores through to pop albums. Today, studios such as Abbey Road continually evolve with modern technology, which is incredibly sophisticated and wide-ranging in its creative possibilities. Any music can be imported as digital material and used seamlessly with real sounds.

RECORDING TECHNIQUES

Before starting a recording, it is a good idea to make a plan of which instruments are to be played on every track. A *track sheet* is often used to plan the overall structure of the music and the role of guitar parts in relation to the music as a whole. The desired sound will be set up with an electric or acoustic guitar, and the source of the sound – an amplifier or an acoustic instrument – will be recorded. At the start of a track, a count-in containing one or two bars of beats should be recorded. This gives the musician advance warning of when he or she should start to play.

INPUT CHANNEL COMPOSITION

Each input channel on the mixing desk has an identical set of functions.

Gain control and pad switch
Different types of microphone and line input rarely have the same output levels. The **gain** is effectively a volume control used to adjust an incoming signal to a level compatible with the mixing desk. The **pad** switch has a similar function, except that it is not variable – it reduces the sensitivity of a microphone input by a specific value, usually one that is outside the range of the gain.

Phantom powering
Some types of microphone require DC power to operate. The **phantom** switch, providing between 12 and 48 volts, provides this power from the desk.

Equalization
Equalization (or tone) controls come in a number of forms. The most common types allow low, middle, and high frequencies to be adjusted. They can be used to change the brightness of the treble and the presence in the middle and bass range, which can make a piece of music sound fuller or less defined. High- and low-pass filters can be used to cut out any unwanted frequencies above or below specified levels.

Sound processing/auxiliary send
Where sound processing is required, the **auxiliary send** controls the amount of the original signal being sent into an external unit. Effects inputs can be set either before or after the equalization stage. It is also possible to create a loop (see p. 172) using the channel's **insert point**.

Channel grouping
Group sends route the signal from specific channels into one or more other channels. An example of their use is in drum-sound production, where the individual sounds are grouped into two channels, producing a stereo sub-mix. These channels are then used to control the volume of the drums relative to the rest of the mix.

Mute and solo switches
The **mute** switch simply prevents the entire signal from the channel being heard. The **solo** switch is used to isolate individual tracks within a mix.

Panning
The **pan** control is used to feed the signal through to the left and right master output channels, controlling the position of the sound in the stereo "field."

Channel fader
The sliding faders usually found at the bottom of the desk control the volume for each channel.

OVERDUBBING TRACKS

The technique in which a number of tracks are played back, allowing the musician to listen to them and to play and record additional material, is known as *overdubbing*. In this instance, the computer or tape machine plays back material from certain tracks and simultaneously records material on new tracks. This is usually achieved by running the guitar into a new input channel on the mixing desk and assigning the signal to a new track.

MONITORING

Foldback monitoring for recording is usually heard through headphones. This enables players to hear the sound of their own instruments and other instruments via the mixing desk, while adding a melody or rhythm part. These instruments may be playing live at the same time, or they may be on tracks that have been previously recorded. Monitoring controls are placed in line with the input controls for each channel or in a separate bank on the desk.

RECORDING WITH MICROPHONES

After experimenting with sound settings in the studio, the guitar amplifier will be recorded using microphones placed in a number of positions. They can be situated near the combo or cabinet speakers (*close miking*), or at a distance, picking up room sound (*ambient miking*). Microphones have widely differing characteristics, and the position in which they are placed in relation to the sound source is important. The distance of the microphone, the angle in relation to the speaker, its relationship to the acoustics of the room, and its

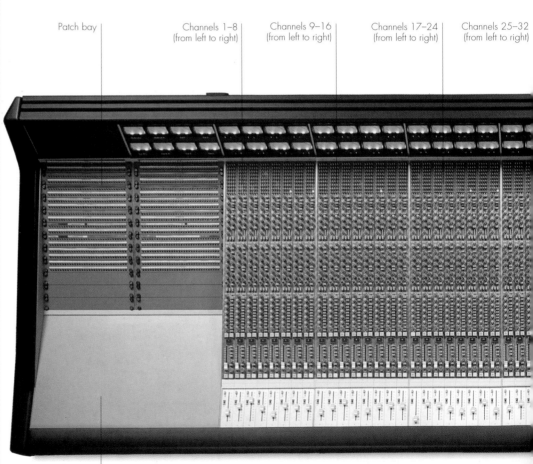

Patch bay — Channels 1–8 (from left to right) — Channels 9–16 (from left to right) — Channels 17–24 (from left to right) — Channels 25–32 (from left to right)

Engineer's table

Solid State Logic console
The Solid State Logic SL4064 G is a 48-32-48 mixing console. The desk has forty-eight channel modules: both the input and the output controls — as well as separate compressor, limiter, expander, and noise gate modules — are contained within each channel module. A computer keyboard, with a VDU, housed in the center of the console, is used to control any of the individual settings for each channel. This "Total Recall" system can memorize and store specific mixes, moving the faders automatically during playback. The main record and transport controls for the tape machines can also be operated from the console. If necessary, the system is expandable to sixty-four tracks.

directional capacities determine the quality and color of the recorded sound. If the signal from the guitar is split, and played through more than one amplifier at the same time, it is possible for each sound to be recorded onto a separate channel and then mixed down and edited at a later stage.

DIRECT INPUT AND SIMULATORS

Direct input evolved partly through the need to separate out instruments so that their sound did not spill during live playing. Where several microphones are used to record instruments playing together at the same time, separating screens or booths are used. However, rather than being played through an amplifier, the guitar can be plugged into either a DI *box* or the mixing console, where preamp gain

takes the signal to tape. In recent years, DI boxes have been replaced by *speaker simulators* (see p. 171), which run the signal from a guitar amplifier output straight into the desk. The speaker simulator takes the line output from the amplifier; imparts a filtered sound, giving the characteristics of a speaker cabinet; and reduces the signal down to line level, where it is then fed into the desk. Some producers prefer to use a mixture of both systems, recording speaker simulator on one channel and a miked-up speaker cabinet on another.

ACOUSTIC RECORDING

An acoustic guitar usually has one or more microphones positioned to pick up the direction of the sound. Minor movements with a microphone can lead to tonal imbalance or left-hand playing

noise. Acoustic instruments often benefit from a room with reflective surfaces to give a live sound. Classical recordings are often made with a pair of microphones running to a portable DAT machine: churches or other buildings that enhance the acoustics are often used for this purpose.

DROPPING-IN

It is not necessary to record a piece of music from start to finish: a section on one track can be *dropped in* (or *punched in*) by listening to the track, switching the computer or tape machine *in* to record mode, playing over the section, and then switching *out* of record mode. With skill and care, it is possible to replace single notes and chords. This technique is widely used for correcting mistakes without having to repeat an entire section.

Visual display unit The settings for each channel can be displayed on this small screen.

Channels 33–40 (from left to right)

Channels 41–48 (from left to right)

Multi-track routing The patching system provides the link between the mixing console and the recording machines.

Back panel The rear of the mixing console houses a series of sockets. These include separate line and microphone inputs, outputs, and insert points for connecting to peripheral effects.

VU meters Channel volume and tape input levels are indicated by a series of VU meters.

Dynamics controls Each channel has compressor, limiter, expander, and noise gate functions.

Equalization section Each channel of the console features four-band parametric equalization and "hi/lo" filters.

Auxiliary send bank The console features four mono sends and one stereo auxiliary send. These controls "send" a signal from the channel into a sound-processing unit.

Blank panels Additional groups of channels can be added as they are required.

QWERTY keyboard

Computer-controlled automation system

Master output fader

Channel fader The volume for an individual channel is controlled by this fader.

Pan control This controls the position of the channel in the stereo spectrum.

Solo button This switch allows an individual channel to be heard by cutting out the other channels.

RECORDING THE GUITAR

The first step in recording any guitar is to be sure the strings are new enough to produce good tone and intonation. Consider, too, the room acoustics – these largely define the sound and cannot be removed. So it is safer to record "dry," often as simple as placing acoustically absorbent material near the instrument.

The type of microphone is crucial. A small diaphragm condenser (pencil microphone) is ideal for acoustic guitar, because it is sensitive yet not prone to boom. A dynamic microphone can reproduce a tougher quality of tone and reject unwanted sound. For electric guitars a combination of dynamic and condenser microphones is typical. With acoustic guitar, place the microphone in front of the 12th fret and 8–12 in

(20–30 cm) away. Make a test recording and listen back, comparing it to the actual sound of the guitar. If it lacks bass, bring the microphone closer to the soundhole. If it lacks definition, move it farther away. With electric guitar, a dynamic microphone such as a Shure SM 57 is often placed close to the amplifier, off-center from the speaker cone. Movements of just an inch or two affect the sound, which brightens toward the center and is intensely bright in the middle. Experiment with test recordings, moving the mic until the sound is right, and consider the amplifier settings. If the recording is to be a solo guitar, ambient microphones create a bigger sound. Each microphone has a separate track and can be blended and panned with the close microphone to broaden and liven the image.

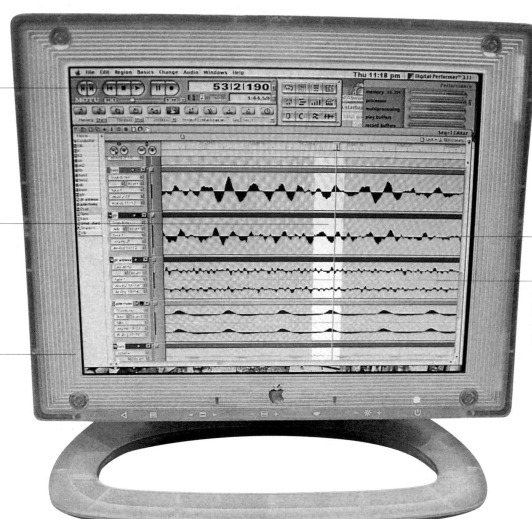

Transport buttons The panel controls the basic functions of the sequencer, such as play, record, and locate. The numerical readout displays time in bars and beats as well as hours, minutes, and seconds.

Yellow bar This indicates a highlighted area ready to be edited, cut, trimmed or otherwise processed.

Computer power The computer, here an Apple Mac running Digital Performer, is an indispensable tool for detailed editing and manipulation of audio, such as repairing mistakes in a performance with cutting, pasting, dropping in, or even retuning.

Waveform This represents one-100th of a second of the sound captured by a condenser microphone 12 in (30 cm) from the 12th fret of an acoustic guitar.

Stereo waveform This shows the sound captured by two equidistant ambient microphones a stride away, pointing to the bridge of the guitar.

The computer
Computers have closed the gap between home recording and the professional studio, making commercial-quality recordings possible in a home environment. A software program such as Digital Performer, Logic Audio, or ProTools has the capability of replicating an entire recording studio in virtual form, including the mixer and multitrack recorder, as well as outboard effects such as reverb delay and chorus.

Hooking up
The microphone is routed to the computer via a preamp, which boosts the output level, and an audio interface, which converts the signal into digital form for storage and manipulation. Both of these stages have a substantial effect on the recorded quality.

GLOSSARY OF EFFECTS

AUTOMATIC DOUBLE TRACKING A delay-based effect usually referred to as "ADT." The effect is created on digital or analog units capable of producing a fast single repeat of a signal. It is sometimes referred to as "doubling."

BYPASS Most effect units can be bypassed by switching the signal to a route where the sound is not processed.

CHORUS This is a delay-based effect (between 15 and 35 milliseconds) designed to simulate what happens when two instruments play the same part. With real-life double tracking, there are always slight differences in timing and pitch between the parts – chorus re-creates this effect electronically. For example, a 6-string guitar can be chorused to sound more like a 12-string guitar. Most units offer "Modulation" (rate) and "Depth" controls. A number of combos exist with built-in chorus, often in stereo, with an amplifier and a speaker for each channel.

COMPRESSOR Using compression, quiet notes are boosted in level, while louder signals – such as a heavily struck chord – are reduced in level. The unit averages-out the natural differences in level as you play, making finger-picked passages sound smoother, and giving a feeling of "flow" to clean lead passages. The controls – usually Threshold and Compression – allow for a wide array of effects. With heavy compression, the percussive front end of a heavily picked note is taken away to give a softer start; as the note fades, the unit increases volume, keeping the level virtually constant.

DELAY When sound is reflected from a distant surface, a delayed version of the original is heard later. Echo units copy this natural effect by either analog or digital means. Solid-state units store the signal electronically; analog devices pass the signal down a long chain repeatedly until it is needed; while digital units encode the signal in digital form, store it in memory until it is required, then decode it. Digital units can offer stereo operation, allowing multitapped signals to be placed left, right, and center-stage or even appear to bounce from one side to the other.

DIGITAL EFFECTS Almost every effect can now be produced digitally. When using digital effects, a signal is converted to binary code – a series of ones and zeros – so that it can be processed in a variety of ways and converted back to an analog signal.

DISTORTION When extra gain and distortion cannot be achieved by an amplifier, traditionally a distortion pedal (or fuzzbox/overdriver) is used. A clean signal is plugged in, and a distorted, sustaining sound is produced. Many early fuzzboxes were simply crude trigger mechanisms, so that no matter how you played, the same "buzzy," square-wave sound would result. Modern pedals allow the amount of distortion to be more easily controlled. Some units include preamp valves to give good tone and dynamics coupled with genuine valve overdrive. Digitally produced distortion, although increasingly common, is generally thought to be too harsh for the tastes of most guitarists.

ENHANCERS This device processes an audio signal to improve the sound and definition. The early enhancers, called "aural exciters," boosted a harmonic element in the music to produce a brighter effect. Other systems use phase correction to place signals precisely in phase so that frequencies are not lost as a result of phase cancellation.

EXPANDER The opposite effect of compression is called expansion. These units are used to increase the dynamic range of a signal.

FLANGER A delay-based effect that originated with tape recorders. The tape was slowed down by pressing the fingers against the reel, and the sound produced was mixed with a normal signal from a second tape recorder. The flanging sound is created electronically by playing back a delayed signal of up to 20 milliseconds, with controlled pitch modulation, against the original signal. The "feedback" or "regeneration" control found on some flanging units creates an unusual pitch-modulated sound. The effect can be produced on most modern digital delay lines.

GRAPHIC EQUALIZER A graphic equalizer is a tone control that divides the sound spectrum into frequency bands, allowing the level of each band to be boosted or cut separately. The word graphic refers to the fact that it is possible to see at a glance what particular "shape" is being used. For example, a V shape boosts the top and bottom ends, while the opposite response adds mid-range warmth. Although the tonal emphasis can be changed, it is not possible to improve the basic quality of tone.

HARMONIZER Also known as a "pitch-shifter," the effect has two main uses. It can enrich the sound of a guitar, using a harmonizer to add overtones that are in harmony with the original signal and sound similar to **chorus**. The harmonizer can also generate a harmony note. Until recently, only fixed-interval harmonies were possible; however, new "intelligent" units allow the player to select specific types of scale, which result in automatically adjusted harmonies.

LESLIE CABINET The Leslie is a rotary speaker cabinet designed for use with an organ. In the 1960s, players such as Jimi Hendrix found that by feeding the guitar signal through a Leslie cabinet they could produce a delicate, ethereal sound. Today, the effect is simulated electronically.

MIDI Musical Instrument Digital Interface (MIDI) was developed in 1981 by the Sequential Circuits company as a universal interfacing system for synthesizers and sequencers. MIDI is widely used within effects units as a way of controlling parameters or stored settings from either footswitches or sequencers.

MULTIEFFECTS UNITS There is an increasing trend toward single units that are capable of producing reverb, phasing, flanging, chorus, delay, harmonizing, and many other effects. These units are generally digital, MIDI-controllable, and capable of chaining effects together and storing settings.

OCTAVE DIVIDER This analog effect (an early forerunner of the harmonizer) added a single note either an interval of an octave above or an octave below the original signal.

PANNING The location of a signal within a stereo "field." It can also refer to the dynamic behavior of the signal – for example, where echo repeats are "panned" from left to right.

PHASING If two identical versions of a signal are "out of phase," so that the peaks in one precisely coincide with the troughs in the other, the two signals will cancel each other out, leading – in theory – to silence. If the signals are partially out of phase, a characteristic coloration to the sound will result. Phasing can be achieved electronically, the results varying from a mild "whooshing" to sounds reminiscent of a jet plane.

PREAMPLIFIER To help overload the input stages of the amplifier, a "preamp" can be used to generate extra gain. The preamp often acts as a tone control when used in conjunction with a main amplifier. It can also be used to boost the signal when used with amplified acoustic instruments.

REVERBERATION A "reverb" unit mimics the natural effect of overlapping sound reflections caused by sound bouncing around an interior space such as a room. Spring reverb is the traditional effect built into many guitar amplifiers, but digital reverb (offering fine control of the many parameters involved, and a crisp, bright sound) is now more common.

STEREO CHORUS This term can refer to a **chorus** effect that is panned over stereo outputs to give the impression of spatial movement. It can also describe the sound created by playing a dry signal through one channel and a chorused signal through the other.

TAPE ECHO The traditional method of producing delay. The original signal is recorded on tape and played back slightly later by one or more replay heads, giving either a single repeat or "multitap" effects. Feeding the delayed signal back to the recording head gives a heavily textured sound.

TONE PEDAL See **WAH-WAH PEDAL**.

TREBLE BOOSTER In the early 1960s, many of the cheaper amplifiers and guitars lacked the top-end produced by high-quality equipment. To overcome this, small battery-powered treble boosters were used.

TREMOLO This rhythmic pulsing effect is obtained by modulating the volume of the signal. It was built into many early combos, being relatively easy to engineer with valve circuitry, and could give anything from a fast rippling sound to a deep throbbing effect. Note that Fender always called their tremolo effect "vibrato" – this is technically incorrect (see below).

VIBRATO This effect is obtained by modulating the pitch of the signal. The sound produced can vary from a subtle enhancement to an extreme variation. Early valve combos such as the Vox AC30 offered vibrato as well as tremolo; however, the feature is more often seen on chorus pedals or digital multieffects units.

VOLUME PEDAL This passive device allows players to vary the volume at will while continuing to play. Its main use (apart from altering overall volume level) is as a "swell" pedal; a particularly attractive effect may be achieved by eliminating the percussive attack at the beginning of notes and chords, letting them "float in." This also works well with string bends and harmonics.

WAH-WAH PEDAL This foot-operated tone control came into vogue in the late 1960s. When the pedal is flat, a high-treble sound is produced; raising the pedal gradually increases the bass sound. It can be used in several ways: rocking it gently back and forth while playing produces a "talking guitar" effect or a soft "wah" sound, while a fast, "chopping" effect is used by many funk players. It can also be set to an in-between position to select a certain tone. MIDI-controlled, rack-mounted auto-wah devices have recently been developed.

String ties at the bridge (above)
Pass approximately 3 in (7.5 cm) of the string through the front of the tie block situated at the back end of the bridge unit. Pull the end of the string back over the tie block, passing it under the string's original point of entry. Wrap the end around itself to hold the string in place. This should be done twice for wound strings and four times for treble strings. Finally, secure the tie by stretching the string toward the headstock. It is important to ensure that the final wrap is positioned at the back of the tie block.

NYLON-STRING GUITARS

The suggested methods for the string ties on the bridge and capstan of a nylon-string guitar are illustrated below. It is useful to make a small knot at the very end of the treble strings, after the tie at the bridge. This stops the string slipping through the bridge if the string tie fails: the "whipping" effect of a tensioned string slipping can cause considerable damage to the body. Some wound strings have an inch or so of loose winding at one end: this section should not be used at any of the string ties. It takes a few days for new strings to settle fully. The plain treble strings improve with age, becoming brighter and louder as the nylon hardens under tension. These can last a long time before being replaced. The wound strings, however, will deteriorate and lose tone more rapidly; for this reason, many players change the bass strings more frequently.

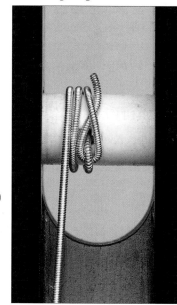

Stringing the capstan (right)
Turn the machine head until the capstan hole is at ninety degrees to the headstock face, and thread the string down through the capstan hole. Bring the string end around the back of the capstan and thread the string beneath itself, forming a knot.

Nylon-string headstock (left)
To achieve the optimum angle between the capstan and the nut, the 1st and 6th strings on a nylon-string acoustic guitar should be wound toward the outer side of the headstock: the opposite direction to the other four strings.

FLAMENCO GUITARS

Flamenco guitars are usually fitted with friction pegs rather than geared machine heads. If the pegs do not fit tightly enough, accurate tuning will become difficult – *peg paste* used by violinists can be applied to improve grip. Stringing at the headstock is the same as for a nylon-string guitar.

FLATTOP ACOUSTICS

On a flattop acoustic guitar, the string tension is taken by the hardwood bridge plate glued to the underside of the top, immediately below the bridge. There are two types of bridge pin commonly used. One type has a recess running down one side to accommodate the string. The second type has no recess – instead, there is a slot cut at the leading side of the pin hole in the bridge where the string sits. Always fully de-tune a string before removing the bridge pin. Use the facility provided on the string winder to lever the pin gently from the bridge. Pins should fit snugly in their holes: modification may be necessary if they are too tight or too loose. Bend the ball end of the new string slightly to one side to fit under the bridge plate, as illustrated. Refit the bridge pin and ensure that it remains properly seated when tuning to pitch. Some makers use an alternative to the pin bridge, similar in principle to the bridge on a nylon-string guitar. Here the ball ends are retained at the back edge of the bridge. When restringing, it is advisable to protect the top of the guitar immediately behind the bridge to avoid dents and scratches as the string is pulled through.

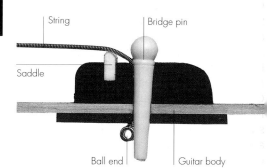

Bridge pin cross section
*This cross section shows the type of bridge used on a flattop acoustic guitar. Note that the purpose of the bridge pin is to hold the ball end in position under the bridge plate, **not** to take the string tension.*

ARCHTOP GUITARS

Traditionally, a tailpiece retains the strings on this type of guitar. Some tailpieces are hinged and will fall onto the guitar top if all the strings are removed, so again protection between the tailpiece and top is recommended. The bridge is not usually attached to the top but held in position by the string tension. As the position and seating of the bridge is critical, it is essential that it is relocated correctly when restringing. Changing the strings individually is advisable because this avoids bridge movement. When tuning to pitch, check that there is no forward tilting on the bridge and that it remains in perfect contact with the top of the guitar. When stringing at the headstock of an archtop guitar, follow exactly the same procedure as for the electric guitar.

CLEANING THE BODY

It is important that any agents used for cleaning should be compatible with the type of body finish. Preventing dirt from accumulating by wiping after use is the best way to keep a guitar clean. For all wiping and polishing, use a clean 100% cotton cloth. Extensive cleaning may be carried out with a clean cloth moistened with warm water. The finish should then be buffed with a dry cloth. Cellulose and synthetic finishes can be cleaned with purpose-made guitar polish. Do not use

Body cleaner   String cleaner

Cleaning cloth   Buffing cloth

Cleaning fluids
A wide variety of specialized cleaning and polishing fluids are available for the body and strings.

cleaning agents that contain silicone – this can permeate the finish, making future refinishing work extremely difficult. Wax polish may also have an adverse effect – it can become sticky in warm temperatures, attracting more dirt. Waxes used in guitar polish are emulsified and blended with cleaning agents, thus avoiding these problems. French polish finishes, commonly found on high-quality classical guitars, are very delicate and should be cleaned by wiping lightly with a barely damp cloth or chamois, followed by buffing with a dry cloth. Never use abrasive cleaners or regular guitar polishes on this type of finish. Exceptionally soiled synthetic finishes can be "revived" with a liquid burnishing cream containing a mild abrasive. This should be used rarely, as the abrasives not only cut through the dirt but also remove some of the lacquer. Cotton wool is good for applying this type of cream, working in small areas at a time and rubbing in a circular motion, finishing in the direction of the wood grain. A liquid glaze cream can then be applied to remove rubbing marks before buffing with a clean, dry cloth. Dust can accumulate inside the

Routine cleaning
It is a good idea getting into the habit of cleaning a guitar regularly after use.

body of acoustic guitars, and it can attract and trap moisture and affect the sound. This can be removed by periodically vacuuming or blowing through the sound hole.

HARDWARE

Plated metal parts should also regularly be cleaned. Chrome cleaners or burnishing cream can be used for cleaning chrome- and nickel-plated parts. Gold-plated parts should be wiped clean with a soft cloth. Corrosion can usually be remedied by removing and soaking the affected parts in penetrating oil. Be sure to wipe off the excess oil before refitting. Finally, a small artists' brush is useful for keeping tremolo units, bridges, and other small parts free from dust. Regular cleaning will not only prolong the life of your guitar but also keep it sounding, feeling, and looking its best.

CLEANING STRINGS

Strings must be clean in order to produce a good tone and accurate tuning. Dirt and grease build up rapidly while playing, and the salt from perspiration causes corrosion if left on the strings, even for short periods. Clean the strings after use with a dry lint-free cloth. This can be wrapped under the strings and drawn along their entire length a few times. Some players prefer to clean each string individually, lifting the string from the nut slot and continuing past the nut. String lubricants can prevent corrosion and keep the strings in good condition. If you use one of these, be sure to remove any surplus. Note: String lubricants should never be used on nylon strings.

THE FINGERBOARD

Keeping the strings clean also prevents dirt and grease from building up on the fingerboard. Each time the strings are changed, wipe the fingerboard with a dry, clean cloth. On ebony or rosewood fingerboards, a little lemon oil can be applied to help loosen grease and dirt. This also "feeds" the wood, preventing it from becoming too dry. The oil should be left on for a few minutes, then cleaned off with a dry cloth. A heavily soiled fingerboard will be far more difficult to clean. In this case, leave the lemon oil on a little longer, then wipe it off and clean the fretboard and frets with very fine steel wool, working with a small circular motion and finishing with the grain. Remove residual dirt from the fret sides by wrapping a cloth moistened with lemon oil around a flatpick (or thumbnail) and running it along each side where the fret meets the fingerboard. Finally, vigorously polish the whole fingerboard with a clean, dry cloth. Lacquered maple fingerboards can be cleaned in a similar way, although steel wool should not be used unless a matte finish is desired. Note: When using steel wool on electric guitars, mask the pick-ups to prevent steel particles from being attracted to the magnets.

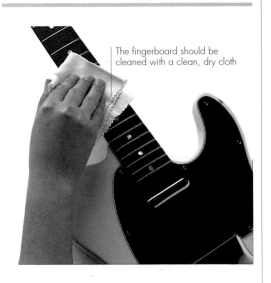

The fingerboard should be cleaned with a clean, dry cloth

SETTING UP

The term *setting up* describes adjustments made to achieve the best possible sound and playing action. There is no definitive setup; ultimately the aim should be to accommodate the individual player's style and technique within the adjustment limitations of the instrument. For the purposes of describing the elements of the setup, it is assumed that the instrument is in a reasonably good condition throughout and free from structural defects. The actual feel and sound of the guitar are the best guides to help you to assess the existing setup condition, so you will gradually become more discriminating as you gain playing experience. The guidelines shown over the next two pages are intended to help you assess the kind of setting-up work that may be required. It is recommended that most of the work involved in setting up be carried out by a specialist, although many players may wish to make simple adjustments themselves. Measurements can be made using a fine-graded steel rule and a set of feeler gauges. To begin with, strings of the desired gauge must be installed and tuned to the correct pitch.

ACTION

The term *action* refers to the playability of the guitar. Many factors contribute to the action, but essentially it is determined by the height of the strings above the frets. This is usually measured between the top of the 12th fret and the bottom of the string: for electric guitars the average figure ranges from 0.05 to 0.08 in (0.13 to 0.2 cm), and for acoustics, 0.08 to 0.11 in (0.2 to 0.28 cm). On electric guitars, the bridge saddles and/or bridge are adjustable and can simply be raised or lowered to adjust the action. On flattop acoustic guitars, the saddle is usually preformed from bone or synthetic material, and the action can be lowered by accurately filing the bottom of the saddle.

Saddle screws are used to adjust the bridge

Measuring the action
Place a ruler on top of the 12th fret and measure the distance to the bottom of the string. Ensure that the ruler is of the type where the scale starts at the tip.

Adjusting the action
Action is changed by altering the height of the saddles on the bridge. Turning the saddle screws clockwise usually raises the height of the saddle; this increases the space between the string and the fret.

NUT

The nut governs the height of the open strings above the 1st fret. Measurements are taken from the top of the 1st fret to the bottom of the string: for electric guitars these range on average from 0.01 to 0.02 in (0.025 to 0.05 cm), and for acoustics, 0.015 to 0.03 in (0.035 to 0.065 cm). Adjustments are made by either refiling the nut slots or replacing the nut. It is essential that the string slots in the nut are filed at a precise angle to provide the string with a clean "take-off" point, and that each slot is proportional to the string diameter. The material used for the nut affects the sound quality of the open strings. Bone or hard synthetic materials are commonly used. Teflon or graphite-based materials are recommended when using a nonlocking tremolo system.

CAMBER

The setting of the individual string heights at the bridge and nut must conform with the *camber*, or the radius of the fingerboard. This is checked by measuring the height of each string at the 12th fret and the 1st fret. You will notice that the action is set highest on the bass side. This is because the heavier strings need greater clearance to vibrate freely. The camber of the bridge and nut should be set so that the action of each string gradually increases from the 1st to the 6th strings. On electric guitars with individually adjustable saddles, this can easily be set. On flattop acoustic guitars, the saddle crown can be carefully reworked or, if necessary, a new saddle can be made for the guitar. Classical and Flamenco guitars normally have no bridge and fingerboard camber.

MEASURING NECK RELIEF

Neck relief is the curve along the length of the neck. Looking along the length of the fingerboard from the nut or bridge will give an indication of the curve. Relief is measured by holding the string down at the first and last frets and measuring the gap between the bottom of the string and the top of the fret. At the deepest point of the curve, usually around the 7th or 8th fret, this averages from 0.005 to 0.020 in (0.015 to 0.05 cm).

Feeler gauge
The measurement should be made at the deepest point of the curve.

Last fret The string should also be held down at the last fret while the measurement is being made.

Capo When making the relief measurements, a capo can be used to hold down the strings at the 1st fret.

INTONATION

For the intonation to be as accurate as possible, the vibrating length of the string must be set proportionally to scale length, action, and string gauge. Without correctly set intonation, accurate tuning over the entire fingerboard cannot be achieved. It is important to install new strings prior to adjusting the intonation, as well as checking that nut height, relief, and action are correctly adjusted and that the frets are in a reasonable condition. On most electric guitars, adjustable saddles allow each string to be intonated individually. Tune to pitch and compare the note produced by the open string with that produced at the 12th fret. If the 12th-fret note is flat, the string length must be shortened by moving the saddle closer to the nut. If the 12th-fret note is sharp, the opposite adjustment must be made. The adjustments are continued until the

two notes are in tune. An electronic tuner is useful for setting the intonation, but, if it is done by ear, it may be preferable to use for comparison the harmonic produced above the 12th fret instead of the open string. Most acoustic guitars have a fixed saddle, in which case intonation adjustments are best left to a specialist.

FRET CONDITION

Ideally, frets should be of uniform height and properly fitted; however, because frets are being constantly worn, maintenance will be necessary. Frets can be *reprofiled* several times but eventually will need replacing by a specialist. Fret height can be checked by holding a string down on two adjacent frets and using a *feeler gauge* to measure the gap between the fingerboard and the bottom of the string. Measurements should be taken where fret wear is most apparent on the fingerboard. Refretting may be needed if this reading is less than 0.025 in (0.6 mm).

Fret wear Excessively worn frets will almost certainly need replacing.

TRUSS ROD

The truss rod reinforces the neck against string tension. Most rods are adjusted by means of a hex, or slotted nut, situated at the heel or headstock end of the neck. Slackening the rod by turning the nut counterclockwise increases relief; tightening it decreases relief. Although this is simple in principle, in practice the results can be very complex, and specialist attention is recommended. The many different types of truss rod, together with the quality and types of timber

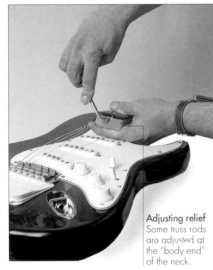

Adjusting relief Some truss rods are adjusted at the "body end" of the neck.

used for the neck and fingerboard, will produce varying results from adjustment. Even the necks of two apparently identical instruments may behave in different ways when similar adjustments are made. With this in mind, you may wish to attempt some minor adjustments to improve the action or test different string gauges. If so, first check the relief (see p. 184). If there is no relief, the neck may be convex – the rod should be slackened until relief is obtained. Adjustments should be made in increments of a half-turn of the hex/slotted nut, and the relief rechecked. Adjustments greater than a full turn in either direction are not recommended. Finally, remember that the action at the nut and bridge will be affected by truss-rod adjustment.

Headstock end Truss rods with adjustment at the headstock end are often made with allen keys.

STORAGE AND TRANSPORTATION CHECKLIST

• Keep the guitar in its case when it is not being used. A good-quality hardshell case is best.
• Avoid exposing the guitar to extremes of temperature. If traveling in exceptionally hot conditions, de-tune the strings.
• If moving the guitar from cold to warm surroundings or vice versa, leave it in the case and allow it to acclimatize for as long as possible.
• Periodically check the instrument thoroughly for signs of climatic effects, such as a noticeable change of the action, splits and cracks, protruding fret ends, lacquer cracking, movement in glue joints, and distortion of the woods. Any problems of this kind should be dealt with by a specialist as soon as possible.
• If traveling by air, where possible arrange with the airline in advance to take the instrument on board as hand luggage. If this is not possible and the guitar travels in the cargo hold, a good-quality flight case should be used. The string tension should always be slackened for air transport.
• Insure the instrument against loss or damage.
• If storing the guitar for long periods, first clean it thoroughly and slacken the strings, leaving a minimum amount of tension.
• Store its case in a safe place of reasonably constant temperature and humidity. Do not store in attics, lofts, or basements.

GLOSSARY

ACCENT An emphasized note or chord.

ACCIDENTAL A symbol used to raise or lower the pitch of a note.

ACOUSTIC GUITAR A classical or steel-string instrument with a sound chamber.

ACTION The height of the strings in relation to the frets and the fingerboard.

AEOLIAN MODE The mode starting on the sixth degree of the major scale.

AMPLIFIER Electronic device for boosting the signal from a pickup or microphone.

ARCHTOP An instrument with a curved top and back carved or made from laminated wood.

ARPEGGIO A succession of chord tones.

AUGMENTED An augmented chord is a major triad with a raised fifth. Certain intervals raised by a semitone are termed augmented.

AVANT GARDE Modern experimental music often featuring modified instruments, unusual techniques, and improvisation with atonality.

BAR A bar or measure is a section of music for grouping note values over a given length of time.

BARRE Method of placing the first or other fingers across the strings to hold down adjacent chord notes.

BASS NOTE The lowest pitched note in a chord or harmonic movement.

BELLY Term applied to an archtop soundboard.

BIGSBY A type of tremolo or vibrato unit.

BINDING A continuous strip of wood around the edge of a guitar body.

BLUES A term applied to an expressive form of North American folk music.

BOTTLENECK A technique for sliding a metal bar or tube along the strings to play notes and chords.

BOUT A term applied to the upper and lower section of the guitar body.

BRACING Strips of wood underneath an acoustic soundboard for support and tonal distribution.

BRIDGE Section for fixing and supporting the strings on an acoustic guitar. The method of supporting the strings on an electric or acoustic guitar.

CAMBER Curvature of the fingerboard, often referred to as the radius.

CAPO A device clamped to the strings with a screw or a strong elastic strip. It holds the strings across any of the lower fret positions enabling open strings on higher fret positions to be played. It also lowers the action.

CHORD Two or more notes sounded together.

CHROMATIC Full scale including all twelve notes a semitone apart within an octave.

CLASSICAL Standard compositional repertoire played on a classical instrument.

CLEF Symbol for fixing the staff at a given pitch.

COMPOUND INTERVAL Interval larger than one octave.

CONTROLS Normally rotary pots or switches used to control electrical signals.

COUNTERPOINT Two or more lines of melody played at the same time.

COURSE Normally a pair of strings placed together to be played with normal fingering.

CUTAWAY A section of the body cut away to give access to the upper part or register of the fingerboard.

CYCLE Series of related musical structures, e.g., the cycle of keys.

DIATONIC The seven-note major and minor scale system.

DIMINISHED Term applied to a minor chord with a lowered 5th and a chord comprising of minor 3rd intervals. Scale composed of successive tones and semitones.

DOBRO A type of resonator guitar.

DOMINANT The note or chord on the fifth degree of a diatonic scale. This is often marked with the Roman numeral **V**.

DORIAN MODE The mode starting on the second degree of the major scale.

DREADNOUGHT A large acoustic steel-string guitar.

EFFECT The result of some form of processing to modify sound.

EQUALIZER A control for filtering frequencies to modify tone.

EXTEMPORISATION *see improvisation*

FEEDBACK A sound produced by a string or microphone picking up and amplifying its own signal from a loudspeaker.

"F"-HOLE Ornamental sound holes on archtop and thinline electric guitars.

FINGERBOARD Wooden section with mounted frets for stopping the strings with the left hand. Also called a fretboard.

FIXED MELODIC MINOR This is an Aeolian mode with a raised sixth and seventh in both the ascending and descending form.

FLAMENCO The indigenous music and dance of Andalusia in Southern Spain.

FLAT Symbol (♭) used for lowering a note by a semitone. A double-flat (♭♭) moves the note down by two semitones (one tone).

FLATPICK Object for sriking the strings held by the right hand. Also known as a pick or plectrum.

FLATTOP A steel-string guitar with a flat soundboard.

FREQUENCY The number of cycles per second, which determines pitch.

FRET Metal strips placed across the fingerboard to determine semitonal spacing.

FRICTION PEG A round wooden peg to hold each string on a solid headstock.

GOLPEADOR A type of pickguard for tapping rhythms on flamenco guitars.

HAMMER A technique for sounding notes with the left-hand fingers.

HARMONIC These are upper parts of a note, related to the fundamental which are played by touching a string at certain points.

HARMONIC MINOR An Aeolian mode with a raised seventh.

HARMONY The simultaneous relationship and order of musical notes.

HEADSTOCK Section for mounting the machine heads or pegs.

HEAVY METAL Intense guitar-based rock music played at high volume and speed, often featuring sustain, overdrive, virtuoso playing.

HEEL A reinforced section supporting the neck where it joins the body.

IMPROVISATION Creative process of composing music or soloing ad lib.

INTABULATION Music in tablature form.

INTERVAL The distance between two notes.

INVERSION The order of notes in a chord from the bass note.

IONIAN MODE Another term for the major scale.

JAZZ North American vocal and instrumental music which has evolved over the past hundred years with a wide diversity of forms and styles.

KEY The reference pitch for a diatonic system.

LEAD A cable for carrying electrical signals. Also a term for single note playing and soloing.

LEADING NOTE The note or chord on the seventh degree of the major scale. Often marked with the Roman numeral **VII**.

LEDGER LINE Small line for placing notes above and below the staff.

LEGATO A smooth, even approach to playing consecutive notes.

LIGADO Term for hammering and pulling-off notes.

LINE A succession of single notes.

LOCRIAN MODE The mode starting on the seventh degree of the major scale.

LUTHIER A guitar maker. Usually associated with the construction of classical instruments.

LYDIAN MODE The mode starting on the fourth degree of the major scale.

MACHINE HEAD Mechanical device for adjusting pitch.

MAJOR Chord with a major third between the root and the third. Scale with major and perfect intervals.

MEDIANT The note or chord on the third degree of the major scale. Often marked with the Roman numeral III.

MELODIC MINOR This is an Aeolian mode with a raised sixth and seventh in an ascending form, and a normal Aeolian mode in its descending form.

MELODY Single notes in a recognizable pattern.

MINOR Chord with a minor third between the root and the third. Scale with minor and perfect intervals.

MIXING Method for controlling and blending recorded sounds.

MIXOLYDIAN MODE The mode starting on the fifth degree of the major scale.

MODE A scale.

MODULATION Movement from a section of music in one key to another key.

MULTITRACKING Storing separate tracks on a reel of tape.

NATURAL Symbol (♮) for cancelling the effect of a sharp or flat.

NUT Point at which the strings are supported as they run from the fingerboard to the headstock.

OCTAVE An interval of twelve semitones. The same note vibrating mathematically related frequencies.

PENTATONIC A five-note scale.

PHRASE A musical sentence.

PHRYGIAN MODE The mode starting on the third degree of the major scale.

PICKGUARD A plate for protecting the guitar body.

PICKUP A coil wound with fine wire which converts the sound into electrical signals.

PIMA Letter names for the right-hand fingers, derived from the Spanish language.

PITCH The frequency of a note.

PLANTILLA The outline shape of a classical guitar.

POLEPIECE Individual metal poles under each string on a pickup.

POT Potentiometer for controlling a signal.

PREAMP A signal-boosting device.

PSYCHEDELIA Drug-based popular music featuring various types of sound treatment, multi-textured sound layers, and unusual forms. Pioneered by British and American groups during the late 1960s.

PULL-OFF Left-hand technique for sounding a note.

PURFLING Decorative inlays next to the binding.

RASGUEADO Method of strumming used by flamenco guitarists.

RELATIVE MINOR The minor system starting on the sixth degree of the major scale.

REST A period of silence.

RHYTHM A pattern of notes and accents.

RIBS The sides of the guitar.

ROCK Music derived from blues and country music in the 1950s.

ROOT The letter-name reference note for a chord.

ROSETTE The circular decoration round the soundhole.

SADDLE(S) The point on the bridge for supporting the strings.

SCALE The string length between the nut and the saddle.

SEQUENCE Often a term for a song or a chordal pattern.

SHAPE The outline form of a chord on the fingerboard.

SHARP Symbol (♯) for raising a note by a semitone. A double-sharp (✕) is used to raise a note by two semitones (one tone).

SLIDE Method for sliding in pitch between notes.

SOL-FA A system of one-syllable abbreviations for scale notes. The notes are Do-Re-Me-Fa-Sol-La-Ti-Do.

SOLO An improvised passage over music.

SOLID-STATE The use of modern transistors.

SOUNDBOARD The top or table of the guitar.

SOUNDHOLE Normally a circular section cut out of the top to allow sound and energy to project from the soundchamber.

SPACE The gap between the lines on a staff.

SPEAKER Circular cone for projecting amplified sound.

STAFF A grid for placing music.

STRUM Method for striking chords with the right hand.

STUDIO A room for recording or practicing.

SUBDOMINANT The note or chord on the fourth degree of the major scale. This is often marked with the Roman numeral IV.

SUBMEDIANT The note or chord on the sixth degree of the major scale. Often marked with the Roman numeral VI.

SUPERTONIC The note or chord on the second degree of the major scale. Often marked with the Roman numeral II.

SYNCOPATION A rhythm emphasizing offbeats.

SYNTHETIC SCALE A non-diatonic succession of notes.

TABLATURE A method for writing music down showing the position of notes on the frets and strings.

TAILPIECE Metal frame or stud for holding the strings on the body of the guitar.

TEMPO The speed of the music in relation to the beats or pulse.

TIME SIGNATURE Two-tier symbol showing the number of notes and their value in a bar.

TONALITY Relationship to a keynote or pivotal tone for a harmonic system.

TONE 1 A major second. **2** The color or quality of the sound. **3** A note.

TONIC The note or chord on the first degree of a diatonic scale. Often marked marked with the Roman numeral I.

TRANSDUCER A device for transferring energy from one form to another. Used to describe a form of pickup used for amplifying acoustic instruments.

TRANSPOSITION Moving a section or a piece of music to a key with a new pitch.

TREMOLO 1 Used for a mechanical (vibrato) arm for controlling pitch. **2** A sound-processing effect. **3** The fast repetition of a single note. **4** A term for Vibrato.

TRIAD A three-note chord with intervals of thirds in root inversion.

TRITONE This is an interval using three whole-tones (tri-tone). It is normally an augmented fourth, or a diminished fifth.

TRUSS ROD Reinforcing metal rod for stabilizing and adjusting the neck.

TUNERS Machine heads.

VALVE Glass tube which amplifies sound using a cathode and anode.

VIBRATO 1 Used for a mechanical arm for controlling pitch. **2** A sound-processing effect. **3** A technique whereby a fretted note is moved rapidly (a minor fluctuation in pitch) to create an effect or enhance tone.

WHOLE TONE An interval of a major second. A six-note scale using whole tones over an octave.

WOLF NOTE A note that is irregular or weak due to the properties of acoustic resonance.

INDEX

Music titles are in *italics*

ACKNOWLEDGMENTS

THE AUTHOR Richard Chapman would firstly like to thank his agent Julian Alexander, and Christopher Davis and Stephanie Jackson at Dorling Kindersley for their help in bringing about an improved, updated, and expanded version of *The Complete Guitarist*.

I would particularly like to thank the contributors: Bill Puplett for the care and maintenance section, John Seabury, Jim Barber, and Terry Burrows for the majority of the sound and amplification section, and Hugh Manson for material on his electric guitar.

I want to give a special thank-you to Veryan Weston for contributing his fascinating system on pentatonic scales and modulation on page 164.

Both the consultants have been tremendously helpful: guitarist Rafael at www.flamencoguitarist.com for flamenco, and engineer and producer Joe Leach at The Cowshed Recording Studio, www.cowshedstudio.com, for recording techniques.

I wholeheartedly thank the people who have worked on this new edition. They have been great! Adèle Hayward and Karen Self for excellent management, Anna Fischel for constructive support and thoughtful editorial work, Ted Kinsey for thoroughly professional design, Neil Lockley and Kevin Ryan for editorial, design, and general help.
Also Trevor Bounford and his company for his important contribution with music setting and graphic elements.

I would also like to take this opportunity to thank Robert Cornford (1940-83) for his inspiration and encouragement.

Thanks to: The Acoustic Centre; Arbiter; Fiona Austin; Tony Bacon; Stephen Barber; Martin Booth; Sheila Bounford; Trevor Bounford; Nigel Bradley; Dave Brewis; Karen Brock; Alan Buckingham; Dave Burrluck; Rod Butcher ; Steve Byrd; Capitol Records; Carter; Doug Chandler; Paula Chandler at Chandler Guitars ; Carol Chapman; Matthew Chattle; David Clifton; James Coppock at FCN; The Cocteau Twins; Brian Cohen; Pete Cornish; Fin Costello;

Jamie Crompton at Fender Artist Relations; Christopher Dean; Denise ; Paul Fischer; Scott Fischer; Russell Fong; Gerald Garcia; Michael Gee; Dave Gladden; Tracey Hambleton-Miles; Phil Harris; Steve Hart; Vincent Hastwell; Mark Hayward; Steve Hazell; Lol Henderson; Andy Holdsworth; Nick Hooper; Steve Hoyland; Grover Jackson; Katie Johns; Rose Jones; Max Kay; Jane Laing; Joe Leach; Alex Lee; Richard Leyens; Heather McCarry; Pete McPhail; Andy Manson; Neville Martin ; Tom Mates; Roger Mayer; Charles Measures; John Monteleone; Paul Morgan; Nigel Moyse; Tom Nolan; Sean Moore; Alan Murphy; Nigel Osborne ; Nick Peraticos; Les Paul; Colin Pringle at SSL; Mervyn Rhys-Jones; Gurinder Purewall; Rafael; Rose Morris; Nick Rowlands; Iain Scott; Damon Smith; Sally Stockwell; Mike Tamborino; Dawn Terrey; Daniel Thomas; Pat Thomas; Ced Thorose; Dave Townsend; Paul Trynka; Helen Turner at JHS ; Ray Ursell; Jerry Uwins; Mike Vanden; Tina Vaughan; Carey Wallace at Christie's; Simon Wallace; Kevin Walsh; Adam Watson; James Westbrook; David Weston; Larry Wexer; Martin Wheatley; Marty Williamson; Andreas Young.

DORLING KINDERSLEY would like to thank Matthew Ward for new photography; Francessca Agati, Rochele Whyte, Daniel Thomas, and David Weston for modeling on pages 34–35 and 40–41; Margaret McCormack for indexing; Diana Morris for picture research; Mike Tamborino for the John Monteleone guitar on page 22 and Dave Brewis for the Flying V on the Contents page.

Bibliography:
R. Aspen Pittman *The Tube Amp Book* (1982); Tony Bacon *The Ultimate Guitar Book* (Dorling Kindersley, 1991); Ralph Denyer *The Guitar Handbook* (Dorling Kindersley, 1982); Mike Doyle *The History of Marshall Valve Guitar Amplifiers* (New Musical Services, 1982); Tom and Mary Ann Evans *Guitars from the Renaissance to Rock* (Oxford University Press, 1977); George Gruhn and Walter Carter *Gruhn's Guide to Vintage Guitars* (GPI, 1991); Brent Hurtig *Multi-track Recording* (GPI, 1988); Juan Martín *El Arte Flamenco de la Guitarra* (United Music, 1978); Norman Mongan *History of the guitar in jazz* (Oak, 1983); Frederick Noad *Solo Guitar Playing Books 1 and 2* (Macmillan, 1968); Vincent Persichetti *Twentieth Century Harmony* (W W Norton, 1961); Professor Walter Piston *Harmony* (Victor Gollancz, 1941); Nicolas Slonimsky *Thesaurus of Scales and Melodic Patterns* (Scrivener's, 1947) Don Randel *The New Harvard Dictionary of Music* (Harvard University Press, 1986); José Romanillos *Antonio de Torres* (Element, 1987); Harry Shapiro and Caesar Glebbeek *Jimi Hendrix: Electric Gypsy* (Mandarin, 1990); Michael Stimpson *The Guitar* (Oxford University Press, 1988); James Tyler *The Early Guitar* (Oxford University Press, 1980); Tom Wheeler *American Guitars* (Harper and Rowe, 1982).

Photography:
Matthew Ward; Visual 7 Photography; Steve Gorton; Andy Crawford; Tim Ridley.

Computer artwork:
Bounford.com

Picture credits:
p.5 Michael Tamborino: r.
p.6 Rose Jones: tl.
p.7 David Redfern/Redferns: b.
p.14 Finn Costello/Redferns.
p.15 Ashmolean Museum; Matthew Chattel; Edinburgh University Collection.
p.19 Country Music Hall of Fame.
p.22 Michael Tamborino: br.
p.25 Robert Knight/Redferns: bl.
p.27 David Redfern/Redferns: cr.
p.169 Sothebys.
p.190 David Magnus/Rex Features: cl.
p.191 Abbey Road Studios www.abbeyroad.com: br.
p.194 Joe Leach: b.

Music credit:
ALL THE THINGS YOU ARE, by Jerome Kern and Oscar Hammerstein II © 1939 (Renewed) Universal - PolyGram International Publishing, Inc. All Rights Reserved Used by Permission WARNER BROS. PUBLICATIONS U.S. INC., Miami, FL. 33014